Created and Directed by Hans Höfer

INSIGHT GUIDES
NORTHERN CALIFORNIA

Edited by John Wilcock
Managing Editor: Martha Ellen Zenfell

Editorial Director: Brian Bell

HOUGHTON MIFFLIN COMPANY

APA PUBLICATIONS

ABOUT THIS BOOK

Höfer

Zenfell

Wilcock

More than most Americans, the early settlers in Northern California were changed not only by what they had to go through to get to their destination but also by the conditions they found when they finally arrived. Harriett Martineau observed in *Society in America, 1837*, that Americans were "better shaped by providence than by men," a statement that would have some resonance even today among those who feel that going West to begin a new life still has some of the essence of the pioneer about it.

A strong sense of the adventure of discovery remains in Northern California, which lends itself especially well to the approach taken by the award-winning *Insight Guides*, created in 1970 by **Hans Höfer**, founder of Apa Publications and still its moving force. Each book in the 190-title series encourages readers to celebrate the essence of a place rather than try to tailor it to their expectations and is edited in the belief that, without insight into a people's history, character and culture, travel can narrow the mind rather than broaden it.

Insight Guide: Northern California is carefully structured: the first section covers the area's history and culture in a series of magazine-style essays. The main Places section provides a comprehensive run-down on the sights worth seeing, with a little bit of gossip thrown in for good measure. Finally, a fact-packed listings section contains all the information you'll need on travel, hotels, shops, restaurants and opening times. Complementing the text, remarkable photography sets out to communicate directly and provocatively life as it is lived by the locals.

The book has been almost completely rewritten since its first edition in 1984, with new text and new photographs periodically introduced to reflect the ever-changing cultural landscape of California. This fresh, thoroughly overhauled edition was supervised by Insight's West Coast editor **John Wilcock** in Los Angeles and Apa's London-based managing editor **Martha Ellen Zenfell** – colleagues who, though 6,000 miles apart, have collaborated for several years on producing travel books, including *Insight Guides* to Los Angeles, Seattle and Vancouver.

Wilcock, who was born in England, worked for the *New York Times* travel desk and subsequently wrote books about more than a dozen countries. He dates his long acquaintance with California to the visits he made while a columnist for New York's *Village Voice* and to his later editorship of the *Los Angeles Free Press*. "After the crowded freeways around LA," he reports, "driving along the coast north of Mendocino is pure joy. Often you'll find yourself on a two-lane highway with nothing in sight in either direction, except possibly a cow or two. Even they look surprised to see you."

Wilcock's northern exposure was undertaken to follow his hunch that he could find the evidence for an essay called "America's Last Bohemia" about this free-spirited region, and such proved to be the case. He was also responsible for the articles on Herb Caen, Hearst's Castle, cable cars, the Golden Gate Bridge and the hemp initiative. Together with **Howard Rabinowitz**, Wilcock also wrote the essay on the literary scene. Wine expert Rabinowitz, a screenwriter, contributed the piece on "California Wineries." He has lived in the Bay Area for

Davis

Carroll

a number of years and has no plans to quit. As Rudyard Kipling wrote a century ago: "San Francisco has only one drawback. 'Tis hard to leave."

On-site reporting and research in the Northern California area was organized by **Jeffrey Davis**, a Silicon Valley-born freelance writer whose clients include the *New York Times Magazine*. He renewed his early acquaintance with the region while an editor at San Francisco's *Mother Jones*. Davis's experience "working midnight shifts at the local 7-11, by day as a reporter for the *California Aggie* (a campus newspaper) and going to class sometime in between," helped build up his stamina for the task at hand. Davis was assisted by three writers: **Laura Jamison**, **Peter** and **Virginia Maloney**, and **Philip Thayer**.

The lion's share of credit for the original book, much of whose influence remains, goes to editors **Jon Carroll** and **Tracey Johnston**, and project coordinator/photographer **Bret Reed Lundberg**. Many of Lundberg's photographs still grace these pages, along with the work of fellow photographers **Catherine Karnow**, **Bodo Bondzio**, **Kerrick James**, **Lee Foster** and **Jan Whiting**.

Johnston

People are in many ways the most interesting thing about California. "I was attending a dinner the other morning given for the Old Settlers of California,' wrote Will Rogers in 1924. "No one was allowed to attend unless he had been in the state 2½ years." The fun-loving, far-fetched, sometimes frustrating but always fascinating subject of Californians and their culture is covered in this edition by **Karen Klabin**. Another *Mother Jones* staffer, **Julie Petersen**, produced the piece on the high-tech developments in Silicon Valley, an area of which she has first-hand acquaintance as she currently lives there.

Pottenger

The essay "The Great Outdoors" is the work of hyperactive sports man **Sean Wagstaff**, fisherman, kayaker, windsurfer and snow boarder who undoubtedly carries a laptop in his backpack. **Dennis Pottenger**, a former staffer on *Sacramento* magazine, was responsible for the chapter on his hometown. For the past 10 years he has specialized in politics in the state capital, and once wrote a book about the San Francisco football team, the 49ers. About Sacramento he reports, paraphrasing the well-known saying, "Well, there is a *there* there, but it's just so hot sometimes that *there* means home with the air-conditioning on at full blast."

"California, more than any other part of the Union, is a country by itself," said James Bryce in 1888. For this reason, a small debt must be paid to the small army of other people who made this book possible. Despite a thorough rewrite, *IG: Northern California* still carries some traces of its earlier edition, whose contributors include **Steve Rubenstein**, **Kief Hillsbery**, **Paul Cohen**, **Phil Garlington**, **Paul Ciotti**, **Frank Robertson**, **Tom Chaffin** and **Tom De Vries**. The book's extensive history is a melding of the work of **Tom Cole**, **Joan Talmage Weiss** and **Matthew Parfitt**, coordinated by editor Wilcock.

In Apa Publications' London editorial office, **Elaine Read** spent the build-up to her wedding putting the manuscript through a variety of computers, while **Mary Morton** proofread and indexed the text.

—*Apa Publications*

CONTENTS

CONTENTS

TRAVEL TIPS

Northern California is the product of a myth – a single, improbable myth of a land of gold – that for less than a century inspired and dominated a ragtag society of men and women who saw the myth spring to life. From the time in January 1848 when a man named James Marshall picked up a few bits of shiny metal out of a river in the Sierra Nevada there was an explosion of greed, energy and longing that changed the world. California was created by it and San Francisco transformed from a droopy backwater into a busy, world-famous dream city.

Northern California is a watery place. Between 35 and 50 ft (11–16 meters) of snow falls each year in the Sierra, and it is the runoff from the snowpack that sustains the vast agricultural fields of the Central Valley. Gravity leads the Sierra meltwater down and westward toward the ocean. Along the way, the 250-mile (400-km) Sacramento River collects most of those waters as it courses down the great valley from its source near the Mount Shasta volcano, close to the Oregon border. But Northern California's Coast Range, lower than the Sierra, though monumental in its own right, is a rampart against the inland water's seaward escape.

The Central Valley might be a stupendous lake if it weren't for a single breach in the Coast Range: San Francisco Bay's sublime Golden Gate. It's scarcely necessary to draw attention here to the world's most famous bridge, and behind it one of the world's most beautiful cities.

Early immigration to this region was hindered by the desert of the Great Basin, created by those moisture-blocking mountains and it wasn't until the Transcontinental Railroad was completed in 1869 that the Sierra Nevada was partially tamed. "Give me men to match my mountains" reads an inscription in the State Capitol in Sacramento, and in due time the heroes arrived, building the region that aims one day to become a state of its own. They were rough and tough, some of those early arrivals, maybe best summarized by the piece of doggerel quoted by John Steinbeck in his 1962 book *Travels With Charley:*

> The miner came in forty-nine
> The whores in fifty-one
> And when they got together
> They made the native son.

Today the newcomers still pour in, some ironically from the warmer and more populated southern part of the state, attracted no longer by the gold or even entirely by the Golden Gate but by the untrammeled open spaces and scenic splendor of an area still relatively unexplored. If that hearty Victorian do-gooder Horace Greeley were still alive today, his advice might well be, "Go north, young man."

Preceding pages: the gnarled trunk of a bristlecone pine; the ghost town of Bodie; a man's best friend; room with a view; Big Sur beer and supplies; watching for the waves; San Francisco with smoke. **Left**, view from Yosemite Valley.

par Franquelin d'après Choris.

Danse des habitans de Califor

Pl. III

Lith. de Langlumé r de l'Abbaye N. 4

à la mission de s.ᵗ Francisco.

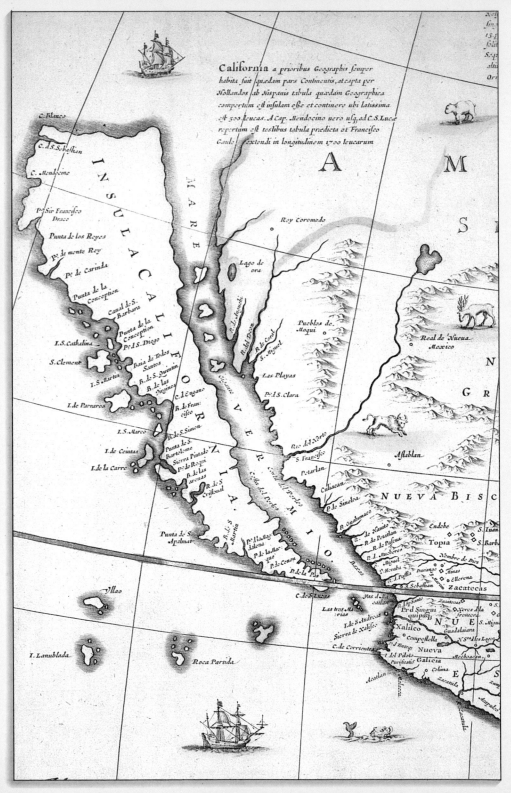

BEGINNINGS

The first tenants of the rich land that became California were the tribes that through the centuries crossed the land bridge of the Bering Strait and slowly filtered down into the North American continent. So many died soon after white people arrived that anthropologists have had to rely on patchy mission records for their estimates – a reasonable guess being that 230,000 Native Americans originally inhabited the northern region.

The land around the Bay probably supported more humans than any other California locale but one area not much frequented was where San Francisco now stands. This was a sandy, windy, desolate place compared to the mild slopes of Mount Tamalpais or the woods of the southern peninsula. San Francisco today, in fact, has more trees and wildlife than at any time in its history.

Customs, talents and preoccupations varied from tribe to tribe, each with separate identities and distinct languages. The Miwoks and Ohlones around the San Francisco Bay moved in short nomadic spurts, sometimes trekking from their ancestral shell mound up to the lush oak groves on what are now the Berkeley Hills where they ground acorns into rich and oily meal, and socialized warily. Then they would pack up for the meadowland and its rich harvest of deer and elk, at each stop along the trail being greeted and heartened by ancient landmarks: a venerable oak, a mossy boulder, a lively stream, a soft meadow.

Simple life: California tribes led a simple life. Their igloo-shaped homes of reed provided breezy shelter in summer, with deerskin roofs for protection during the rainy season. When temperatures dropped, open fires were built indoors, holes in the roof allowing the smoke to escape. In warm weather, the men and children were naked except for ornamental jewelry such as necklaces, earrings, bracelets and anklets. They kept warm when they needed to with robes of yellow cedar bark or crudely tanned pelts.

Preceding pages: dancing for priests at a San Francisco mission. **Left,** map drawn in 1638 by a Dutchman, Joannes Jansson. **Right,** Father Junipéro Serra.

Some groups practiced tattooing. The women wore two-piece aprons of deerskins or reeds.

The Miwok, Ohlone and Wituk Indians, among others, occupied much of northern California, living in the kind of harmony with the land that the most ecologically-conscious can only dream of today. This tribal lifestyle continued and prospered for 10,000 years with few major changes and, by our standards, with hard times and few possessions. The arrival of white people bewildered them, but their acquisition of manu-

factured articles such as guns, metal utensils, axes, knives, blankets and cloth led inevitably to a decline of the native arts and crafts. With the coming of the immigrant wagons and the encroachment of white settlements, warfare became a unifying force.

Tribes that had formerly been hostile to one another often united against the intruders. But even this did not save them, and in the end they were overwhelmed. The culture of all Native Americans was radically changed. They had survived earthquakes and droughts, but the whites proved too strong for them.

Once the Europeans arrived, the tribes'

decline was assured. Regarding the Indians as little better than animals compared with "the people of reason" (themselves), within a century the avaricious newcomers virtually obliterated the culture and ravaged the environment. The city of San Francisco was built on greed and gold, which are often synonymous.

Early explorers: Exactly what Sir Francis Drake discovered in 1579 during his voyage around the world in the *Golden Hind* has never been established with certainty. Drake had a mission from Elizabeth I to "annoy" the Spanish provinces and had been obediently causing havoc up and down the west coast of Mexico. (Yet in his gentlemanly

manner of operation, he had killed not one person.) Apparently Drake passed by the bay's entrance without venturing inside or even noticing an opening. But his log shows that he did anchor just north of the bay and sent several landing parties ashore. It seems that one of these groups left behind the small brass plate that was discovered only in 1936 near what is now Drake's Bay.

It was rumors of riches that had enticed the Spaniards from the beginning. The early explorers were seeking a Northwest Passage that would lead them to the Orient and its valuable spice trade. Hernando Cortés, the conqueror of Mexico, had ordered a series of

expeditions up the coast of Baja California – at the time thought to be an island – but it was not until 1542 that Juan Rodriguez Cabrillo discovered the land to the north. Cabrillo even passed by these shores without noticing the immense natural harbor that is now San Francisco Bay. But of course it may well have been concealed in fog, as it so often still is today.

Later, Gaspar de Portolá, on his northern expedition to find a suitable harbor, also missed its significance, thinking it to be an open gulf. But another explorer, Jose Francisco Ortega, reported it as "a great arm of the sea extending to the southeast farther than the eye could see." It wasn't, however, until the visit of Captain Juan Bautista de Anza six years later that a decision was made to build a mission here at Yerba Buena.

The mission, a little chapel with a thatch roof, was founded on October 9, 1776, by Fray Palóu. The chapel was named Mission Dolores after the nearby creek. Palóu acted for the renowned "Apostle of California," Fray Junípero Serra, who was directly responsible for founding nine of the eventual 21 Californian missions, and personally baptized thousands of Indians. *Presidios* (garrisons), like the one nearby, were customarily built at strategic points to protect a mission against hostile tribes or foreign colonists.

Remote outpost: By the end of the century the population remained under 1,000. The garrison was strong enough to sustain attacks by hostile Indians but would have easily fallen to attacks from the sea had there been any. But northern California was still a remote outpost and held little appeal for foreign adventurers.

Ironically, the Gold Rush that eventually ended the region's isolation might have come a century earlier if the Indians' discovery of the precious metal had been acted upon at the time. Instead, the Spanish *padres* to whom it was shown advised silence on the matter, reasoning correctly that knowledge of its existence would bring an unmanageable influx of invaders.

After the 16th-century discoveries of California variously by Hernando Cortés, Juan Rodriguez Cabrillo and Sebastian Vizcaíno, there followed another century and a half of lassitude until the overland arrival in 1769 of Gaspar de Portolá from Baja. Crossing the Santa Ana Rivér and exchanging gifts with friendly tribes, de Portolá's band passed the bubbling tar pits of La Brea, through the mountains at Sepulveda Pass to Lake Encino, and headed northwards to open up the route to Monterey.

"The three diarists in the party agree that the practical discovery of most significance was the advantageous site on the Los Angeles river," noted John Caughey in a volume published by the California Historical Society to mark the city's bi-centennial. "Equally important were the numerous able-bodied, alert and amiable Indians because Spanish policy looked towards preserving, Christianizing, Hispanizing and engrossing the natives as a major element in the Spanish role in enslaving hundreds of coastal Indians into an endless round of work and prayer. Father Junípero Serra, a tireless zealot who stood a mere 5ft 2ins (1.6 meters) in height, was personally responsible for establishing the first seven missions (San Diego, San Carlos, San Antonio, San Gabriel, San Luis Obispo, San Francisco and San Juan Capistrano), most of which were destroyed in the severe 1812 earthquake.

As early as 1775 the Indians rebelled: in an uprising at the San Diego mission one of the Franciscans was killed. But abolishing age-old tribal customs and introducing a complex religious structure centered around endless work eventually converted the Indians

Habitants de Californie

colony now to be established."

Time-tested methods: Over the centuries Spain had developed a standard method for settling new territory, using the sword to cut down any opposition from the natives and pacifying the area with the introduction of Christianity. This was the approach used in California where between 1769 and early in the next century a chain of 21 Franciscan missions was established between San Diego and Sonoma. These played the major

Left, Sir Francis Drake's 1579 voyage around the world included a landing just to the north of San Francisco. **Above**, early Californian inhabitants.

into obedient servants. The object of every mission was to become self-sufficient, to which end its subjects became cooks, blacksmiths, farmers, tanners, vintners or underpaid laborers. Indian men were taught to tend cattle; women to sew.

White diseases such as measles and chicken pox killed thousands. Hundreds more fell ill with venereal diseases and the Indians developed a mortal fear of mission life. But benevolent despotism kept thousands of Indians in the missions and it was their labor that made the system successful. Not until the Mexican government's secularization decrees of 1834 were the Indians freed – only to exchange their status for that of underpaid peons on the vast ranches. Today, peppering the coastline and inland areas, are ruins of these once-dominant communities, each with its own unique features.

There are many who believe that for all the good it brought, the mission system promoted outright slavery under the guise of piety, and was at least partly responsible for the ultimate destruction of California's Native American population. Even after the missions had been secularized, pillage of the environment continued for the rest of the century: forests were cut down, hunting lands confiscated and mining wastes ruined the once-pure salmon streams. The missions themselves were parcelled out to political favorites by the Mexican government, 8 million acres (3.2 million hectares) fragmented into 800 privately owned ranchos and sold for as little as 23¢ per acre.

In theory, the Secularization Act of 1834 gave lay administrators and Indians the right to ownership of the missions and their property; a potential ranchero could ask for as many as 50,000 acres (20,000 hectares). In practice, the acts were barely observed: Indians were driven out into the world of poverty and helplessness, ill-equipped to deal with white men's laws. Some returned to the hills, others indentured themselves as ranch hands or turned to drinking and gambling.

Meanwhile, the orange groves and the productive gardens were either cleared or plowed under, and the "string of pearls" (the mission areas) transformed into a patchwork quilt of ranches.

By the end of the 18th century, foreign officials were beginning to show a discreet interest in the region. In 1792, the English sailor George Vancouver scouted the coast, bringing the first (white) American visitor, John Green, to the shores of California. The Russian trading post and garrison only 50 miles (80 km) to the north at Bodega Bay was also engendering a certain nervousness on the part of the Californians; the Russians eventually left in 1841. By this time Mexico had declared its independence from Spain and the secularization of the missions had begun. Life in the area remained, for the most part, uneventful.

When a certain Captain Beecher visited this part of northern California in 1826, five years after Mexico had declared its independence from Spain, he noted among the residents only ennui. "Some of them," he wrote, "were ingenious and clever men but they had been so long excluded from the civilized world that their ideas and their politics, like the maps pinned against the wall, bore the date 1772 as near as I could read for the fly specks."

It wasn't until 20 years after his visit that the US flag was raised, the same year (1846) that Samuel Brannan arrived with a group of 230 Mormons to colonize the region that was then renamed San Francisco. There was also some apprehension about the growing signs of interest by France and Britain in the American west, and especially the value to a foreign power of San Francisco Bay, which an American diplomat, Waddy Thompson, described as "capacious enough to receive the navies of all the world."

But the immediate problem lay nearer to home. When President James K. Polk took office in 1845, he pledged to acquire California by any means. He felt pressured by the English financial interests which plotted to exchange $26 million of defaulted Mexican bonds for the rich land of California. On May 13, 1846, Polk surprised no one by declaring war on Mexico. News of the war had not reached California by mid-June when a group of settlers stormed General Mariano Vallejo's Sonoma estate. Vallejo soothed the men with brandy and watched as they raised their hastily sewn Bear Flag over Sonoma's Plaza.

The Bear Flag Revolt is sanctified in California history – the flag now being the official state flag – but, for all its drama, it was immaterial. Within a few weeks Commodore John Sloat arrived to usher California into the Union.

Most of the fighting in the War of American Conquest took place in the south. The war in the north effectively ended on July 9, 1846, when 70 sailors and marines from the ship *Portsmouth* marched ashore in Yerba Buena village and raised the Stars and Stripes in the central plaza.

The Treaty of Guadalupe Hidalgo, which came into force on July 4 (US Independence Day), 1848, ended the Mexican War. By this treaty, California became a territory of the United States of America.

Right, detail from artist Louis Storey's 18th-century painting of early American life.

Lith. de Langlumé, r de l'Abbaye N.4

de Californie.

ON STONE BY F. PALMER.

Entered according to Act of Congress in the year 1851 by

Clarkes Point.   Rincon Point.   Happy Valley   Long Wharf (building.)

VIEW OF SAN FRAN

TAKEN FROM TELEGRAPH HILL, APRIL 1850, BY Wᵐ B. Mᶜ

Published by N. Currier, N.Y.

CISCO, CALIFORNIA.

TRIE, DRAUGHTSMAN OF THE U. S. SURVEYING EXPEDITION.

Capt. Sutter's account of the first
discovery of the Gold.

"I was writing one afternoon," said the Captain,
"just after my siesta, engaged, by the bye, in
writing a letter to a relation of mine at Lucern,
when I was interrupted by Mr. Marshal a gent-
leman with whom I had frequent business
transactions - bursting hurriedly into the
room. From the unusual agitation in his
manner I imagined that something serious
had occured, and, as we involuntarely do in
this part of the world, I at once glanced to
see if my rifle was in its proper place. You
should know that the mere appearance of Mr.
Marshal at that moment in the Fort, was quite
enough to surprise me, as he had but two days
before left the place to make some alterations in a
mill for sawing pine planks, which he had just
run up for me, some miles higher up the Ameri-
canos. When he had recovered himself a little, he
told me that, however great my surprise might be
at his unexpected reappearance, it would be much
greater when I heard the intelligence he had come to
bring me. 'Intelligence,' he added, 'which if properly
profited by, would put both of us in possession of
unheard-of-wealth- millions and millions of dollars, in
fact.' I frankly own, when I heard this that I thought
something had touched Marshall's brain, when suddenly all my
misgivings were put an end to by his flinging on the table a
handful of scales of pure virgin gold. I was fairly thunderstruck
and asked him to explain what all this meant, when he went on to say, that
according to my instructions, he had thrown the mill-wheel out of gear, to let the whole
body of the water in the dam find a passage through the tail race, which was previously
to narrow to allow the water to run off in sufficient quantity, whereby the wheel was prevented from
efficiently performing its work. By this alteration the narrow channel was considerably enlarged, and a mass
of sand & gravel carried off by the force of the torrent. Early in the morning after this took place, Mr. Marshal
was walking along the left Bank of the stream when he perceived something which he at first took for a piece of
opal - a clair transparent stone, very common here - glittering on one of the spots laid bare by the sudden crumb-
ling away of the bank. He paid no attention to this; but while he was giving directions to the workmen, having
observed several similar glittering fragments, his curiosity was so far excited, that he stooped down & picked
on of them up. ' Do you know,' said Mr. Marshal to me, 'I positively debated within myself two or three times
whether I should take the trouble to bend my back to pick up one of the pieces, and had decided on not doing
so when farther on, another glittering morsel caught my eye - the largest of the pieces now before you. I
condescended to pick it up, and to my astonishment found that it was a thin scale of what appears to
be pure gold.' He then gathered some twenty or thirty pieces which on examination convinced him that
his suppositions were right. His first impression was, that this gold had been lost or buried there, by
some early Indian tribe - perhaps some of those mysterious inhabitants of the west, of whom we have no
account, but who dwelt on this continent centuries ago, and built those cities and temples, the ruins
of which are scattered about these solidary wilds. On proceeding, however, to examine the neighbouring
soil, he discovered that it was more or less auriferous. This at once decided him. He mounted his
horse, and rode down to me as fast as it could carry him with the news.
At the conclusion of Mr Marshals account, and when I had convinced myself, from the specimens he
had brought with him, that it was not exagerated, I felt as much excited as himself. I eagerly inquired
if he had shown the gold to the workpeople at the mill and was glad to hear that he had not spoken to a
single person about it. We agreed not to mention the circumstance to any one and arranged to set off
early the next day for the mill. On our arrival, just before sundown, we poked the sand about in
various places, and before long succeeded in collecting between us more than an ounce of gold,
mixed up with a good deal of sand. I stayed at Mr Marshall's that night, and the next day we proceeded
some little distance up the south Fork, and found that gold existed along the whole course, not
only in the bed of the main stream, where the had subsided but in every little dried-up creek
and ravine. Indeed I think it is more plentiful in these latter places, for I myself, with nothing
more than a small knife, picked out from dry gorge, a little way up the mountain, a solid
lump of gold which weighed nearly an ounce and a half.
Notwithstanding our precautions not to be observed, as soon we came back to the mill, we noticed
by the excitement of the working people that we had been dogged about, an to complet our disappointment, one of the indians who had worked at the gold mine in the neighbourhood of La Paz
cried out in showing to us some specimens picked up by himself, — Oro! — Oro — Oro !!!—

30

In 1848, James Marshall stood by a mill in the Sierra Nevada foothills, on the banks of the American River. Marshall, a contractor, had just built the mill for another man, John Augustus Sutter. The mill was one of Sutter's screwier ideas for he was a man, one contemporary wrote, with a disastrous "mania for undertaking too much."

Born in Switzerland in 1803, Sutter arrived in San Francisco in 1839. Despite a disorderly career as a Swiss Army officer and dry-goods merchant, he somehow impressed Alta California's authorities enough to offer him the largest possible land grant, nearly 50,000 acres (about 20,000 hectares) of the Central Valley. Naming it "New Helvetia" and using Indians as serf labor, Sutter set out to create a semi-independent barony.

Sutter's Fort, at what is now Sacramento, was often the first stop for bedraggled overlanders after their harrowing Sierra crossing. Sutter gloried in providing comfort and goods (at a price) to California's new settlers. He planted wheat and fruit orchards, bought out the Russians at Fort Ross, lent his aid to several of Northern California's jostling factions, and in 1847 decided to build the sawmill that was his ultimate undoing.

Marshall, who had been hired to oversee the mill's construction, peered into the mill race on January 24, 1848, and noticed a bit of shiny material, one of the millions of smithereens of gold that had been tumbling down the streams of the Sierra for millennia.

He took the nugget to Sutter and the pair, applying "every test of their ingenuity and the American Encyclopaedia," decided that it was indeed gold. They raced back up to the sawmill, poked and panned awhile, and found more. They tried to keep the find a secret, but the news, of course, changed the nature of this peaceable pastoral region forever. (Today, a recreation of the mill stands at Coloma, 50-odd miles (80 km) east of Sacramento.)

By the end of May the word "gold" was all over California: the editor of *The Californian*

announced the suspension of his newspaper because his entire staff had quit. "The whole country from San Francisco to Los Angeles and from the sea shore to the base of the Sierra Nevada," he wrote, "resounds with the sordid cry of GOLD! GOLD! GOLD! – while the field is left half-planted, the house half-built and everything neglected but the manufacture of shovels and pick-axes…"

The Western world had been waiting for the myth to come to life for centuries. The Spanish had uprooted and discarded more

A GOLD HUNTER ON HIS WAY TO CALIFORNIA, VIA, ST LOUIS.

than one civilization looking for the country of gold. The myth had grown into a prophecy. San Francisco was left nearly deserted, its shops stripped of axes, pans, tents, beans, soda crackers, picks and whatever else might conceivably be of use. Monterey, San Jose, all of Northern California's mission towns and farms joined in the scramble. Gold fever worked its way to Utah and Oregon, where "two-thirds of the able-bodied men were on their way to the diggings."

Ships in the Pacific spread the word to Peru, Chile, Hawaii and Australia. Lt L. Loeser carried a "small chest… containing $3,000 worth of gold in lumps and scales"

Preceding pages: early view of San Francisco. **Left**, John Sutter's account of the discovery of gold in his sawmill. **Right**, satirical portrait of a California gold-seeker.

back to Washington, DC, where it was exhibited at the War Office, increasing greed in the Capital. On December 2, President Polk told Congress that the "extraordinary accounts" were true. A few days later the *New York Herald* summed it up: "The El Dorado of the old Spaniards is discovered at last."

Hundreds of thousands of reveries were fixed on the fabled Mother Lode, which ran for 120 miles (190 km) from north of Sutter's Mill to Mariposa in the south. "Forty-niners," (as the Gold Rush devotees were called) first worked the streams of the Klamath Mountains in the far north: later, the southern deserts had their share of miners and boom towns. But the Mother Lode's wooden hills

hard. In 1849, $10 million of gold was mined in California; the next year, four times that. Almost 50,000 prospectors arrived in the state in 1850 and in 1852, the pinnacle of the Gold Rush, $80 million wound up in someone's pockets.

The Sierra streams did much of the miner's work for him. The rushing waters eroded the hillsides and sent placer gold (from dust to nugget size) rushing downstream. A miner crouched by the streambank, scooped up a panful of gravel, shifting, and turning his pan as the debris washed out and the gold sank to the bottom. Later, sluices were built and holes were dug. Finally hydraulic mining took over, although this was banned in 1884

and deep valleys were the great centers of the raucous, short-lived argonaut civilization.

Claims were limited: Gold Rush mining, especially in the early days before the streams were panned out, was a simple affair. The Mother Lode was owned by the federal government, and claims were limited to the ground a man and his fellows could actually work. Thus, stockpiling claims was impossible and hiring a work force was unlikely. There was scant reason to make another man rich when one's own wealth-spouting claim was so easily achieved.

There was definitely gold in "them thar hills;" it was keeping it that seemed to be

after causing dramatic ecological damage to the foothills.

The endless disputes over water rights, which still continue, mostly date back to the days of the gold prospectors when miners whose claims were staked far from stream beds collaborated to build ditches funnelling water from sources whose "riparian rights" (i.e. owning the adjoining land) were in conflict with "appropriation rights."

The introduction of hydraulic mining bringing streams of water to bear on hillsides intensified the problem. The extensive network of canals and flumes which eventually brought water a long way from its original source came to be worth more than the claims it served, but the conflicting arguments over who had a prior right to the water were never entirely solved. (As the mines petered out, however, the great agribusinesses of the state's central valleys gained the lions' share.)

Winners became losers: As easy as it was to find, the Mother Lode's gold was easier for naive young men to lose, whether to rapacious traders, or in gambling halls and bawdy-houses. But for most it was a grand adventure. Many returned home sheepishly but full of stories for their grandchildren.

California as It Is and as It May Be, Or, A Guide to the Goldfields was the title of the first book to be published in San Francisco

connected with it; some men who two years ago had not a cent in their pockets, count by thousands now…"

For most of the '49ers, life was rough, ready and expensive. Eggs from the Farallone Islands sold for $1 apiece. Real-estate speculation was epidemic. Each boatload of grinning '49ers represented another batch of customers. As the city burst from the boundaries of Yerba Buena Cove, "water lots" sold for crazy prices on the expectation they could be made habitable with landfill. They were correct: much of today's downtown San Francisco is built on landfill.

Not civic-minded: Most of California's new tenants – fixed on their golden dreams – had

(in 1849). In it author F.B. Wierzbicki wrote that the city looked like it had only been built to endure for a day, so fast had been its growth and so flimsy its construction. "The town has led the van in growth … there is nothing like it on record. From eight to ten thousand may be afloat on the streets and hundreds arrive daily; many live in shanties, many in tents and many the best way they can… The freaks of fortune are equally as remarkable in this place as everything else

Left, *Life at the Mines,* **a late 19th-century drawing. Above left, Sutter's Fort before the discovery of on-site gold. Above right, panning and posing.**

little desire to pour the foundation for the orderly society that would surely follow the Gold Rush. The popular conception was that the foothills were crammed with gold. "Ages will not exhaust the supply," Bayard Taylor wrote. In the end, the winners in the great money-scramble were those shrewd enough to take the time to sink roots by establishing businesses and buying land, taking easy advantage of the '49ers' disdain for tomorrow. Each fire, for instance, was an opportunity for the arising bourgeoisie to build new, more solid buildings.

The early arrivals made instant fortunes from merely washing the abundant nuggets out of a stream, or scraping the gold dust from easily accessible veins in the rock. It was estimated that the area was yielding as much as $50,000 worth of the precious metal each day.

But as the risks increased, the supply dried up and prices of everything skyrocketed. The real necessities of life were buckets, shovels, rockers, dippers, pans. Miners mostly lived in tents, sleeping on blankets atop pine needles, but for those who needed a roof overhead, the rental of a hut in town cost $3,000.

It wasn't long before those who serviced the prospectors grew considerably richer than most of the laboring class. Levi Strauss arrived from Germany to sell tents but ended

up turning his supply of canvas into durable trousers. In 1850 a gold digger wrote home: "You can scarcely form a conception of what a dirty business this gold digging is… A little fat pork, a cup of tea or coffee and a slice or two of miserable bread form the repast of the miners."

Paid on delivery: Women understandably were in short supply. Hundreds of prostitutes would board ships in Mexico and South America, knowing that their fares would be paid on arrival by captains selling them to the highest bidder. In his book *Madams of San Francisco*, Curt Gentry points out that although speculators tended to import large

quantities of anything saleable, sometimes the market would be glutted and the speculators out of pocket. "There was safety in the importation of women," he explained. "They might become spoiled but nobody ever found it necessary to throw one away."

Hookers, prospectors, merchants and adventurers alike – all seemed to regard San Francisco as their personal mecca. It had become a city in which unprecedented numbers of people thought they saw their future. In later years, Edwin Màrkham, comparing the city to Venice and Athens "in having strange memories" said it was unlike the other places "in being lit from within by a large and luminous hope."

When Sam Brannan, early colonizer of San Francisco, ambled down Montgomery Street with his vial of gold, the town's population had been less than 1,000. By 1850, with the madness in full swing, it was more than 30,000.

Bayard Taylor, a reporter for the *New York Tribune*, described the atmosphere as a "perpetual carnival." What he found when he returned from four months in the diggings was not the town of "tents and canvas houses with a show of frame buildings" that he had left but "an actual metropolis, displaying street after street of well-built edifice… lofty hotels, gaudy with verandahs and balconies… finished with home luxury and aristocratic restaurants presented daily their long bills of fare, rich with the choicest technicalities of Parisian cuisine."

In 1853, the Gold Rush began to wind down. Real-estate values fell 20–30 percent. Immigration slowed to a trickle and merchants were cornered by massive oversupplies ordered during the heady days when it seemed the boom would last for ever.

The men who started the Gold Rush, John Sutter and James Marshall, were only two of the many eventual losers in the great game. Marshall ended his days in 1885 near the site of his discovery, broken-down, weepy, shaking his fist at fate. Sutter, whose barony was overrun just as he had feared, kept up a brave front for some years. But history had swept him aside, too, and he died in 1880 after years of futile petitions to Congress for restitution to be made.

<u>Left</u>, Sam Brannan, an early colonizer of San Francisco. <u>Right</u>, romantic view of the Gold Rush.

None of California's new towns, much less San Francisco, were built with much care or foresight. Pre-Gold Rush street plans, based on tight grids, were expanded out from flat Yerba Buena Cove with a flick of pen on ruler, jauntily ignoring the city's hills – which is why San Francisco's streets barge up and down those hills, rather than gracefully following their contours. Most buildings were hasty wooden edifices, and between 1849 and 1851, six major fires ravaged San Francisco. Sacramento, smaller, marginally quieter, also had its share of blazes.

In San Francisco, hoodlums (a word coined in late 19th-century San Francisco) had organized themselves into gangs like the Sydney Ducks and the Hounds. At least some of the city's fires were set by these gangs, as well as routine robberies and beatings. In 1851, the forces of social stability asserted their constitutional right to "acquire, possess and defend property" by warring against the criminal elements.

The robbery and beating in early 1851 of a merchant named C.J. Jensen inflamed the righteous, especially Mormon colonizer Sam Brannan – a man who, according to historian Josiah Royce, was "always in love with shedding the blood of the wicked." Newspapers like the *Alta* brought up the specter of lynch law, and Brannan shouted that the time had come to bypass "the quibbles of the law, the insecurity of the prisons, and the laxity of those who pretend to administer justice."

A Committee of Vigilance was formed; soon a Sydney Duck named John Jenkins was hanged for stealing a safe. Within two weeks Sacramento also had its vigilante corps and other California towns followed their lead. California's first bout of vigilantism put a damper on crime only for a while.

Taxing the gamblers: Already in debt and lacking funds to keep law and order, much less provide shelter or health care for the Gold Rush newcomers, San Francisco cast around for a way to raise funds. The city came upon the idea of a steep tax on gamblers, of whom there seemed to be an unlimited supply. "Gambling saloons glittering like fairy palaces… suddenly sprang into existence, studding nearly all sides of the plaza and every street in its neighborhood," a historian recorded. "All was mad, feverish mirth where fortunes were lost and won on the green cloth in the twinkling of an eye." As much as $60,000 was bet on the turn of a card. The new license fees paid for police and the upkeep of a brig – moored at Battery

and Jackson streets – used as a city jail.

A more perfect Union: California was rushed into the Union on September 9, 1850. In November 1849, it had already formed a state government and drafted a constitution which guaranteed the right to "enjoying and defending life and liberty, acquiring, possessing and protecting property, and pursuing and obtaining happiness," a typically Californian mix of the sublime and practical.

Such dreams were not for everybody however. Soon to suffer from marginalization and racist attitudes were the Chinese, thousands of whom had poured into northern California from the gold fields after their

Preceding pages: rough and rowdy San Francisco. Left, an imposing-looking vigilante committee membership certificate. Right, a graphic re-creation of an 1856 execution.

(mostly-unappreciated) labor building the railroads had been completed. The Central Pacific alone discharged 12,000 laborers on completion of its tracks in 1870.

A major hazard in hastily-built San Francisco was fire, where most buildings were constructed of wood and cloth and where ocean winds constantly fanned the flames of wood-burning stoves and oil lamps used for heating and light. Half a dozen major conflagrations broke out in successive years, each of them destroying several blocks at a time, but each followed by sturdier rebuilding.

By 1854, with a library, churches, schools and theaters among the many substantial stone or brick buildings, and horse-drawn controversial move that aroused many critics, but it did serve its purpose in banishing from the city most of the undesirable elements. Within months it was disbanded and electors had voted in a new city government.

Whatever chance California had of becoming placid was swept away in 1859 by yet another torrent of riches flowing down the Sierra slope. This time it was silver, not gold, that geared up the rush.

The Silver Rush: One of the most comfortless outposts of the Gold Rush had been centered around Nevada's Sun Mountain on the dry eastern slope of the Sierra near Lake Tahoe. There was a little gold up in the Virginia Range, but eking a living out of the

streetcars traversing the now-tidy streets, it was becoming clear that the Gold Rush was coming to an end. Immigrants were still arriving, along with boatloads of supplies that could no longer be paid for, but shops and businesses were going bankrupt and the streets were filling with penniless and now jobless ex-miners.

Outlaw town: About the only people still sitting pretty were the gaming bosses whose money had thoroughly corrupted the city government. The gunning down of James King, a prominent editor whose *Evening Bulletin* had targeted police and the courts, brought a revival of the vigilantes. It was a area's irritating bluish clay was wicked work. In June 1859 a sample of that "blue stuff" found its way to Melville Atwood, an assayist in Grass Valley. He found an astounding $3,876 worth of silver in that sample of ore.

At first it appeared that the Silver Rush would mimic the Gold Rush of a decade earlier. "Our towns are near depleted," wrote one spectator. "They look as languid as a consumptive girl. What has become of our sinewy and athletic fellow citizens? They are coursing through ravines and over mountaintops," looking for silver.

One of the athletic young men who rushed up to the Virginia Range was Mark Twain. In his marvelous book *Roughing It*, Twain describes how he and his fellow almost-millionaires "expected to find masses of silver lying all about the ground." The problem for Twain and the thousands like him was that the silver was in, not on, the steep and rugged mountains. And getting it out was no matter of poking and panning.

The Silver Rush, it turned out, was a game for capitalists, men with the money to dig tunnels, buy claims, install the expensive machinery and mills that transformed the blue stuff into cash. They were men like William Ralston of the Bank of California in San Francisco, and the four legendary "Bonanza Kings" – James Flood and William

traded shares in San Francisco's Mining Exchange. Fortunes were made and lost in moments as rumors of bonanza or borasca (profitless rock) swept into town. At one time, more speculative money was wrapped up in Comstock mining shares than existed in real form on the whole Pacific Coast.

The Comstock lasted until the 1880s, plumping up California's economy with $400 million the Virginia Range yielded. In San Francisco, Billy Ralston, the Comstock's greatest mine owner, had taken over from Sam Brannan as the city's top booster. (Sam by this time was going broke trying to make his resort at Calistoga into "The Saratoga of the West." He died, dollarless, in 1889.)

O'Brien, former saloon-keepers; and James Fair and John W. Mackay, old miners – whose Consolidated Virginia company regularly disgorged $6 million a month.

The Comstock Lode: As usual, the treasures of the Comstock Lode (named for an old-timer who, in traditional fashion, ended up broke) flowed downslope from the boomtown of Virginia City to San Francisco. By 1863, $40 million of silver had been wrestled out of the tunnels in, around, and through Sun Mountain. Two thousand mining companies

Ralston poured his Comstock money into a myriad of grand schemes: he built the Palace, America's largest city hotel; he bought sugar refineries, lumber, stage and water companies; and as the 1860s drew to a close he prepared for what he and his fellow plutocrats thought would be the capstone to the state's greatness – the long-awaited completion of the Transcontinental Railroad.

Meanwhile, there were the clipper ships, elegant replacements for the sturdy vessels that in the days when reliability was more important than speed took six or eight months to get from Boston to San Francisco. In the year 1849, after President Polk had declared

Left, by 1860 the era of the clipper ship was over.
Above, Market Street, San Francisco, in the 1860s.

that "the abundance of gold in [California] would scarcely command belief," almost 800 ships set off on the lengthy journey from the East Coast. It was a lucrative business.

Author Richard Henry Dana, who had visited California earlier, had called its denizens "an idle thriftless people," an observation lent considerable weight by the lifestyle of so many of the rancheros who found it a simple matter to maintain and even increase their wealth. After the discovery of gold, the sudden influx of prospectors to the northern part of the state created an immense demand for beef, from which ocean-going men from other areas were able to amass big incomes.

In his novel *Two Years Before the Mast*,

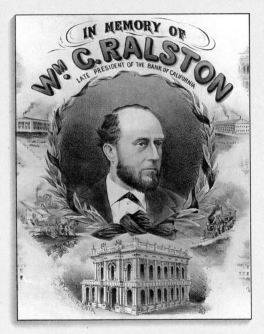

Dana describes how cattle hides and tallow in 500-lb (230-kg) bags were thrown from the cliffs to the waiting ships. Accepted as a basic unit of barter, these hides were turned into rugs, blankets, curtains, sandals, chaps and saddles. Rawhides were twisted into reatas (for roping cattle) or used to lash timbers together. Edible meat not eaten immediately was sun-dried as beef jerky, or pickled for barter with trading ships. All fat was rendered into tallow, the basis for candles and soap.

Yankee trading ships plied up and down the coast, operating like floating department stores offering mahogany furniture, gleam-ing copperware, framed mirrors, Irish linen, silk stockings, silver candlesticks and cashmere shawls. For many of the native-born these were their first amenities from the civilized world. Sometimes the trading ships which survived the precarious Straits of Magellan would stay an entire year, working up and down the coast.

Curious Customs: A genteel contraband soon developed. To reduce import taxes, ships worked in pairs to transfer cargo from one to the other on the open seas. The partially-emptied ship would then make port and submit to a Customs check. With duties paid, it would rejoin its consort and reverse the transfer. Sometimes the Yankee traders unloaded cargoes in lonely coves where it was eventually smuggled ashore. Traders and buyers were happy with this arrangement.

But starting with Donald McKay's *Flying Cloud* in 1851, a trim, fast clipper could make such a journey around Cape Horn in 90 days – and pay for itself in the freight charges on a single run. Within a dozen years, 50 steamers out of San Francisco were carrying passengers and freight both up and down the coast and as far away as China and Australia.

"When this bay comes into our possession," Secretary of State John C. Calhoun had predicted in 1844, "there will spring up the great rival of New York." Before the end of the century San Francisco's port, with its easy access to Arctic waters, was to become the whaling capital of the world.

Concurrent with the development of clippers – and by 1860 their era was over – was the growth of the overland stage. Spurred mostly by the need to deliver the mails, it was financed initially by regional postmasters. For a brief period, the glamour of the Pony Express (relays of boy jockeys, unarmed, dodging Indian ambushes) captured the public imagination, but the intervening Civil War also brought the telegraph system and sending $5 letters lost favor. It was to be another half-century before, on January 25, 1915, a month before the Panama Pacific International Exposition opened, San Francisco's Thomas Watson received the very first transcontinental phone call – from Alexander Graham Bell himself.

Left, city booster Billy Ralston made his fortune from the Silver Rush. **Right**, the westward expansion continues.

EMIGRATION TO
CALIFORNIA !

Do you want to go to California? If so, go and join the Company who intend going out the middle of March, or 1st of April next, under the charge of the California Emigration Society, in a first-rate Clipper Ship. The Society agreeing to find places for all those who wish it upon their arrival in San Francisco. The voyage will probably be made in a few months.— Price of passage will be in the vicinity of

ONE HUNDRED DOLLARS !
CHILDREN IN PROPORTION.

A number of families have already engaged passage. A suitable Female Nurse has been provided, who will take charge of Young Ladies and Children. Good Physicians, both male and female go in the Ship. It is hoped a large number of females will go, as Females are getting almost as good wages as males.

FEMALE NURSES get 25 dollars per week and board. SCHOOL TEACHERS 100 dollars per month. GARDNERS 60 dollars per month and board. LABORERS 4 to 5 dollars per day. BRICKLAYERS 6 dollars per day. HOUSEKEEPERS 40 dollars per month. FARMERS 5 dollars per day. SHOEMAKERS 4 dollars per day. Men and Women COOKS 40 to 60 dollars per month and board. MINERS are making from 3 to 12 dollars per day. FEMALE SERVANTS 30 to 50 dollars per month and board. Washing 3 dollars per dozen. MASONS 6 dollars per day. CARPENTERS 5 dollars per day. ENGINEERS 100 dollars per month, and as the quartz Crushing Mills are getting into operation all through the country, Engineers are very scarce. BLACKSMITHS 90 and 100 dollars per month and board.

The above prices are copied from late papers printed in San Francisco, which can be seen at my office. Having views of some 30 Cities throughout the State of California, I shall be happy to see all who will call at the office of the Society, 28 JOY'S BUILDING, WASHINGTON ST., BOSTON, and examine them. Parties residing out of the City, by enclosing a stamp and sending to the office, will receive a circular giving all the particulars of the voyage.

As Agents are wanted in every town and city of the New England States, Postmasters or Merchants acting as such will be allowed a certain commission on every person they get to join the Company. Good reference required. For further particulars correspond or call at the

SOCIETY'S OFFICE,
28 Joy's Building, Washington St., Boston, Mass.

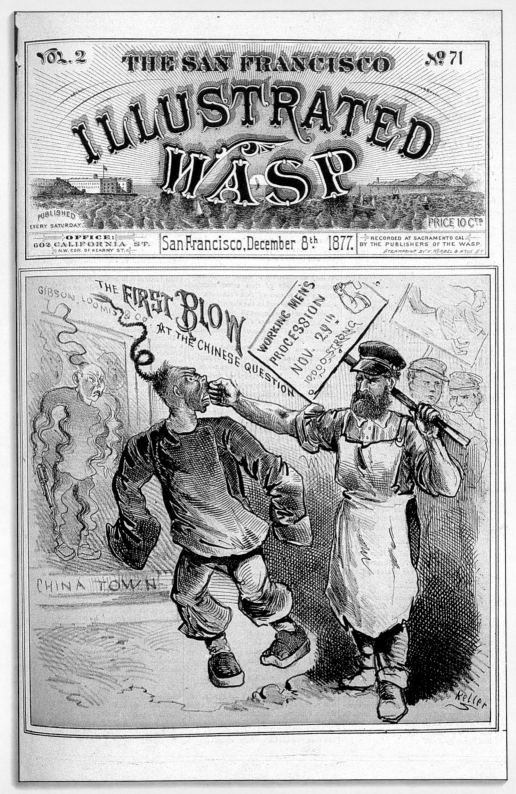

The rush for gold had added a new urgency for contact between the east and west coasts. In addition to those in search of gold itself were hundreds who sought to become part of the boom by shipping supplies and, although regional railroads were an actuality, transcontinental lines were still in the future. It was not until 1853 that the Federal government allocated funds for the study of feasible routes, with California's gold boom making the state a top contender for the terminus over previously favored Oregon.

Plans for a railroad linking the coasts had been floating around for many years. When the Civil War broke out, Congress, intent upon securing California's place in the Union, at last stirred itself. In the winter of 1862, the Pacific Railroad Act granted vast tracts of Western land, low-interest financing and outright subsidies to two companies – the Central Pacific, building from Sacramento, and the Union Pacific, building from the Midwest, specifically Omaha, Nabraska. As it happened, the Civil War largely bypassed California, and the West, but it nonetheless prompted the building of a railroad that brought unexpected havoc to the residents of the state.

On the right track: In his widely read book *Progress and Poverty*, Henry George, a journeyman printer and passionate theorist, had warned that the increasing dominance of the railroads would prove to be a mixed blessing. He predicted that California's immature factories would be undersold by the Eastern manufacturing colossus and that the Central Pacific's ownership of vast parcels of land along its right-of-way would drive prices of much-needed farming land shamefully high.

George even saw the racial tensions that would result from the railroad's importation of thousands of Chinese laborers. "Crocker's Pets," as they were called, flooded the state's job market in the 1870s and became targets for bitter discontent.

George's prophecies began to come true

with the arrival of the first train. In San Francisco, real-estate dealings of $3.5 million a month fell to $1.5 million a month within a year. "California's initial enthusiasm soon gave way to distrust and dislike… an echo of the national conviction that the railroads were responsible for most of the country's economic ills," was the assessment of historian John W. Caughey in his book *California*. "The railroad became a monster, the Octopus. It was a target for criticisms by all those made discontented and bitter by the hard

times of the seventies."

The genius of the Central Pacific was a young engineer named Theodore Dehone Judah, who had built California's first railroad, the 22-mile (35-km) Sacramento Valley line, in 1856. He spent years crafting the crucial route across the Sierra at Donner Pass. Unfortunately for Judah, the Central Pacific's other partners were uncommonly cunning and greedy men.

Charles Crocker, Mark Hopkins, Collis Huntington and Leland Stanford, who became known as "The Big Four," had been lured West by the Gold Rush. They were Sacramento shopkeepers when they invested in Judah's scheme. Shortly after Congress dumped its largesse in their laps, they forced Judah out of the Central Pacific. He died, at the age of 37, in 1863, still trying to wrest control from his former partners.

The Central Pacific made the Big Four almost insanely rich. The government's haste to get the railroad built, and Stanford's political maneuvering, made the Central Pacific the virtual dictator of California politics for years. Between them the railroad barons raised private investment, earned government subsidies, acquired bargain-priced land, imported cheap "coolie" labor from China and by their exploitative and monopolist practices made themselves multi-million-

pus in 1901, no one had to guess at the reference: the Southern Pacific (as it was renamed in 1884) had its greedy tentacles in every corner of the state.

In the beginning, at least, carping at the Big Four's use of the railroad's treasury as a kind of private money preserve was a game for malcontents and socialists. In the mahogany boardrooms of San Francisco's banks, on the editorial pages of its newspapers, in the overheated stock exchange, up and down Montgomery Street, the verdict was the same. The railroad would bring firm and fabulous prosperity to California.

In April 1868, five years after construction had begun on Sacramento's Front Street, the

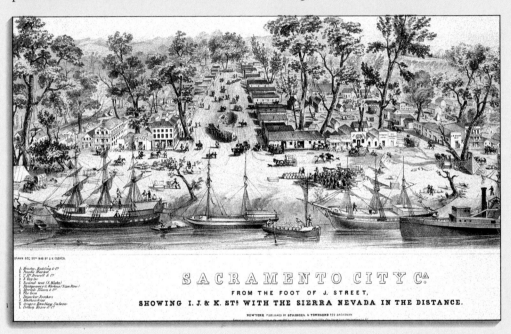

SACRAMENTO CITY C.ᴬ
FROM THE FOOT OF J. STREET,
SHOWING I. J. & K. STˢ WITH THE SIERRA NEVADA IN THE DISTANCE.

aires. In 1869 the Union Pacific and the Central Pacific met for a "joining of the rails" at Promontory, Utah, and in 1876 the Southern Pacific line connected San Francisco and Los Angeles.

Bribed politicians: As the biggest landowners and biggest employers the immensely rich railroad barons were able to manipulate freight rates, control water supplies, keep hundreds of thousands of productive land for themselves and with their wealth subvert politicians and municipalities. It was many years before state regulation of the railroads became the norm rather than the other way around. When Frank Norris wrote *The Octo-*

first Central Pacific train breached the Sierra at Donner Pass. On May 12, 1869, the Golden Spike was driven at Promontory Point, Utah, and the coasts were linked. "San Francisco Annexes the Union" read one San Francisco headline. But the rush of prosperity failed utterly to materialize. Only a few deep thinkers – none of them ensconced in boardrooms – had understood the financial calamity the railroad would bring.

In the winter of 1869–70 a severe drought crippled the state's agriculture. Between 1873 and 1875 more than 250,000 immigrants came to California. Many were factory workers and few could find work. The "Terrible

70s" had arrived, which certainly for William Chapman Ralston were a calamity. As head of the Bank of California in San Francisco, he had presided over the endless boom mentality that was a legacy of the Gold Rush, but by the mid-1870s the full bloom of depression was on the state. On "Black Friday," April 26, 1875, a run on the Bank of California forced it to slam shut its huge oaken doors at Sansome and California streets. Driven into debt by Comstock mining losses and by the failure of the railroad to bring prosperity, Bill Ralston drowned the next day while taking his customary swim in the Bay.

The boom ends: Ralston's death signalled the end of California's booming affluence.

many Hispanics left the Sierra Nevada mines to take up residence in large American cities. This new urban movement, coupled with the friction over gold rights and ranches, spawned a period of "Hispanophobia," a brand of virulent racism exacerbated as Mexican bandits gained notoriety.

Among the most famous *banditos* was Tiburcio Vasquez. Although he became something of a Robin Hood-type folk hero to his Mexican countrymen, this was more a commentary on the state of relations between Mexicans and Americans than a tribute to Vasquez. He had a long career as a cattle rustler and stagecoach robber. Eventually lawmen captured him in Los Angeles in

Those hurt most by the great shrinkage of capital in the 1870s were the state's working people. During the gold and silver booms California's laborers had enjoyed a rare freedom to move easily from job to job and to dictate working conditions. Now, however, with massive unemployment, unionization began to take hold. For the next 60 years, California would suffer recurrent bouts of labor strife.

As the gold and silver rushes wound down,

Left, although Sacramento was the state capital, San Francisco received all the glory. **Above**, Chinese laborers built much of the railroad.

1876 and convicted him of a murder near Tres Pinos, a small community east of Salinas, for which he was hanged.

The depression was slow to disappear, but California was too rich to suffer permanently. In the next few decades it slowly built up its industrial strength to the point where it could compete with the East. After decades of depending on the land to deliver riches in the form of gold or silver, the state developed its agricultural lands as never before. In the Central Valley, wheat, rice and cotton became major cash crops, and California's cattle herds grew from 262,000 to more than 3 million. Towns like Stockton, San Jose and

Monterey were thriving as '49ers set up their shops and sank their roots. In the late 1870s, the splendid Napa Valley began to produce wines in earnest.

From 1860 to 1880, despite the depression, Northern California's population expanded at its greatest rate until the middle 1900s. The six Bay Area counties (San Francisco, Marin, San Mateo, Contra Costa, Alameda and Santa Clara) grew from 84,000 to 350,000. Though San Francisco accounted for most of that growth, the neighboring cities of Oakland (the terminus of the Transcontinental Railroad), Berkeley and San Jose were growing apace.

The Central Valley's population doubled

in those years, as did the population of Napa and Sonoma counties. The rise of agriculture was responsible for the creation of new inland towns like Redding (an artifact of the Big Four) and Modesto (originally to be named for Billy Ralston; when he declined the honor, the town was named instead for his modesty.)

Increasing population and the emerging middle class gave rise to the massive building program of Northern California's trademark Victorian homes. Beautiful redwood houses were erected all over the North, but the decade-long building boom almost transformed San Francisco, with suburbs springing up in all directions. The city's steady expansion from its historic center at Yerba Buena Cove required new ways to be found to transport people from one area to another.

In 1873 an Englishman named Andrew Hallidie unveiled the first of his ingenious cable cars. By 1906, the date of the San Francisco earthquake, 600 cars rolled over 115 miles (185 km) of track. But overhead wires strung up to power a fleet of more modern electric trolleys hastened the demise of cable cars. Today, the system has 30 cars and a mere 10 miles (16 km) of track.

Among the more successful mineowners had been George Hearst, who poured some of his millions into a newspaper, the *San Francisco Chronicle*. In 1887, he turned the paper over to his son, William Randolph, thus initiating what became the largest publishing empire the world had known to date. By the time of his death in 1951, William Randolph Hearst had extended his empire to more than a score of daily papers (including two New York papers and two Chicago papers), 14 US magazines and two British magazines, 11 radio stations and five news services employing a total of 38,000 people. As well as presiding over the magnificent estate known as San Simeon (*see page 203*), Hearst served two terms as congressman for California, but was beaten in his runs for governor, mayor and president. Today he is remembered as the prototype for Orson Welles's *Citizen Kane*.

Insane but beautiful: Since 1854, California's capital had been in Sacramento but it was San Francisco that presided over a rapidly settling, coalescing state. San Francisco's boomtown mentality may have taken a beating, but as the century drew to a close, its historic predilection for high living remained. Author Rudyard Kipling, visiting during the Gilded Age at the end of the century called it "a mad city, inhabited for the most part by perfectly insane people whose women are of a remarkable beauty." Its society had "a captivating rush and whirl. Recklessness is in the air."

The Gilded Age, with all its extravagance and corruption, continued right up to an April morning in 1906, after which nothing was ever the same again.

Left, the seal of the city. **Right**, San Francisco's society had "a captivating rush and whirl."

Long before the new century San Francisco had become California's most prosperous center, a city of 27,000 buildings, a place whose 1,700 architects were perfecting the "tall, narrow rowhouse with vertical lines and a false front to make the house look more imposing," as noted in a book by the city archivist. These characteristically Victorian and Queen Anne-style homes, or those that survived the 1906 fire, still predominate in at least half a dozen neighborhoods today.

A geologist, Andrew Lawson, had discovered and named the San Andreas Fault a dozen years previously, yet, despite two earthquakes in the 1890s, there had been very little notice taken. When the Big One arrived in 1906, there had been scant warning except for the strange nervousness of dogs and horses on the previous evening.

An earthquake measuring 8.25 on the Richter Scale preceded the fire that shook Northern Californians from their beds at 5.12am on Wednesday, April 18 When the San Andreas Fault lurched that morning it sent terrifying jolts through an area 210 miles (338 km) long and 30 miles (48 km) wide, from San Juan Bautista in the south to Fort Bragg in the north. Other towns like San Jose and Point Reyes Station near Drake's Bay suffered more from the initial shock than San Francisco. Church bells jangled chaotically, dishes fell, windows shattered, dogs barked, Enrico Caruso (appearing locally in *Carmen*) was scared voiceless, and San Francisco's new City Hall crumbled. In 48 seconds it was all over. The city lay in ruins.

No prior warning: The subsequent fire destroyed 28,000 buildings over more than 4 sq. miles (7 sq. km). It killed 315 people; the bodies of 352 more were never found. The city had experienced many earthquakes before but none on this scale. Because it housed over 40 percent of the state's population (it is now less than 4 percent), the effect was cataclysmic. There had been no prior warning of, or preparations for, this major upheaval. Only an unearthly low rumble preceded fissures opening up and spreading wavelike across the city.

With its alarm system destroyed, the Fire Department lacked coordination. When the brigades did arrive they found mangled mains lacking any water supply. The situation was worst in the area south of Market Street where expert demolition work might have prevented the fire from spreading. Experts were lacking, and improvisations by the commandant of the Presidio, Brigadier General Frederick Funston, who had leaped in unauthorized to fill the gap in authority served only to destroy scores of beautiful Victorian mansions along Van Ness Avenue and to spread the fire still further.

Hundreds were dead or still trapped in smoking ruins, 500 city blocks were leveled and a handful of people had been shot or bayoneted by Funston's inexperienced militia who had poured into the streets to keep order and prevent looting. Golden Gate Park became the home of as many as 300,000 people for at least the next few weeks. Cooking inside the tents was banned, sanitation was rudimentary, water was in short supply and rats (and the threat of the bubonic plague) a lingering menace.

Fighting back: But there was a will to recover. A Committee of Forty on the Reconstruction of San Francisco was formed to define the tasks to be done and A.P. Giannini's tiny Bank of Italy, making loans to small businesses intent on rebuilding, was at the forefront of those reviving the city's fortunes. The bank was later to become the Bank of America, the country's largest.

Aid poured in from all over the world, $8 million worth within weeks. Even the much-reviled Southern Pacific Railroad pitched in generously, freighting in supplies without charge, offering free passage out of the city and putting heavy equipment and cranes to work on clearing the debris.

"While the ruins were still smoking on top of a heap of collapsed walls," wrote the photographer Arnold Genthe, "a sign would announce: 'On this site will be erected a six-storey office building to be ready for occupancy in the fall'."

San Francisco's renaissance was inevita-

Preceding pages: the aftermath of the 1906 earthquake. **Left**, the Panama Pacific Exposition, held in San Francisco in 1915.

ble. The new, improved, taller buildings of Montgomery Street, the Wall Street of the West, were needed to process all the money churned out by the state's industries, farms and banks. The Port of San Francisco was still one of the world's busiest harbors. San Francisco's historic business of making business was unstoppable.

In 1911 San Francisco elected a new mayor, James "Sunny Jim" Rolph, a purveyor of goodwill whose reign encompassed some of the city's giddiest times. The 1915 Panama Pacific International Exposition, which occupied 600 acres (240 hectares) of reclaimed land in what is now the marina, is still considered one of the greatest of the world's fairs.

open, 19 million visitors came to marvel at the latest fashions and inventions. The distant war in Europe had few repercussions in the Bay City beyond boosting industry, manufacturing and mining, with a consequent steep drop in local employment when World War I finally came to an end.

Major labor troubles typified the Depression years and those which followed, culminating in the General Strike of 1934 when the International Longshoremen's Union immobilized traffic in the port. During one demonstration, two strikers were killed and 100 people – police and strikers – were injured.

In 1933, the year that Alcatraz island became the site of what was for 30 years to be

Today only one vestige remains: the Palace of Fine Arts, intended by its architect, Bernard Maybeck, to impart a certain "sadness modified by the feeling that beauty has a soothing influence." It was saved from gradual decay by civic benefactors in the 1960s.

Two events in successive years held great significance for San Francisco: the first was the opening of the Panama Canal in 1914, which cut days off the ocean route from the east while making the long journey around Cape Horn obsolete. Then, on January 25, 1915, the Panama Pacific International Exposition opened in the city.

During the year that the exposition was

America's most famous prison, ground was broken for the Golden Gate Bridge, although it wasn't dedicated until four years later, six months after the even longer (4½-mile/7-km) Bay Bridge joined San Francisco to Oakland. Two years later, the city celebrated the opening with the Golden Gate International Exposition, attended by 17 million.

The bridge, more than any other single structure, created the city's romantic image. "To pass through the portals of the Golden Gate," wrote Allan Dunn, "is to cross the threshold of adventure." And Gene Fowler asserted: "Every man should be allowed to love two cities; his own and San Francisco."

It is not surprising that the founders of the United Nations came here in 1945 after World War II was over, for their first conference.

But even with the thousands of new workers to staff the wartime factories and the bustling port, as well as numbers of servicemen who had remained behind when the war was over, the city's population was still only 700,000 – less than half that of its rival 450 miles (730 km) to the south.

In the summer of 1920, San Francisco's population of 508,000 was surpassed for the first time by Los Angeles, initiating a furious jealousy that still exists. The southern portion of the state was "the world's closest approach to bedlam and babel," sneered

George Creel, with columnist Westbrook Pegler urging that it "be declared incompetent and placed in charge of a guardian."

During the 1930s, troubles broke out in the great central valleys of the state which, with ample supplies of water for irrigation combined with skilful techniques developed by the new agribusiness barons, were bidding to feed the world. The workers, mostly Mexican and Filipino and long exploited by brutal bosses, staged spontaneous strikes which were met not with an improvement in their

Left, the Golden Gate Bridge was dedicated in 1937. **Above**, a cartoonist ponders the next quake.

condition but by arrests under the oppressive Criminal Syndicalism Act. But sending strikers to jail merely served to anger the others, and more strikes followed.

Gradually, with the sympathy of writers such as Carey McWilliams, who documented the story in *Factories in the Field,* and John Steinbeck, whose subsequent best-seller *The Grapes of Wrath* became a popular movie, public outrage grew. Steinbeck wrote of the "curious attitude" towards a group necessary for the success of the state's agriculture and yet who were greeted with "this hatred of the stranger [that] occurs in the whole range of human history" as if they were dirty, diseased and ignorant.

And yet, he wrote, most were "small farmers who had lost their farms or farmhands who have lived with the family in the old American way... They are resourceful and intelligent Americans who have gone through the hell of the drought, have seen their lands wither and die and the top soil blown away, and this to a man who has owned his land is a curious and terrible pain."

Many of the migrants, of course, were the famous Okies, about 400,000 of them from Oklahoma or neighboring states in the midwestern "dustbelt." As a result of his campaign to help them (after a short-lived attempt by the state to turn them back), Cary McWilliams was appointed to head a Division of Immigration and Housing. The mandated improvements to some of the labor camps cost the growers almost $1 million; it is unsurprising that they reacted with a PR campaign to discredit both authors and introduced into the state legislature a bill to abolish McWilliams' department.

Some of the fall-out carried over into opposition to the campaign of another "muckraking" author, Upton Sinclair, whose 1934 End Poverty in California (EPIC) campaign was successfully savaged by a rightwing coalition that included the *Los Angeles Times'* Harry Chandler, rival publisher William Randolph Hearst, Texas oilmen, and MGM's Louis B. Mayer who joined other movie tycoons in churning out fake newsreels attacking this "Moscow agent." Responding to the studios' threat to move to Florida if he was elected governor, Sinclair pointed out that they couldn't have moved if they'd wanted to because their investment in California was much too large.

World War II gave a tremendous boost to California's aircraft industry which increased statewide from under 10,000 to more than 300,000. When the war was over, a gradual shift in the industry's workers from mainly blue-collar laborers to scientists and technicians meant, as historian Bruce Henstell wrote, that "aeronautics was replaced by something called aerospace."

The war had plunged California into a spasm of activity. Twenty-three million tons of war supplies and 1½ million men and women passed through the Golden Gate during the war's 46 months. The ports of San Francisco, Sausalito, Oakland, Vallejo and Alameda were busy around the clock building and repairing ships, and loading supplies for the war machine.

In the Bay Area alone, the federal government spent $3 billion on shipbuilding. A dramatic new wave of immigration swept into the region as new factories needed new workers – 100,000 at the Kaiser Yards in Richmond, 90,000 more at Sausalito. Within two years of America's entry into the war the number of wage earners in San Francisco almost tripled. The federal government doled out $83 million in contracts to the California Institute of Technology (Cal Tech) alone.

War aids economy: Even though 750,000 Californians left for military service, the state's wage earners in California increased by nearly a million in the first half of the decade. After the war, the great suburban sprawl got underway as war workers and their families settled down to enjoy post-war prosperity. Nevertheless, the war had a tremendous impact on the local economy – "as great as any event since the Gold Rush," wrote historian Oscar Lewis.

And even before the war, San Francisco, with its obvious ties to Oriental ports, had begun to harbor a large component of immigrants. At least 110,000 *Nisei* (second-generation Japanese) had been unfairly rounded up and sent to detention camps in the xeno-

Protest is part of Californian life. Preceding pages: logging is the issue of the 1990s. Left, against everything in the '80s. Right, Caesar Chavez, celebrated Hispanic activist of the '70s.

phobic early days after Pearl Harbor. Although accused of no crime, they lived behind barbed wire and under military guard. Americans of Japanese heritage were estimated to have lost $365 million in property from having to sell their homes at under market prices at this time.

Immigrants were not limited to the Japanese. In the first 30 years of the 20th century, nearly 10 percent of the population of Mexico migrated to the southwestern United States, with Texas and California receiving the larg-

est share. In California, their numbers went from 8,000 to 370,000, with most of them recruited to harvest cotton, cantaloupe and lettuce crops. Working the fields until the harvest was over and then returning across the border to their families, the migrants' transient status often rendered them a semi-homeless community.

Eventually settling in Northern and Southern California *barrios*, (communities), where cheap rentals were available but where there were no zoning requirements – no sewers, no paved roadways or street lighting – they would often succumb to illnesses such as tuberculosis. The late Hispanic activist Cacsar Chavez, well-known leader in the 1970s of the United Farmer Workers Union, lived in such a *barrio* in Santa Clara country just 50 miles (80 km) south of San Francisco. During the 1940s, "enforced rotation" of migrant workers and the mass deportation of unemployed aliens was suggested. Nevertheless, immigrants continued to pour into the state.

Freedom: As a new, almost instant society, California has always felt free to experiment. Many of its newcomers, from the "Anglo hordes" of the 1840s to Gold Rush adventurers to the geniuses of Silicon Valley today (*see page 101*), have come to the state to escape the burdens of conformity else-

declaimers and pavement philosophers who became known as the beatniks.

Led by writers Allen Ginsberg and Jack Kerouac and supported by Lawrence Ferlinghetti of North Beach's City Lights Bookstore, the Beats exemplified a life style centered around poetry readings, marijuana and dropping out of the mainstream. This was a potently attractive lifestyle which came to have wide appeal, and soon brought a stream of youthful admirers to the coffee houses and taverns of North Beach and, in the following decade, to the streets of the Haight-Ashbury district.

In the 1950s the Beats seemed titillating and somehow significant, a tempting combi-

where. The great majority of Californians have always been settled and, to one degree or another, God-fearing. But the anti-conformists – the colorful, sometimes crazy minority – have given California its name for verve and drive.

In the 1950s and 1960s, according to author Mike Davis, Los Angeles became "the capital of youth" but it was in San Francisco that the first stirrings of post-war protest and florid eccentricity were most acutely felt. While the American nation was settled into a prosperous torpor, the city's historically Italian North Beach area became the haunt of a loosely defined group of poets, writers,

nation for the nation's press, who ogled at their rambling poetry readings, sniffed at the light marijuana breezes drifting out of the North Beach coffee houses, and wondered if civilization could stand such a limpid assault. The beatniks, it seems, mostly wanted America to go away. But it wouldn't, of course, and before long "Beat" had become a fashion and North Beach had transformed itself into a tourist attraction.

The Beats, though, had struck a nerve of dissatisfaction and alienation in America. Though it was never a coherent movement, it produced juice-stirring works like Allen Ginsberg's *Howl* and Jack Kerouac's *On the*

Road. That inspired alienation gave rise to two parallel, dissimilar, but oddly congruent movements: the angry politics of the New Left and the woozy love fest of the hippies.

Watering them down: The first great protest of the protest-rich 1960s took place in San Francisco in the decade's first year. In mid-May, the House Un-American Activities Committee opened a series of hearings in City Hall. When hundreds of demonstrators met the committee in the rotunda, the police reacted furiously, turning water hoses and billy clubs on the formerly peaceful crowds. Dozens of battered protesters were carted off to jail, but the angry shouts in City Hall about police brutality made international headlines.

and purposes, with the writers and protesters clustered around Max Scherr's *Berkeley Barb*, one of America's five earliest "underground" papers. Scherr, a bearded radical who had previously operated a bar called Steppenwolf, took to the streets himself to sell his paper which, at its peak, reached a circulation of 100,000 – an astonishingly high figure for a newspaper that was largely put together by a group of amateurs in a crowded kitchen.

Stimulated by the burgeoning rock music scene and steered by underground newspapers, thousands of gaudily dressed hippies descended on Golden Gate Park the first day of January 1966, to celebrate what was termed

Over on the Berkeley campus of the University of California, the locus of dissent was the Free Speech Movement, which kept up a steady assault against racism, materialism and what the students regarded as the stifling effects of the "multiversity" itself, and its aid, support and encouragement to the Vietnam war machine.

Anti-war protests, which eventually spread around the world, began here, for all intents

a Be-In. Among those who addressed the 100,000-strong gathering were Ginsberg, psychedelic drug guru Tim Leary ("Turn On, Tune In, Drop Out"), Mario Savo and other representatives of the Free Speech Movement from Berkeley, plus a daredevil parachutist who droppped from the clouds into the center of the gathering.

The resultant publicity made Haight-Ashbury irresistible to disaffected kids from all over the globe, substantial numbers of whom began to clog San Francisco's streets, with predictable results. The euphoria was short-lived, and within a year it was all over, with begging, drug-dealing and exploitation

The 1950s were personified by the Beats. Far left, Jack Kerouac. Left, Allen Ginsberg. Above, Janis Joplin performs in the Polo Fields, Golden Gate Park, in 1967, during the Summer of Love.

by greedy landlords the most notable side effects. It was from the Haight-Ashbury district that the notorious mass-murderer Charles Manson recruited some of his most earnest disciples.

The movement reached its apogee in 1967's celebrated "Summer of Love," when the days and nights were filled with sex, drugs and a pot-laced breeze, and music was provided by Janis Joplin, Jimi Hendrix, Jefferson Airplane and the Grateful Dead – all of them living in Haight-Ashbury at the time.

At first, San Francisco was amused by the hippies. But as altogether too many sons and daughters of respected citizens took to marijuana-induced meandering, as the LSD hys-

Gay abandon: No one knows the exact number of gay people living in the city, although officials speculate endlessly. Current estimates suggest that there are at least 100,000, or almost one in seven of the total population of San Francisco. The sprawling Castro district houses many well-heeled professionals; bohemians congregate in SoMa (South of Market); young transients poured into tight jeans hustle on Polk Street and in the Tenderloin district, while an affluent pocket of three-piece-suited gay business executives can be found in very, very proper Pacific Heights.

For years, the city has had gay and lesbian supervisors, police officers, congressional

teria took flight, sympathy began to evaporate. Sometimes the legacy of political activism created bizarre mutations, like the Symbionese Liberation Army, which kidnapped William Randolph Hearst's granddaughter Patricia in 1974.

Nevertheless, the hippie movement and the New Left helped to change the American lifestyle, especially in San Francisco, whose heterogeneous population – 46 percent white, 29 percent Asian, 14 percent Hispanic, 11 percent black – is generally regarded as being more tolerant than that of other cities. Nowhere is this more visible than in San Francisco's loud, proud gay community.

aides and bureaucrats, as well as judges on the Municipal Court. These are hard-won battles, however. In 1978, former Supervisor Dan White, the city's most anti-gay politician, gunned down Supervisor Harvey Milk and Mayor George Moscone in City Hall. The moderate prison sentence imposed on White (five years only) sparked off the massive gay "White Night" riots which gained worldwide headlines and contributed substantially to San Francisco's image as a bastion of liberalism.

Its tolerant outlook, relative prosperity and beautiful setting make San Francisco a highly desirable city in which to live. When *San*

Francisco Chronicle columnist Alice Kahn wrote in the early 1980s about Young Urban Professionals, coining the acronym "Yuppies," she was describing perfectly the ideal San Francisco resident.

Into the future: Californians have at last started to take a look at their relentless exploitation of the environment, and developers still pit their wits and legal expertise against the environmentalists. Yet these "eco-freaks" now have a vocal constituency. The Sierra Club has become caretaker of the wilderness; the Coastal Commission reviews all construction near the coastline; and all plans for major construction must be preceded by a federal environment impact re-

have fought long and hard against "Manhattanization." In the always-independent northern counties such as Mendocino, Sonoma, Humboldt and Del Norte, the "tree-huggers" (as their lumber industry opponents disparagingly termed them) began to escalate their battles to save the redwoods from what had become mass harvesting.

Their numbers were swelled by a tide of "immigrants" from San Francisco and the southern part of the state, all seeking a hideaway in what for centuries had been a peaceful wildnerness.

Although the center of the state's power has moved south towards Los Angeles, California in general is on the leading edge of the

port. Nuclear power plants at San Onofre and Mount Diablo (near San Francisco) also have strict legal controls. New voices are not only speaking; they are being heard.

The northern part of the state is the center of the state's ecology movement, not only the Sierra Club, but also Friends of the Earth and the whale-savers of the Greenpeace Foundation. Towns such as Petaluma have passed no-growth ordinances and San Franciscans

Left, in the 1980s San Francisco was home to the first yuppies and the largest gay parades. **Above**, ecology and back-to-basics living are themes to take Northern Californians into the next century.

future. With the high technology of nearby Silicon Valley and San Francisco's acknowledged lead in such emerging developments as Virtual Reality, Northern California is definitely a significant player. Simultaneously it shares with the rest of the state a fascination and involvement with consciousness expansion, Eastern philosophy and exploring new lifestyles.

New Yorkers sometimes scornfully claim to be too busy *living* their lives to have time to think about how to improve them. But are the lifestyles that Californians are currently trying to improve necessarily the lifestyles that others will choose to embrace?

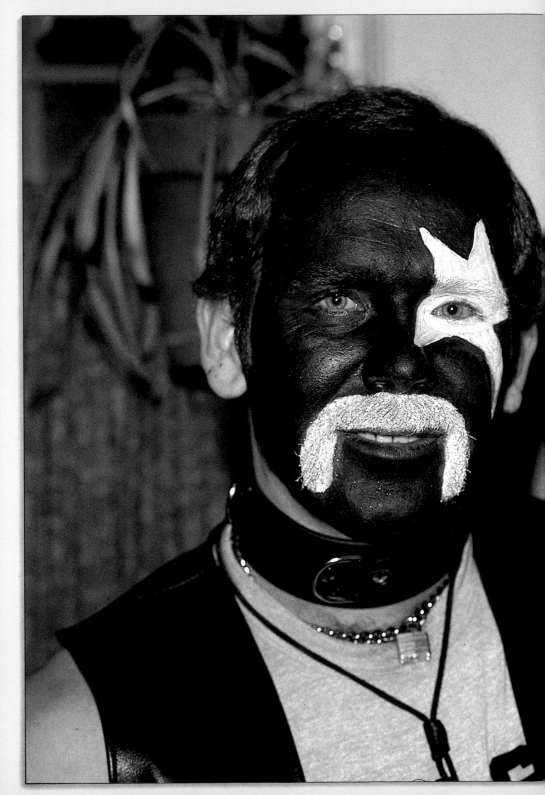

California, the third largest state in the union, ranks highest in number of inhabitants but perhaps what is less appreciated is that no other part of America can claim such an ethnically diverse population. In at least one school district, for example, the pupils speak a total of over 90 different languages.

From the onset of the industrialized era, the state's population has been melded by boom cycles of immigration: Mexicans, Anglos from the Midwest, the Chinese and Japanese, African Americans from the South, Russians, Armenians, Asian Indians, Koreans, Salvadorans, Iranians, Filipinos, Samoans, Vietnamese. Almost half a century ago historian Carey McWilliams was already referring to southern California as an "archipelago of social and ethnic islands, economically interrelated but culturally disparate."

When California joined the Union in 1850, it was considered to be the final frontier, a land promising spiritual and social riches. Pioneers armed with little more than faith came in search of sunshine, fertile soil, and freedom from oppression. Like the grape vines and citrus trees, the people could bloom under the gentle sun. Boosters furiously sold the fable of the Golden State to the rest of the union, a dream that more than a century later has yet to lose its tenacious hold on the imagination.

Mixing began early: The miscegenation of cultures had an early start two centuries ago when Spanish Franciscan monks arrived to set up a string of missions throughout the state spreading a Catholic hand across the souls of the heathen indigenous peoples. In 1834, the state having passed from Spanish to Mexican rule, a proclamation was issued providing for the secularization of the missions.

Before the end of the century, the American Indian population had been decimated and their offspring, the Mestizos, found themselves pushed southward by an influx of miners flooding the foothills of the Sierra Nevada mountain range. The development and growth of California's industries throughout the 19th century brought a tide of immigration. The Chinese initially came as railroad workers on the Central Pacific construction gangs before branching into agriculture and fishing. African Americans also came as railroad employees, in smaller numbers at first and then, during World War II, to fill manufacturing and service jobs. And

towards the turn of the century, Japanese immigrants arrived in search of opportunities in the produce industry, which they eventually came to dominate.

By 1851 there were 25,000 Chinese working in California mines, the majority of them settling later in San Francisco. These Chinese fortune seekers shared a common dream that *Gum San*, the Gold Mountain, would provide them healthy fortunes with which they could return home and rejoin their anxious families. The first Chinese men to come to San Francisco and Northern California during the Gold Rush were called "coolies" – workers willing to do hard labor for signifi-

Preceding pages. cultural diversity in California as represented by the Oakland Women's Rowing Club, gays painted to thrill, and performance artists posing for a portrait. <u>Left</u>, Yurok Indian salmon festival in Klamath. <u>Right</u>, a Mexican Aztec dancer.

cantly lower wages than whites. This term came from the Chinese phrase *ku li*, meaning "bitter strength."

Wherever new gold strikes were made, Chinese workers formed communities. In San Francisco they lived in crude, segregated barracks in a section called Chinatown, which provided goods and services, often at significantly cheaper prices than those of their white competitors, to both the Chinese and non-Chinese population. Space was precious. San Francisco landlords added on verandas and makeshift back rooms to already dilapidated wooden buildings. The community began to grow, and thrive.

In the 1860s, as the Gold Rush was dying

out, so many Chinese miners got jobs on the railroads – at half the pay of whites – that eventually they formed 90 percent of the Central Pacific's workforce. One newspaper of the time reported that 20,000 lbs (9,000 kg) of bones were collected from shallow graves along the tracks where Chinese workers had died. The bones were sent home to China for burial.

Chinese labor filled many jobs until various exclusion laws forced them out, after which other Asians began take their place. Anti-Chinese sentiment became widespread late in the century, and resulted in such violent events as one in 1869 in which a

Chinese crab fisherman in San Francisco was branded with a hot iron. By 1900 Japanese immigrants were underbidding Chinese in the canneries.

From 1890 to 1940 the Chinese both locally and throughout the United States faced harsh discrimination. Laws were created which prohibited them from marrying non-Asians, becoming citizens, holding skilled jobs and owning property. When San Francisco's immigration station on Angel Island was opened in 1910, it had separate facilities for Asians. Conditions were similar to prisons of the day with new arrivals subjected to humiliating physical examinations and long months of waiting without any idea of whether they would be allowed to enter the city. Many Asians in fact, primarily Chinese and Japanese, were turned back and had to board ships for the long journey home.

The number of Japanese in the United States increased fourfold to 25,000 between 1900 and 1910 with many of these Japanese immigrants settling in the San Francisco area. While some fought during World War II on the side of the United States and against their mother country, thousands here at home were detained in concentration camps. Reparations from the US government forty years later did little to erase the bitter memories, but went a long way in securing a permanent place for the Japanese in American culture. Today, roughly 12,000 Japanese now live in the city, most concentrated in the area called Japantown.

The Philippines had been under the American flag since the end of the Spanish-American War and many Filipinos came to the US without restriction in the 1920s to work on California farms. Revised immigration laws in 1952 brought another wave of Filipino immigration and recent census figures show Filipinos to be among the city's fastest-growing "Asian-Pacific" immigrant groups.

Now, following a wave of Koreans – many in possession of enough capital to start businesses – refugees from Kampuchea, Vietnam and Laos are settling in San Francisco in record numbers

Enter the Okies: Nothing, however, compared to the tidal wave of Anglos from the Midwest during the 1880s (and then again – fleeing the parched dustbowl farms of the prairies – in the 1920s). First they established major colonies around the San Francisco and Sacramento areas and then spread southwards with visions of manifest destiny.

But destiny's capricious nature has a habit of throwing a dash of irony into the stew. During the 1980s, hundreds of thousands of Mexicans and Central Americans fleeing civil strife and political persecution immigrated, both legally and illegally, to California. By the year 2020 – some say sooner – it is estimated the number of Latinos in California will surpass that of Anglos, becoming once again the majority ethnic group.

The mix has understandably had significant political implications. More than at any time in the history of the state, multiculturalism is beginning to be reflected in the as most other ethnic communities – tend to be ·more spread out, making voting blocs more difficult).

Nevertheless, although Latinos in California are heavily involved in community activism, they are vastly under-represented politically, one reason being that the number of Latinos who are citizens, and therefore capable of voting, is much smaller than the actual population. For many years, the only notable Hispanic leader was the late César Chavez, the widely admired president of the United Farm Workers of America who gained fame during the early 1970s for his battle to gain decent working conditions for the mostly Mexican farm laborers.

offices of elected and appointed officials: mayors and congressional representatives, city council members and police chiefs. As a consequence of lawsuits brought by such groups as the Mexican American Legal Defense and Education Fund and the American Civil Liberties Union in the past decade, districts have been reshaped to give African Americans and Latinos a chance to elect representatives of their communities. (Asian-American populations in California – as well

Left, Asian acrobatics. **Above**, Cathy Lee, the last descendant of a notable Chinese family in the north.

San Francisco is the nation's 13th largest city, with a population of about 725,000, fit snugly into 47 sq. miles (120 sq. km). According to the 1990 census, 46 percent of the city's population are white, 29 percent Asian (more than half of which are Chinese), 14 percent Hispanic, and 11 percent black.

Black power: It is African Americans who have probably had the most success with forming community and political organizations. Groups ranging from the Black Panthers (which originated in Oakland) to Recycling Black Dollars have made great strides in forwarding black causes. But California's African-American population has been declining in the past few years with a consequent stagnation in their political progress. With notable exceptions, most of the influential African-American politicians were elected in the fervor of the civil rights movement of the 1960s and '70s.

Some non-whites have become police chiefs around the state, with a commitment to revamping police departments with long histories of repression of and blatant racism towards minorities. They are transforming the relationship between law-enforcement departments and the public by installing community-based policing programs – taking cops out of the isolation of police cars and putting them on foot patrol, where they can

tion in 1860, and by 1863 the campaign had been successful.

Following World War II the tremendous influx of blacks from the South into the Bay Area to work in shipyards and defense industries during the war helped to create a housing shortage in San Francisco. Today, the black population of San Francisco has dropped to 76,000, with most of the departed moving to the suburbs that have begun to push the Bay Area's outer limits into the San Joaquin Valley, the wine regions of Sonoma and Napa counties, and south from San Jose and the Peninsula.

Regrettable racist past: Although a historically progressive state, California has had its

better interact with the local people.

Thousands of free blacks were among the '49ers who made their way to California in search of instant riches. One such black pioneer, J.B. Sanderson, became famous for starting schools in San Francisco for poor Indian, Asian and black children who were barred from public schools. He had to teach in these schools until replacements could be found. In the city, black settlers took action to secure their civil rights. A "Franchise League" was formed to campaign for the repeal of a law forbidding blacks the right to testify in trials involving whites. Five hundred white San Franciscans signed the peti-

ignominious periods of violent racism, including the October 1871 riot in LA when a mob of Anglos lynched 19 innocent Chinese and beat dozens of others. Early in World War II the notorious Executive Order 9066 authorized the internment of all Japanese on the West Coast – most of whom lost everything they owned. It was during that same decade that African Americans who escaped the repression of the Deep South found that they themselves were barred from living in certain neighborhoods by restrictive housing covenants.

As a result, clusters of ethnic communities formed where people could be protected and cultures preserved – San Francisco's famous Chinatown being one such example. Now considered a charming tourist attraction, Chinatown developed out of necessity as a refuge from abuse: until the 1960s when immigration laws changed, the Chinese had been subjected to severe and continual harassment and discriminatory legislation had deprived them of eligibility for citizenship, ensuring that they had no legal recourse.

In California's sprawling metropolitan areas, many without any recognizable center, it has often been the churches and temples that have served as the nexus of a community – spiritually, socially and politically. It is perhaps the necessity of asserting one's iden-

Multi-culturalism in California is a fact, not something to be argued by theorists. Ideas, language, art – these are generated from the streets, by the co-mingling of people's needs and desires. Rap music, for example, has been linked to the malaise that occurred after the Watts rebellion in 1965. Assembled from the shards of the uprising, the Watts art renaissance delivered up a number of visionaries, including a group called the Watts Prophets who performed the spoken word. Theirs was the poetry of frustration, self-assertion and, unlike some contemporary rap, hope. Graffiti art also arrived on the heels of disenfranchisement.

"Tagging" (initialing) property provided

tity in this Babel-like sea of cultures that has made California the state in which more trends and artistic movements take flight. East-coast pundits have long joked about California's lack of culture. To be sure, it is a culture without a face – without *one* face, anyway. It is as much a refined performance of *Swan Lake* at San Francisco's War Memorial Opera House as a *barrio* mural spray-painted by teenaged graffiti artists.

Left, a Vietnamese immigrant harvests pickles near Gilroy; elderly man in Chinatown's Stockton Street, San Francisco. **Above**, a father with his adopted son; black power on the prowl.

inner-city teens – primarily Latino – with a voice that the larger culture refused to hear. Today, rap's impact on the media and advertising has been palpable. And Anglo kids from conservative areas, infatuated with the image of defiance, have been known to don "gangsta wear," the cartoonishly oversized, fall-down clothing of gangmembers, rappers and taggers.

Leaning towards the exotic Far East (or West, depending on one's point of view), California inevitably adopted the customs of Asian immigrants. Health-conscious Californians submit to strenuous programs of yoga and meditation. Beat Generation writers, who tumbled around San Francisco in the '50s, derived much of their inspiration from Buddhism and Japanese and Chinese poetry.

The experience of facing society as "other" in California has produced some of America's finest writers and artists of the last half-century, including playwright William Saroyan, who grew up in an Armenian enclave of grape-growers and farmers in Fresno; poet and novelist Alice Walker, best known for *The Color Purple*; essayist Richard Rodriguez, who writes about gay and Latino assimilation and the politics of multi-culturalism; Filipino-born artist Manuel Ocampo, whose paintings often depict symbols of racism and brutish imperialism; theater

artist Anna Deavere Smith, whose performance piece *Twilight: Los Angeles, 1992* concerned the riots that devastated the city, told through the voices of the people who experienced it; and novelist Amy Tan, who found the characters of her acclaimed *Joy Luck Club* in the Chinatown (San Francisco) of her childhood.

Musical break: Music has often provided the best opportunity for people of color to bring their talent to the wider world. This is especially true of African Americans, from jazz-musician Charles Mingus playing his bass in the bars of LA's Central Avenue to Michael Jackson's sell-out performances at 100,000-seat arenas. One of the most remarkable signs of the times, not only in music but in a larger cultural context, has been the high ratings radio stations have achieved by playing contemporary *ranchera* and *banda* music, the Spanish equivalent of country and western.

Of course, nothing brought more focus to California than the film and TV industry. Its history, however, is notoriously unvariegated. With notable exceptions, few non-Anglos have been given the chance to produce or direct their ideas. Hopefully, young filmmakers like John Singleton, writer-director of the highly successful *Boyz N the Hood,* will make it easier for artists of diverse backgrounds to find outlets for their work.

In the past few years, Californians have set upon the concept of multi-culturalism like a pitbull to the mailman's pantleg, arguing about its meaning in stores, educational institutions, businesses and government. Around the state, celebrations honoring California's multi-ethnicity have cheered their way into the streets in the hopes that unity and goodwill would abound. Oakland's three-day mulitcultural Festival at the Lake in June, for example, is followed almost immediately by San Francisco's Ethnic Dance Festival with its dazzling array of dance, music, costume and tradition from 40 countries. The annual Ramona Pageant in Hemet, a performance based on the 1884 best-selling novel by Helen Hunt Jackson, boasts a cast of 350 and a slightly romanticized version of California's mission era. Jackson's *Ramona* is a story about an Indian sheepherder, Alessandro, and his half-breed wife, Ramona – about the ruin of their lives by Anglo cruelty and greed.

Mingling of styles: What has become more and more evident, though, is that the people of California have slowly amalgamated each other's habits and styles, epicures and mannerisms. While most California towns and suburbs do tend to stay relatively homogeneous, pockets of cultures border one another, stiched by the colorful religions and customs of its people. California is hip-hop and cha-cha wrapped in a gold-flecked sari.

California epitomizes the best and worst of what being a truly multi-ethnic society can mean. There are some, like San Jose State University professor Shelby Steele, who believe that the obsession with tribalism is a leading factor in causing the sometimes bitter divisiveness throughout the state; viewing others always through the prism of your culture deepens the trenches and hinders society's gains. It's the cult of "other."

Critics of this argument say that recognition of California's many ethnic groups is the first step towards peaceful coexistence. Promoting minorities to meaningful positions in public policy – whether it be through affirmative action or some nebulous sense of political correctness – will eventually mitigate the issue.

Today, politicians and economists have once again latched onto the issue of immigration, blaming illegal aliens for Califor-

areas as the former Yugoslavia. What is evident, however, is not that the hope for multi-culturalism is withering, but that it is being realized.

At the very least from an economical standpoint, many business and political leaders are making a concerted effort to adapt to California's quickly shifting landscape. Neighborhoods that had previously been abandoned after the flight of the whites are now being targeted for revitalization according to the new communities they serve.

California urban theorists like Mike Davis, author of *City of Quartz: Excavating the Future in Los Angeles*, have proposed the idea of neighborhood planning councils in

nia's staggering debt. Even in liberal San Francisco, where law enforcement is prohibited from reporting illegal aliens to the Immigration and Naturalization Services (INS), there's been an uproar about the growing number of Central Americans standing on street corners attempting to get hired out for menial work.

It has been suggested by the media that California is becoming dangerously Balkanized, that the cities especially are starting to resemble such racially and ethnically driven

Left, black is beautiful. **Above**, a multi-ethnic college band plays at a football match in Berkeley.

order to give responsibility to the many ethnic populations that are not adequately represented. The basic premise is that a rotating group of representatives elected from each neighborhood would convene on issues concerning their community – including revitalization, law enforcement and public safety, business development, education, health, and arts programs. They would then meet with their city council member or county supervisor. Bringing an additional level of representation to the local citizens might help to render impotent the power-breaking restructuring of districts. Maybe this, at least in California, is the future of democracy.

Bohemian might not be the most precise word to describe the lifestyle of a large number of Northern Californians. A real description, too long even for a bumper sticker, would be more like: Don't Tread On Me–Get Off My Back–Leave Me Alone–The Less Government the Better–Tree Hugging–Whale Preserving–Support the Hemp Initiative folk.

Local papers in the region are filled with battle cries for everything from legalizing marijuana for medical purposes and encouraging the growth of hemp (from which marijuana is derived) to making paper and garments, to supporting such causes as the Wild Horse Sanctuary which was set up to rescue these endangered animals from their decimation by greedy ranchers.

In *Cash Crop*, one of his numerous books about the region, Ray Raphael theorizes that "geographical isolation has considerable bearing on lifestyle and to such settlers the very concept of a civil authority seemed to have little relevance. An illegal activity in this context was seen as no special sin, as long as it didn't harm anyone. This concept of 'legality' derives directly from the logic of survival not from arbitrary edicts issued from afar. Herein lies the essence of rural anarchy, the rugged individualism and frontier spirit which goes right to the heart of the mythic American West."

Ecology is of course the major concern of Northern California's activists, and involvement is widespread: as many as 70 groups to be found in the region around Mount Diablo, northeast of San Francisco Bay, where one-third of the readers' letters to local papers concern the environment.

Walnut Creek's Stephen Barbata says: "There is still an optimism here that we can, in fact, take care of our community – a healthy attitude given the cynicism that is so pervasive in the nation and the state…" Tens of thousands turn out for the local Earth Day celebrations whose coordinator, Harvey Green, aims to get everybody working to-

gether. "The end goal," he says, "is to get business and environmentalists to talk to each other and understand they have a mutual interest in a sound, clean and healthy environment."

The further north one goes, however, the more problematical this becomes. In Humboldt County, which begins about 150 miles (240 km) north of San Francisco and runs up to the Oregon border, thousands owe their jobs to the logging industry whose appetite, opponents say, is insatiable and

which has little sentiment for the old-growth redwood trees.

Forest strippers: As old as the Christian era and topping 300 feet (90 meters) or more, many redwoods have been acquired by the state but most of the rest are privately owned – almost 200,000 acres (80,000 hectares) by the giant Pacific Lumber Company alone. The company is accused of stripping the forests at an ever-increasing rate to pay off the $660 million worth of junk bonds with which the company was acquired. Originally there were 2 million acres (800,000 hectares) of redwoods between Monterey and southern Oregon. Today, after 130 years of

Preceding pages, homesteaders at home in Northern California. **Left**, the drive-thru tree near the activist town of Garberville. **Right**, new bohemian.

logging, over 96 percent of the coastal redwood ecosystem has been destroyed.

Palco, the friendly patronym with which the company styles itself, has been the key target of environmentalists whose legal maneuvers have succeeded in blocking logging – however temporarily – on thousands of acres. The lumber company's chief executive officer, Charles Hurwitz, said about the protesters: "I clearly underestimated what would happen." But the environmental group EPIC (Environmental Protection Information Center) plays rough. EPIC's director Charles Powell says: "People are touched by these forests; many of them feel they are the embodiment of God's wonder."

Nor is it just trees that are in jeopardy. In addition to the famed spotted owl, the state's Fish & Game Department has listed the marbled murrelet (a black, brown and white speckled coastal seabird) as an endangered species. Its numbers have dropped from 60,000 a century ago to less than 9,000 today. Similarly, the coho salmon has been reduced by 90 percent or more in the past half century, and along the Klamath River, beside whose banks live 3,000 members of the Yurok tribe, there are worries about pollution from herbicide spraying. Referring to a growing number of cancer victims, Yurok building contractor Lawrence O'Rourke blames the lumber industry, calling their policies "genocide."

Greed for gold: Not, of course, that this is a new story. A tribal scholar wrote 80 years ago, in the introduction to a book, *To the American Indian*: "With every day the unrelenting subjugation of the faith, values, mores and traditions of the old Yurok society progressed. The old ones watched as the Earth was literally being flushed into the river by the white man in his frenetic search for gold. One can only imagine the impact on their psyches."

The bellicose EPIC, whose largely volunteer staff has filed 18 lawsuits challenging corporate timber practices and negligent government oversight, promotes statewide forestry reform and has helped draft legislation for federal acquisition of unprotected redwood groves. Its headquarters are in the tiny town of Garberville, which more than anywhere outside Berkeley, could be termed "a hotbed of environmental activism."

With a population of barely more than 1,000, Garberville boasts two weekly newspapers and such innovative businesses as Alternative Energy Engineering ("making electricity from solar, wind and water") which ships its products – solar panels, wind turbines, composting toilets – around the world.

Garberville is at the apex of the "Emerald Triangle" (southern Humboldt and Trinity and northern Mendocino counties), the prime growing areas for sinsemilla, the finest marijuana. District attorney Terry Farmer says Garberville was for a while a "town right out of the Wild West."

High Times magazine reported that in one year alone law officers spent more than $2 million and employed 600 people to uproot and destroy 150,000 marijuana plants in the state, two-thirds of them in Humboldt County. Until it was amended, a law allowed confiscation of land on which marijuana was found growing, but locals sometimes thwarted this by refusing to bid at auctions where the land was offered for sale.

On the edge of the redwood forests at Leggett, John Stahl, a printer and papermaker who may be the first American since World War II allowed to legally grow hemp (*see page 291*) founded The Church of the Living Tree. "Timber companies want you to think they are felling trees to build houses and fine furniture," he says, "but the sad truth is that ever-greater percentages of timber harvests are just being chipped up for the pulp mills so that our mail boxes can be stuffed with junk mail. Trees literally hold the Earth together, their roots extending sometimes hundreds of feet into the earth's crust pulling up minerals, nutrients and water from below as well as sheltering the ground surface from above so that animals and smaller plants and even people can develop a habitat supported by the trees. It is not surprising to me that Northern California is beginning to dry up. When the trees are gone, the earth can no longer hold onto the water."

Lively legislator: Further down US Highway 101, about two hours' drive south of

Joseph Pulitzer: "A newspaper should have no friends."

Ukiah is the site of the Annual Great Russian River Cleanup (22 miles/35 km between Ukiah and Hopland) which brings out hundreds of volunteers. At its first gathering, its people pulled 200 old tires from the river.

Mendocino, the county south of Humboldt, is at least as environmentally active as its northern neighbor. Tree-hugging is popular here, too – more than 100 people were arrested for trying to block logging of a large tract near Albion – but an even greater concern might be summarized as "Don't Carmelize Mendocino" – a reference to "the high-priced aura of commercial-quaint and

Palco's company town of Scotia, is Ukiah, where the sawmill employs 110 workers and pumps $100,000 a day into the local economy. A thorn in the side of just about every kind of authority is Bruce Anderson, the intimidatingly feisty editor of the *Anderson Valley Advertiser*, a tiny hamlet west of Ukiah. "Fanning the Flames of Discontent... Peace to the Cottages, War on the Palaces!" the paper clamors just below its masthead and, emphasizing its independence, a quote from

Left, a law officer with confiscated marijuana. **Above**, looking down on Garberville, once described as a "town right out of the Wild West."

celebrity-chic" displayed by the popular tourist town on the Monterey Peninsula. (Seattle residents express similar sentiments with a bumper sticker reading: *Don't Californicate Washington State*.)

It was Juan Rodriguez Cabrillo who first sighted the cape in 1542. He named it after his patron, Mexican viceroy Antonio de Mendoza, although he didn't disembark. Walt Whitman sang about it in *Leaves of Grass* – "the virgin land, land of the Western shore."

Mendocino began as a logging town shipping redwood to San Francisco's Gold-Rush building boom. Long before the highway was built, the little port had three fancy hotels, 21 rowdy saloons and several whorehouses. After the mill shut down in 1931 the population ebbed away, only to boom again with a 1960s wave of counter-cultural dropouts ranging from Haight-Ashbury hippies to doctors and lawyers.

Most of the century-old structures were still standing and, in inimitable NIMBY ("not in my backyard") style, its newer residents wondered how they could reconcile their dislike of visitors with the obvious benefits of tourism.

Tourists versus trade: It is a dilemma familiar to many of its Northern California neighbors. In Marin County's Mill Valley, tourists spend over $250 million every year, enough

Journalist Mark Dowie packed up years ago, relocating upstate to Inverness, where he finds himself fighting the same anti-tourism battle. Dowie, an investigative reporter and president of the Environmental Action Committee, thinks ideal visitors would be ones with a better appreciation of the "ecology and aesthetic" of the area. "We don't want to build an infrastructure for people to come out and shop. If that's snotty, then I'm snotty. Sausalito was ruined by that."

He's critical, too, of mainstream environmentalists whom he sees as too polite, a movement run by Washington power elites in what he terms a "gentlemanly" fashion.

Together, the Golden Gate National Rec-

to employ 4,000 people in related jobs. Towns such as Sausalito and Tiburon try to discourage tourists, whereas more isolated places such as San Rafael put out glossy brochures to try and lure them in.

One year Sausalito – 60 percent of whose budget comes from tourism – even planned to display a tourist map with Bridgeway (the street of souvenir shops, T-shirts stalls and art galleries bordering the bay) prominently listed, but omitting mention of the parallel street, Caledonia, which is zoned for local stores. The media, of course, wasted no time in making fun of the Street With No Name, and called the idea elitist.

reation Area and the Point Reyes National Seashore region attract 4½ million visitors a year. This figure is estimated to increase by 50 percent before the end of the decade. Dowie and his 12,000 neighbors scattered through West Marin feel outnumbered. Tiny Stinson Beach attracts 800,000 visitors per year in itself, with traffic jams sometimes 10 miles long (16 km) on the narrow highway over the mountains.

Stolen signposts: Bolinas, a tiny village on a dead-end road at the seashore's southern end, is notorious for its disdain toward strangers. At last count, the California highway signs pointing to the town have been stolen

38 times, presumably by what a local paper refers to as "the clandestine Bolinas Border Patrol." It is also assumed that it was the patrol's more militant members who threw eggs at a visiting tourist, an incident that drew a prompt apology from the West Marin Chamber of Commerce. A local farmer William Weber said it showed how hostile Bolinas could be to visitors. "They expect people to be tolerant of them," he said, "but they won't tolerate anyone different from them." And Dave Sobel, owner of the local bakery, added: "My thinking is in order to save paradise, you've got to share it. If people are going to vote for open space and preservation they've got to feel welcome

lawsuits and organizing appeals to politicians to stop Caltrans from spraying herbicides to control weeds along Highway 1. In the end they won. "We respond to the public; when the public speaks we listen," deadpanned a Caltrans spokesman.

Planners are top dogs: Marin, the first county over the bridge from San Francisco, is filled with affluent – and usually independent-minded – activists whose views sometimes clash. Mill Valley's planning director Don Dickenson who describes his town as a bohemian village that contains lots of artists and writers who like to hide away in the woods says it's the planners who make the decisions. "The architects have lots of dreams

(but) it's a fine line between promoting tourism and providing visitor services."

One of the small town's activists, Paul Kayfetz, concentrates on internal affairs, leading a team of people who monitor the activities of developers and meetings of school and public utility boards in an effort to slow growth and have the community control its own destiny instead of being overrun.

Meanwhile, the West Marin Environmental group MOW was spending 11 years filing

Left, Mendocino homesteaders teach their children at home. **Above**, lumber companies are accused of stripping the forests.

that are never accomplished because the planners affect the public policy and what actually occurs." Neon is banned in the town, and signs are restricted in size. "We spend a lot more time here on real petty issues, but that's the kind of town that Mill Valley is," Dickenson explains.

Back in Bolinas, however, minds were on weightier matters. A recent reader of the *Coastal Post* called upon "all Patriots to… institute a massive impeachment, recall or voting campaign to kick out of office all congresspeople and senators, except those who have shown their worth."

That's the spirit.

Among the adventurers lured by tales of fabulous easy-to-find riches who poured into Northern California from the middle of the last century onwards was many an intrepid writer. Not only the itinerant newshound who was always in search of a story (and personal advancement) but the stars of the literary profession, too – talents such as Oscar Wilde, Hans Christian Andersen, Robert Louis Stevenson and Bret Harte.

Some, like Mark Twain, liked it so much they got jobs and stayed awhile; others, of which Jack London was the best known, were native sons who explored the world and kept coming back home. But all left their indelible mark helping to spread universally news of a Golden State whose riches were not only found under the ground.

The hot center: San Francisco, of course, became the mecca – a city that has always held an attraction for writers and has spawned more than a few of its own. Even today, in the neo-Beat cafes of the Mission District and North Beach, you can hear poets spouting their rhythmic verse to local hipsters at open-mike readings. With its jumble of ethnic neighborhoods spilling over into one another the city is alive with languages and cultures. It's a welcoming and romantic literary breeding ground, offering the golden promise of the West.

A bronze plaque in San Francisco's Burritt Alley, just off Union Square reads. "ON APPROXIMATELY THIS SPOT, MILES ARCHER, PARTNER OF SAM SPADE, WAS DONE IN BY BRIGID O'SHAUGHNESSY." The memorial doesn't mention the classic detective story *The Maltese Falcon* or even its author. But leaving the alley and walking toward Powell Street, the mystery is solved as you pass "Dashiell Hammett Street" on the right. It is one of a dozen alleys that in 1988 were renamed, at the suggestion of the celebrated City Lights Bookstore, after prominent writers and artists who lived in the city. They could have added dozens more.

Born near Baltimore in 1894, Dashiell

Hammett – his French mother was named De Chell – dropped out of high school at 14 to help support his family, and shortly after joined the Pinkerton Detective Agency, a five-year experience that provided raw material for the shady characters of his subsequent fiction. In 1921, Hammett moved to San Francisco to marry Josephine Dolan who had nursed him during the tuberculosis that was the legacy of his army days. The couple had planned to return East but they stayed on with Hammett spending his days

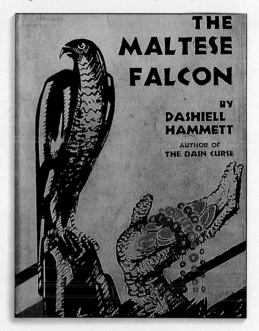

writing advertising copy for Samuels Jewelers at 865 Market (still in business), and by night producing the detective fiction that redefined the American mystery story.

In such hard-boiled novels as *Red Harvest* and *The Dain Curse*, he created an inforgettable character in Sam Spade, the cynical gumshoe always disappearing into a foggy San Francisco night. Aficionados of *The Maltese Falcon* can still stop in at John's Grill, at 63 Ellis (between Powell and Stockton streets), one of the stops on historian Don Herrold's occasional tours of Hammett sites. Established in 1908 and with a second floor Maltese Falcon Dining Room filled with

Preceding pages, Cafe Vesuvio and Jack Kerouac Street. **Left**, City Lights bookstore. **Right**, an early edition by a local hero.

Hammett memorabilia, it is one of the only two restaurants mentioned in the novel that is still operating.

Mark Twain's dream: "San Francisco is a truly fascinating city to live in… The climate is pleasanter when read about than personally experienced," wrote Mark Twain in his 1871 memoir, *Roughing It*. Twain (born Samuel Clemens) arrived from Missouri in 1861, following his brother Orion, a newly appointed secretary to the governor of the Nevada territory. Samuel dreamed of striking it rich in the gold mines but turned to writing humor and travel pieces for Virginia City's *Territorial Enterprise* newspaper, and fast became a celebrity throughout the West.

Other Gold Rush literary figures include Ambrose Bierce, author of the flawlessly cynical *Devil's Dictionary* – "A person who talks when you want him to listen," is how the fierce Bierce defined "bore" – and Bret Harte, who befriended Twain. Both were contributors to the *Golden Era* but Harte was the most popular and best-paid Western writer of his day. In 1870, while living on Monroe Street (on a block where Dashiell Hammett rented a room half a century later), Harte was earning $10,000 a year from the *Atlantic Monthly*, which contained a story of his in just about every issue.

Bierce, famous for his brilliant short stories about the Civil War, was perhaps Ameri-

From 1864 he covered the police, fire, and theater beats for San Francisco's *Morning Call* before writing lampoons and commentaries for the *Golden Era*, the *Chronicle*, and then the *Sacramento Union*. Clemens changed his name while in San Francisco and, as Mark Twain, received international acclaim for his first short story: *The Celebrated Jumping Frog of Calaveras County*. Based on the tale of the miner who added leadshot to a frog's lunch before a contest, the story is honored every spring in the town of Angels Camp where it supposedly took place. Present-day Annie Street (off Market near 3rd) was earlier named after Twain.

ca's first columnist. His Sunday column "Prattles," in William Randolph Hearst's *Examiner*, skewered any and all forms of pomposity with an intensity that earned him the nickname Bitter Bierce. He kept ranting on about corrupt politicians (this was a century ago) and suggesting that they would doubtless enrich themselves in the aftermath of a major earthquake. The iconoclastic philosopher Bierce turned war correspondent in 1913 and went to Mexico to cover bandit Pancho Villa. He was never heard from again; some say he was shot.

The Scots novelist Robert Louis Stevenson is commemorated by the Silverado Museum near Calistoga in the Napa Valley, the scene of his honeymoon in 1880 and where he recuperated from tuberculosis. He's also honored by several monuments in San Francisco to which he traveled from his native Scotland in pursuit of Fanny Osbourne, a married woman he had met and wooed in France. Trying unsuccessfully to support himself with his writing, he spent several impoverished months living in a rented room at 608 Bush Street, waiting for Mrs Osbourne's divorce to be finalized. Stevenson didn't write his major works until after his return to Scotland but a monument in Chinatown's Portsmouth Square depicts the galleon *Hispaniola* which was featured in

adventure he came back to Oakland. Returning from the Klondike with scurvy, he began to write about his experiences on the rugged Alaskan frontier. After immediate success, he continued writing in this vein, producing a slew of best-selling novels such as *The Call of the Wild* (1903) and *The Sea Wolf* (1904) in which he features the Hyde Street Pier.

Jack London Square, as Oakland's waterfront plaza was renamed in 1951, boasts Heinhold's First and Last Chance Saloon, an actual haunt from the two-fisted novelist's own era, where supposedly, he sealed the purchase of his first sloop. London and his wife Charmain eventually moved north to a ranch in Glen Ellen, in Sonoma's wine coun-

his classic pirate novel *Treasure Island*.

Born at the corner of Brannan and Third streets in 1876 as the illegitimate son of an astrologer and a medium, Jack London grew up across the water on the Oakland waterfront. He bought a sloop, the *Razzle Dazzle*, when he was 14 and became an oyster pirate along the shoals of the San Francisco Bay. "Drifting along from job to job," he wrote, "I looked on the world and called it good, every bit of it."

London traveled everywhere, but after each

Left, San Francisco reading list. **Above**, Jack London's Oakland saloon.

try. At the then-incredible cost of $70,000, London built Wolf House only to see it burn down the night before they were about to move in. Since 1959, the ranch has been open to the public as Jack London State Historic Park.

Second in popularity to London early in the century was Chicago-born Frank Norris, who had turned his year of study in Paris to good advantage by selling a precocious story set in medieval France to the *Overland Monthly* while still a student at Berkeley. In his short life – he died aged 42 in 1902 – he produced six novels of which the best known, *The Octopus*, concerns the bullying and ac-

MR SAN FRANCISCO

I t was the *New York Mirror's* Walter Winchell who invented the so-called "three-dot" style of journalism once ubiquitous in American newspapers, but for a generation Herb Caen has been its most famous practitioner. For thousands of San Franciscans, his column is the first thing they read each day and when he shifted from the *San Francisco Chronicle* to the rival *Examiner* (and back again in 1958) tens of thousands of fans are said to have moved with him.

Although Caen maintains he still doesn't know what makes a good item, others have pinpointed "his outstanding ability to take a

wisp of fog, a chance phrase overheard in an elevator, a happy child on a cable car" as major ingredients. Caen says he owes some of his style to an early news editor who admonished him to "be entertaining" because he was easily bored and had "a very short attention span."

He defines a great column as "twenty-four short, snappy items" which can be as varied as an offhand comment about a landmark city building infiltrating its elevators with recorded music, to somebody's recollection of a woman gushing to T.S. Eliot in London about what a wonderful party they were attending and the poet's rejoinder: "Yes, if you can see the essential horror of it." One of his judgments that made the quotation books is: "The trou-

ble with born-again Christians is that they are an even bigger pain the second time around."

Answering one of his critics who accused him of writing "the same column every day" about a city that had died long ago, Caen remarked, "That's accurate. But I'm trapped in this persona I've created... this late version of a Walter Winchell spin-off... it just keeps going along."

Born in Sacramento in 1916, he wrote his first column, "Raisin' Caen," for the student paper while at high school and, apart from his 3½-year stint in the army, has churned out five columns a week for more than half a century. He still types on an old Royal typewriter and usually answers his own telephone, leaving an assistant to deal with the hundreds of weekly tips that pour in from an army of faithful readers and fans.

He strings around 1,000 words together daily with such subheads as "Bay City Beat" or "Caenfetti." His half-century spent documenting the minutiae of what he once termed "Baghdad by the Bay" not only makes him San Francisco's supreme chronicler but also gives his opinions a sort of timeless credence. Comparing *The New Yorker*, under its new editor Tina Brown, with the older version, for example, he remarked offhandedly that he had been a subscriber since 1936 – two years before he began his *Chronicle* column – and added about the glitzier magazine, "There's a hole in there where a soul used to be."

Interviewing him almost a decade ago, magazine writer Ken Kelley observed that in no other American city does a columnist wield such great influence anymore. Caen feels that he didn't get noticed "until I started writing these sort of love poems to San Francisco. I hadn't realized the depth of narcissism in this city... I got this huge reaction to either my bad poetry about the fog coming in through the Golden Gate or the old San Francisco stuff which I used to dig out of old books and papers... To this day people aren't that crazy about the gossip or the political stuff – they like the sentimental stuff the best... (especially) this 'old San Francisco stuff.' Part of it is synthetic after all. Nostalgia is a bad reporter." Caen's nostalgia columns appear in the paper's Sunday edition.

When defining today's typical San Francisco resident, Caen said that it would most likely be somebody who lives in Novato (a neighboring suburb) "or somewhere he can afford the rent. A typical San Franciscan is either an old guy like me who can afford to go on living here or some kids who double or triple up in some place where the rents haven't gone out of sight." ∎

quisitive tactics of the Southern Pacific Railroad against the San Joaquin wheat farmers whose land they virtually stole.

Although Gertrude Stein was born in Allegheny, New York in 1874, the Steins moved west to Oakland in 1880, living for some time on a hilltop farm she later recalled in her 1925 book *The Making of Americans*. After studying at Radcliffe and Harvard she went to Paris.

Stein remained an ex-patriate for years but with her companion Alice B. Toklas revisited the city in 1934 during a US lecture tour, meeting with William Saroyan while staying in style at the Mark Hopkins Hotel. She is still remembered in Oakland, not always

plays, among them *The Iceman Cometh* and *Long Day's Journey Into Night*. He died in Boston in 1953 but Tao House remains.

Twenty miles (32 km) north, at Martinez, is the John Muir house where the Scottish-born conservationist wrote most of his seminal works late in the last century. Muir, whom most regard as the first environmentalist, had been a wealthy fruit rancher before deciding to remind Americans of the importance of the wilderness.

In Monterey, John Steinbeck, Pulitzer Prize-winning author of *The Grapes of Wrath*, brought fame in the 1940s to the sardine fisherfolk with *Cannery Row* while, further down cliff-hugging Highway 1 at Big Sur,

fondly, for disparaging her home town – ("there is no *there* there") – in her 1937 memoir, *Everybody's Autobiography*, but the city, perhaps relishing this distinctive notoriety, endorses the annual event every February 3 that celebrates her birthday.

In the 1930s, just after winning the Nobel Prize, playwright Eugene O'Neill built a home, Tao House, at Danville in the San Ramona Valley, and lived there with his actress wife Carlotta Monterey. It was here O'Neill wrote some of his most famous

Left, columnist Herb Caen. **Above**, Jack London (left) and John Steinbeck.

Henry Miller had set up house after writing all those dirty books in Paris: the green-jacketed Olympic Press novels that until the 1960s Americans had to smuggle in from Tijuana. Miller died in 1980, but near to his old home his friend Emil White set up the Henry Miller Memorial Library to honor the most influential writer of his time.

In the mid-1950s, the writing emerging from the cafes of North Beach commanded national and international attention as the arbiter of another cultural revolution. The "Beat Generation" had been first defined on the East Coast a decade earlier, with Jack Kerouac, Allen Ginsberg and John Clellon

Holmes experimenting with spontaneous writing based on the rhythms of jazz and be-bop. But it wasn't until Kerouac and Ginsberg came West in 1954 and 1955, encountering writers Lawrence Ferlinghetti, Gary Snyder, Michael McClure and others, that the Beats galvanized a literary movement.

It came together in San Francisco on October 7, 1955, at a poetry reading at the Six Gallery, an artists' cooperative. Organized by Kenneth Rexroth, the "Six Poets at the Six Gallery" reading featured Rexroth, Snyder, McClure, Ginsberg, Philip Whalen and Philip Lamantia and introduced the first public reading of Ginsberg's incendiary poem, *Howl*. Kerouac recounts the event in his

novel *The Dharma Bums*.

The poem created a sensation when published in 1956 and was immediately confiscated by US Customs officials as "obscene" literature. Ferlinghetti's City Lights bookstore, America's first paperback bookstore and the publisher of *Howl & Other Poems*, faced criminal charges. The ensuing trial (which City Lights won) brought the Beats to national prominence, as did Kerouac's book *On The Road*, published in 1957.

Many quintessential Beat hangouts, such as the Co-Existence Bagel Shop and the Place, are long gone, but City Lights (just up from Jack Kerouac Street), in the heart of North Beach, still carries a wide range of Beat writings. Nearby Café Vesuvio, which opened in 1949, still retains the same Bohemian feel it had in the 1950s. Welsh poet Dylan Thomas favored this bar during his visits to the city. Caffe Trieste, on Vallejo, was (and continues to be) a favorite among the writers. On Saturday mornings, you can hear live opera performed here.

The '60s and beyond: As the beatniks gave way to the hippies, so were the Beats followed by The Merry Pranksters. Led by Ken Kesey, author of *One Flew Over The Cuckoo's Nest* and *Sometimes A Great Notion*, the Pranksters were early experimenters with hallucinogens and organized several massive LSD-tinged gatherings, or "Acid Tests," among them the legendary Trips Festival in January 1966. Held at Longshoreman's Hall in Fisherman's Wharf, the event reportedly drew 20,000 adventurous souls.

Tom Wolfe's *The Electric Kool-Aid Acid Test* recounts the Pranksters' exploits in detail. At the time, San Francisco was also home to *Rolling Stone* magazine and its "gonzo" correspondent, Hunter S. Thompson. Thompson lived in the Haight-Ashbury district during the mid-1960s when he was researching *Hell's Angels*, his off-kilter look at the motorcycle gang.

In the 1970s, playwright (and now movie star) Sam Shepard produced his influential plays *Angel City* and *Curse of the Starving Class* at the Magic Theater, currently housed at Fort Mason. Armistead Maupin, a North Carolina native who relocated to San Francisco in 1971, offered a serial called "Tales of the City" in the *San Francisco Chronicle* beginning in 1976. Detailing the lives of young gay and straight San Franciscans, the series was embraced by the public, published in several volumes of best-selling books and later in a TV series.

Several acclaimed women authors have also lived and worked in San Francisco – and will no doubt someday have some city streets named in their honor. Among the likely honorees are Alice Walker, Alice Adams and Amy Tan. The journalist Joan Didion was born and raised not far away in the town of Sacramento (*see page 235*).

Left, Ambrose Bierce. **Right**, writer/conservationist John Muir with Theodore Roosevelt at Yosemite National Park.

Though you won't find its name on any map – and its exact location is disputable – Silicon Valley definitely exists, and to trace its history is to trace the evolution of contemporary culture. This valley, which stretches about 20 miles (32 km) from the lower San Francisco peninsula to San Jose, nurtured many of the technological advances that have shot the world into the electronic age. Having exhausted the frontier they settled, the valley's inventive minds have turned to creating their own horizons.

Silicon Valley embodies the very definition of high tech America, but with a new Californian state of consciousness. Endowed with the enterprising spirit of pioneers, it is a place where international giants in the electronics and computer industries got their first break in suburban garages, and where futuristic dreams are manufactured into reality.

Palo Alto, home to Stanford University, lies at the heart of this region both as a physical intersection and high-tech magnet. The valley is bounded to the east by the bay and to the west by the mountains thrust up by massive land shifts along the San Andreas Fault. Traversed by Highway 101 and pinched off by the foothills just beyond San Jose, it spreads north toward San Francisco, consuming a number of small cities in its wake.

High-tech: An estimated 7,000 high-tech businesses dealing in everything from microscopic transistors to networked computer systems are located here. The valley embraces nearly 15 cities, including Mountain View, home of the United States Navy's Moffett Field and NASA/Ames Research Center, a revitalized San Jose (now America's 11th largest city) and several suburban communities like Cupertino and Sunnyvale, which have grown so densely populated that it's nearly impossible to tell where one begins and the other ends. Industrial office parks and silicon chip factories now dominate where acres of fruit orchards once blanketed the land. At intervals along this major highway tiny orchards peek from between rows of identical tract houses – reminders of the region's rural roots.

Before the silicon chip existed, this land was known as Santa Clara Valley. It was first settled in the mid 1800s, not by fortune seekers of the 1849 Gold Rush but by farmers who found wealth in the area's rich soil. In 1851, the first significant contribution to the future incarnation of the valley was made when Stanford University was established

by railroad tycoon Leland Stanford near Palo Alto. The high-tech atmosphere of the area was further cultivated by Palo Alto native Lee DeForest, who in 1906 invented a three-element vacuum tube that provided the spark for the development of electronics. A marker in front of his former residence at 913 Emerson Street commemorates the house as the "birthplace" of this industry.

In the early years, America's brightest technical minds migrated to Stanford's engineering school to study radio, the valley's first high-tech industry. When they finished school, they stayed – and a thriving radio, telephone, and telegraph industry emerged.

Preceding pages: church at Stanford University, home of the high-tech revolution. **Left,** "virtual reality" drinks at a San Francisco nightclub. **Right,** the microchip originated in California's Silicon Valley.

In 1938, two Stanford students living at 367 Addison Street – David Packard and William Hewlett – founded what would one day be one of the world's high-tech corporate giants: Hewlett-Packard. That house is now a state historical monument.

With World War II, San Francisco also became the center of West Coast military activity. From Highway 101 near Mountain View, you can see the empty hull of a dirigible hangar marking Moffett Naval Air Station. In 1940, NASA (National Aeronautics and Space Administration) leased space at Moffett. This facility, NASA/Ames Research Center, was for many years the focus of the country's astrophysical research, and still

Clara Valley. Noyce, known to many as the father of Silicon Valley, founded Intel in 1968, foreshadowing the personal computer revolution.

One discovery begat another. Along with Intel and Fairchild, companies like Advanced Micro Devices and National Semiconductor grew to be internationally known magnets of high-tech. Those companies, in turn, brought exponential population growth to the valley.

The 1970s was the decade of the Silicon Valley rush. The electronics industry was flourishing and the time was ripe to apply the new technology. In 1972, Nolan Bushnell founded Atari in yet another garage – this one at 3572 Gibson Avenue in Santa Clara.

houses the world's largest wind tunnel. Ames became a touchstone not only for the electronics and engineering communities of Silicon Valley, but an early testing ground for the exploration of the latest Silicon Valley frontier – "Virtual Reality."

In 1956, valley native William Schockley returned home after receiving the Nobel Prize for developing the electronic transistor. He intended to build an empire, but the eight young engineers he had hired all left to form the Fairchild Semiconductor Company. It was here that Bob Noyce, in 1959, developed the miniature semiconductor set into silicon that would change the face of bucolic Santa

Bushnell created the world's first videogame, called Pong, or electronic ping-pong. Simple though it was, it ignited the modern video-game craze. More important, high technology had finally found a way into people's living rooms, not just into industrial mainframe computers.

Atari and several other valley successors gave the average American family their first of many brushes with technology. In just a decade, Atari grew from a counter-cultural garage brand to a small high-tech empire, eventually to be owned by Warner, one of America's largest entertainment giants.

In the hands of a new generation, the shape

of high-technology was molded in new ways during the late 1970s and early 1980s. Teenage techno-jocks hooked on video games began fiddling with chip boards and microprocessors to see what they could do. In the last of the great valley garages – at 2066 Crist Drive in Cupertino – Steve Jobs and Steve Wozniak turned out their first micro computer. In 1982, the two formed Apple. A legend was born, and the personal computer revolution began. Now a sprawling green glass and stucco complex, Apple's headquarters (still located in Cupertino, but now at 20525 Mariani Avenue off Highway 101) is one of the few companies that allows visitors past the front door.

gently on a new kind of computer game that seemed to create a new dimension in which humans and computers could coexist. Some called it "electronic LSD," others simply regarded it as another of the valley's undiscovered technological wonders. Most know it as Virtual Reality.

Imagine you fly with your fingers. When you point up, you rise high above trees, clouds, above a towering white marble pillar with a huge red ruby beaming like a lighthouse. Point your finger toward the ruby and you swoosh down inside of it and everywhere you look, red light glows. Point down and you are at the base of a column, point left and you pass unscathed through the marble

Obsolete but influential: During the 1980s, personal computers replaced video games as the entertainment of choice. Atari became extinct, like many Silicon Valley giants before and after it, but not without launching the careers of a new generation of explorers. What would be next? In Atari's Sunnyvale research laboratory, engineers were beginning their advance on the next high-tech frontier that would fascinate the modern world. Researchers worked dili-

walls to find yourself standing on an oriental rug which moves endlessly like a motorized kaleidoscope. Welcome to the fantastic world of Virtual Reality.

This strange realm is a comparatively recent step in the evolution of computer-generated graphics. Rather than simply viewing graphics on a flat screen, Virtual Reality users immerse themselves in a completely artificial environment, which has approximately the look and feel of real life.

Gearing up for the experience requires looking like a creature from outer space. One essential is the video-goggle, or head-mounted display, inset with two miniature

Left, Steve Wozniak was co-founder of Apple Computer; computers 1980s-style. **Above**, trade shows do a brisk business.

liquid crystal screens. The views of the two screens are slightly different, producing the 3-D effect of normal vision. The headset also senses the movements of your head and reports this information back to the computer. The computer then creates moving images on the screens that mimic your shifting point of view. Also essential is a way of navigating your way through this world. This is done by a "data glove," laced with sensors that measure finger movements.

The glove commands the computer to move or stop, and can also mimic the actions of picking up an object, opening a door or throwing a ball as they happen (or are dramatized) in real life. Body suits – as sensitive to

tual Reality into underground pop-culture.

Various scientists, computer programmers and theorists across the country were independently developing and perfecting specific components of Virtual Reality, but it was in Silicon Valley in the late 1980s that it all came together. NASA/Ames Research Center in Mountain View was the first site of a fully functional Virtual Reality testbed. In typical valley fashion, a group of America's foremost researchers – many of them natives of the area – assembled to manufacture the future. Ames Research Center concentrated on developing more useful applications for the technology, particularly in the areas of space exploration. Among other achieve-

movement as data gloves – come next.

Inner space: Imagine that a good computer programmer can build you any world you want, no matter how fantastic, unreal, exotic, or mundane. You can live in a multiple-story mansion, walk on Mars, fly around in a molecule or take a virtual-tour of the whole of San Francisco. The possibilities are endless – but realities are slow to follow. The American media quickly dubbed this infinite supply of computer-generated hallucinations "electronic LSD" – in some ways a fitting name for an experience that emanated from the San Francisco Bay Area with its hippie counter-culture history. The hype thrust Vir-

ments, researchers hoped to develop Telepresence, a device through which an earthbound person could control a robot located in space – or on another planet.

NASA/Ames Research Center soon launched more Virtual Reality ventures, including VPL Research of Redwood City. Every legend has its hero, and Virtual Reality has Jaron Lanier. As the chief executive of VPL, Lanier embodied the spirit of Silicon Valley at its most eccentric. The youthful, dreadlocked zealot embraced both the usefulness and high-entertainment value of Virtual Reality. His company did much to launch the private exploration of virtual worlds. As a result VPL became the principal suppliers of Virtual Reality headsets and gloves to companies around the world.

The total cost for a VPL system can easily reach $300,000, but the race is on to develop affordable VR tools – playthings for every household. Like so many Silicon Valley pioneers, however, Lanier's VPL was ill-fated. Its foreign parent-company scooped up all the patents and kicked employees out on the streets. In its place, several new companies in the Bay Area (some started by former VPL employees) have sprung up to carry on the research. Jaron Lanier still remains a local techno-saint.

Worldwide applications: The Virtual Reality

everything from shoes to houses to cities. Designers can view their product before they make it, streamlining the building process and saving thousands of dollars in time-wasting, costly mistakes.

The medical establishment plans to employ Virtual Reality in the preparation for rare surgical procedures and for medical training. And drug researchers are using the new technology to develop better pharmaceuticals and to increase the efficiency and safety of the development process. But in the end, it will probably be the entertainment value of Virtual Reality that will drive full-scale development by private corporations. There's big money to be made in the interna-

research that started in Silicon Valley touched off a budding industry around the world. In Tokyo, the Matsushita Electric Works uses Virtual Reality to assist customers in building the kitchen of their dreams. Prospective buyers wearing headsets can try out different floor-plans, rearrange appliances at whim and even resize the cabinets. In London, Virtual Reality is being used to train drivers of public transportation vehicles. In a similar fashion, VR can also be a design aid in

tional entertainment industry, the kind of money needed to continue important research in all applications of Virtual Reality.

Silicon Valley continues to mutate. Speculation has mounted about whether it has passed its prime. But with so many companies, it's hard to believe this area will be a ghost town soon. Regardless of its future, this technological Mesopotamia has provided the tools for a new generation – computers, software programs, and a staggering array of electronics. The techno-trailblazers who live here have moved on to conquering virtual worlds, ensuring an endless supply of new "valleys" and, perhaps, new civilizations.

Left, Apple's headquarters are still located in Cupertino. **Above,** hackers and phreaks on San Francisco's streets.

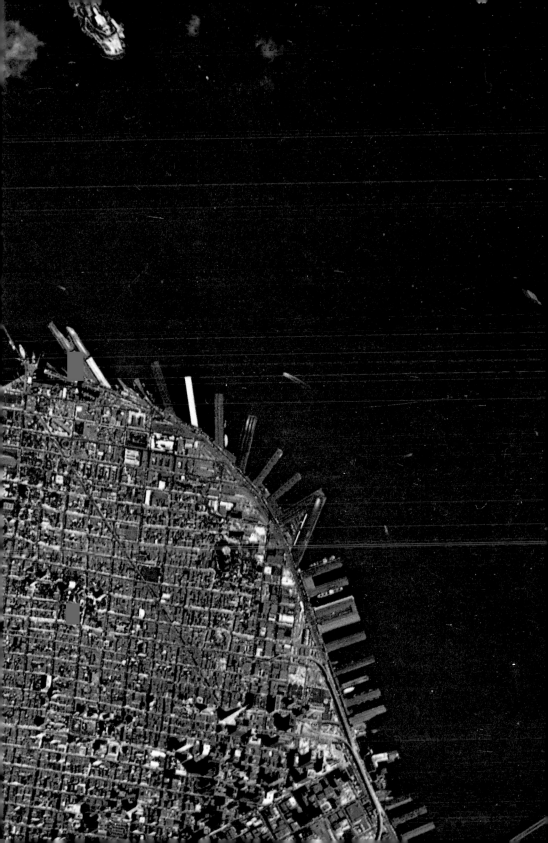

EARTHQUAKES AND HOT SPRINGS

California, with all your faults, we love you still… only you don't stay still long enough.
—Romeo Martel, earthquake engineer

For years, doomsayers have predicted "The Big One," the earthquake that will once and for all send California slipping and sliding into the Pacific. There is a long-standing joke that says smart Californians are investing in beachfront property – in Nevada.

Earthquakes, indeed, have played a major role in creating this state and are still a geological force to be reckoned with. The shaking and quaking occur because the region straddles two plates of land that scrape against each other. The suture that separates the Pacific and North American plates is the infamous San Andreas Fault, a 650-mile (1,050-km) earthquake zone that has been trembling for about 65 million years. The land on the west side of the fault strains northward, while the land on the east side moves ever south. Because San Francisco is east of the fault, and Los Angeles is west, the two cities actually move closer with every slip of the fault – about 2 inches (5 cm) a year.

Search for solutions: California scientists recently announced their intention of drilling a hole many miles deep into the San Andreas Fault zone to see if they can learn more about earthquakes. They have poured skepticism on critics who suggest that such activity might hasten the advent of "the Big One," pointing to a similar project underway near the Czech border in Germany which has the participation of more than 100 scientists. Geothermal drilling has also been tried without adverse efects in California's Imperial Valley although at lesser depths. One of the potential sites under consideration for the $50 million project is Point Arena in Northern California.

The 1906 San Francisco earthquake which measured 8.25 was the biggest since 1857; the 1994 quake further south in the San Fernando Valley (6.6) is the biggest since.

Earthquake terrain often contains hot springs. That's certainly the case in California, where scores of bubbling mineral springs were soothing weary bodies long before Europeans arrived. Carbonated springs are so relaxing that Johannes Brahms is said to have composed an entire symphony while bathing in the carbonated baths of Baden Baden in Germany's Black Forest.

Long before the end of the century California had almost 80 mineral water resorts, with the biggest concentration around Calistoga in the Napa Valley. In 1860 pio-

neer publisher and entrepreneur Sam Brannan first tapped the 212°F (100°C) waters to found Indian Springs Spa at a spot where the Wapoo Indians had bathed for hundreds of years. Brannan, the state's first millionaire, boasted this would become the "Caligosta of Sarafornia" a play on the famous Saratoga Springs back East which became a favorite of President Franklin D. Roosevelt. The Sam Brannan cottage, with period furnishings, is still preserved on Wapoo Avenue.

There is a curious connection between earthquakes and hot springs in Calistoga where the eruption of the famous Old Faithful geyser is said to forecast the imminence

Preceding pages, San Francisco's terrain as photographed by NASA. **Left**, Lassen Volcanic National Park. **Right**, Calistoga's geyser.

of an earthquake by blowing off more frequently than its regular eruptions which occur every 40 minutes.

At a score of spas in the Calistoga area, the tradition is to soak for about ten minutes in a mud bath consisting of volcanic ash, peat moss and the local mineral water hot out of the ground. Next after a shower to rinse off the mud, comes 20 minutes in an individual hot tub of jet-activated water. A short steam bath and soothing massage rounds off the health treatment.

Clinical studies show that the presence of invisible carbon dioxide gas in spa waters helps to expand capillaries near the surface of the skin producing a feeling of warmth and

for medicinal healing. Grace Hudson, a local artist who became world famous for the hundreds of paintings she made of Pomo Indians before her death in 1937, was a frequent visitor. (Her work is on show in a museum in Ukiah.)

Bubbling up at a rate of 65 gallons a minute from a depth of up to 25,000 feet (7,600 meters) into a natural rock grotto, the Vichy Springs water runs through redwood pipes to 14 individual outdoor and indoor tubs. Guests can sip the healthful warm water, tagged "champagne" because the natural carbonation makes the 90°F (32°C) water sweet and bubbly, not bitter. It contains such minerals as sodium, potassium, calcium,

well being similar to the warm glow experienced after vigorous excercise. The waters are said to have therapeutic value for rheumatism, ulcers and gout.

Possibly the best-known northern spa is Ukiah's 700-acre (280-hectare) Vichy Springs Resort (named after the naturally carbonated springs in France first discovered by Julius Caesar) whose visitors have included Ulysses S. Grant, Theodore Roosevelt, Mark Twain and Robert Louis Stevenson. Jack London called it "my favorite summer home."

The springs were well known to Pomo Indians who regarded them as a holy place

magnesium, iron sulfate, chloride, bicarbonate and silica.

In 1884, the springs advertised that it had the largest bath tubs and the most water of any spa. It cost $10 a week to stay at the resort. The two original cottages built in 1854 and which still accommodate overnight guests are the oldest structures still standing in Mendocino County. During World War I the resort was remodeled, with the addition of a bowling alley, beauty shop and sports facilities for tennis, croquet and other amusements.

Tassajara in Monterey County has the hottest springs in the nation, up to 140°F

(60°C), with its waters also the richest in mineral content. Early visitors after the resort opened in 1884 were General Sherman and the violinist Ignace Paderewski. In 1967, the 160-acre (65-hectare) site was acquired for conversion to a Zen monastery by followers of the Zen master Shunryu Suzuki who operate it as a resort between May and September. No music is allowed, so the soothing sound of Tassajara Creek is a constant background for bird songs and the ringing of bells from the meditation hall. Tassajara cookbooks have sold more half a million copies.

In California's unique geography, high mountain peaks and low desert valleys are within unusually close proximity. For exam-

million years ago, is in a period of emergence. Because of this uplifting, and unlike America's East Coast, there are only a few navigable rivers or inland estuaries. (Apart from San Diego, the only other natural harbors in the state are San Francisco and Humboldt in the north). This uplifting also leaves a coastline that is often rugged. Bartolomeo Ferrelo, who arrived at California's shores with Juan Cabrillo's expedition of 1542–43, described mountains "that rise to the sky, and against which the sea beats and which appear as if they would fall on the ships."

San Francisco Bay is the keystone to Northern California's history. It was formed by the tilting and sinking of the earth caused by the

ple, Mount Whitney in the Sierra Nevada range at 14,494 feet (4,418 meters) is the tallest peak in the contiguous United States, yet it's only 60 miles (100 km) away from the lowest point in North America, Death Valley, at 282 feet (86 meters) below sea level. This is within a state that is 780 miles (1,260 km) long and from 150–350 miles (240–560 km) wide.

In geological years, the state is still a baby. The coastline, where volcanoes continued to belch out smoke and lava until only 15–20

Left, thermal activity at Bumpass Hell, Lassen Park. Above, eating after the 1906 earthquake.

San Andreas Fault, one of the many deadly rifts that marble the state. Those faults, and the vagaries of drifting continents, created a dip in the Coast Range and a valley behind it. The Sacramento River carved its way through that valley canyon for millennia, reaching the sea some miles from what today is the Golden Gate.

The Bay as we know it wasn't formed until the end of the last Ice Age (or during a pause in the glacial period; no one is quite sure). About 25,000 years ago the ice caps of the north began melting and the earth's sea level gradually rose. Decade by decade the ocean expanded until it overflowed into the fault and the river-created valley, filling it and making it into a bay.

Ring of fire: About 130 million years ago, the land that is now California lay beneath the water, part of the "ring of fire" that created the Pacific Basin. Four out of every five earthquakes in the world occur in this ring. To the east of the ocean was North America, to the west was Cascadia. Debris washed down from these shores to form layer upon layer of sedimentary rock, building up the land. But there were also weak spots – faults – in this new crust, and the evolving land strained in different directions.

The quakes and volcanoes folded and

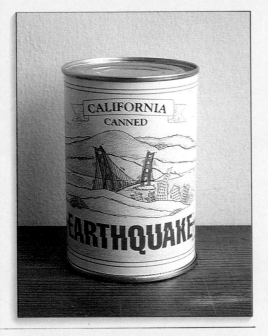

molded the newly formed land into two great mountain ranges – the longer Coast Range that runs the length of the state, and the higher Sierra Nevada to the east.

Glaciers played a major role in shaping the Sierra Nevada 3 million years ago. The huge ice sheets were active as recently as 10,000 years ago, and there are still some small ice pockets in the higher elevations. During the Ice Age, some of the glaciers were 40 miles (64 km) long and thousands of feet thick.

When the great sheets of polar ice melted in North America, raising the level of the ocean, salt water was sent coursing through the Coastal Range, carving out deep canyons

and beautiful valleys. Millions of years ago, the desolate Mojave Desert had rustling meadows and life-giving streams. A 600-ft (180-meter) deep lake once existed where Death Valley is today and mountain peaks were made islands in the flood. As the air warmed, the water started to evaporate. The mountains of the Coastal Range and Sierra Nevada kept ocean moisture away from the soon-to-be desert.

Fire and ice: North of California, glaciers also dominate the Cascade range of mountains, which run almost due north all the way to British Columbia in Canada. Here in California, though, only the highest peaks bear these Ice Age relics. The dominant snow-capped Cascade peaks are young volcanoes. The Cascades are like the fire and ice of the Pleistocene. Subduction, the melting of tectonic plates as they dive under the continent, continues to nourish volcanic activity here. But it is the condition of that basalt when it returns to the earth's surface that determines the shape, size and duration of the eruptions.

There are three kinds of lavas and four types of Cascade volcanoes. When volcanic rock flows in a molten stream, it is a *lava flow*. If it erupts in solid chunks, it is *lava rock*. If it explodes into molten fragments that solidify before they reach the ground, it is termed *pyroclastic*.

Volcanoes composed entirely of pyroclastics (from the Greek phrase for "fire-broken") are called *cinder cones*. Usually they are steeply conical and indented by a crater from which the lava erupts. Generically named Cinder Cone in Lassen Volcanic National Park is a textbook example of this type. *Shield volcanoes*, like Prospect Peak in the same park, are especially common at sea and on islands. They are the opposite of cinder cones: formed from highly fluid lava-flow accumulations, shields are gently sloping and low to the ground.

The *composite*, or *stratovolcano*, is the classic Cascade volcano. Examples are Mount St Helens and Mount Shasta. Unlike composites, *dome* volcanoes are produced by a single mass of solid rock that has been pushed up through a vent. If a lava dome forms in a pre-existing crater, as it did on Lassen Peak, it is called a plug dome.

Left, a quake in a can. **Right**, bubbling mud in the Cascade mountain range.

California could be a dozen states, each with its own outdoors personality, its own climate, its own natural wonders. For many Californians, the outdoors is synonymous with activity. It's a big state, the theory goes, and you'll have to keep moving to see it.

While breathtaking scenery and solemn serenity intrude on every scene in California, this outdoors tour adopts the native philosophy: Go where you like, but *do* something when you get there. The naturalist John Muir once sat transfixed by the "window to the Heavens" he found in the high Sierra – to get there, he walked. Today, millions of tourists arriving in the dusty heat of July experience the awesome beauty of Muir's Yosemite Valley through the greasy windows of a tour bus – a dull, forgettable experience.

California has high mountains – the Sierras – that run the length of the state like a spine, north to south, separating forest from desert. Thickly forested on the shoulder, bald as a cue ball on top, polished smooth by the moving glaciers of the last Ice Age, the Sierras are rich in strange, beautiful geology: giant batholith granite domes in Yosemite National Park, Kings Canyon and Desolation Wilderness, with names like El Capitan and Half Dome; the cores and flows of extinct volcanoes named Devil's Postpile and Valley of the Moon.

In the north, the Sierras of Tahoe and Yosemite give way to the foothills where gold sometimes still generates a rush; the hardened ponderosa of pine, madrone and manzanita fall away to the lush, irrigated oasis of the San Joaquin Valley, the low rise of the coastal mountains, then the cool Pacific Ocean. In the valley, through a break in the Coast Range, the Sacramento River and its hundreds of tributaries form a delta that drains through the San Francisco Bay.

There are many ways to enjoy the outdoors of California: the drive along the high winding, seaside cliffs of Highway 1 is spectacular in any part of the state. But once again, you won't regret it if you elevate your

heartbeat – walk, roller-skate, ride a bike, paddle a kayak, climb a 2,000-foot (600-meter) granite face, or "catch a wave." California is rife with outfitters, schools, clubs, rental shops, guides, resorts – and even tour buses – that specialize in outdoor adventure.

The following is just a sampling of activity for hire: backpacking, whitewater rafting, mountain climbing, sea kayaking; back-country skiing, downhill skiing, snowboarding, road and mountain biking, deep sea fishing, dry fly fishing, surfing, wind-surfing, sailing, hot-air ballooning and bird watching. Thrillseekers can try bungee jumping, rock climbing, hang gliding, parachuting, and river kayaking.

The Far North: Still partly populated by native tribes, the far northern corner of the state is home to the legendary Sasquatch – Bigfoot to modern locals – a huge reclusive ape-like creature whose red fur camouflages him among the towering redwood trees and river canyons. The rivers and streams bear names that join in a confluence of Indian mythology and the whims of 19th-century prospectors – Klamath, Ukunom, Trinity, Salmon, Smith. Fishing and floating these rivers is by no means limited to natives; the streams are big and cool in hot summers, and rafting and fishing guides take visitors down many of the most inviting canyons.

Prospectors of adrenaline seek out the thundering rapids of Burnt Ranch Falls on the Trinity, the cataracts of Hells Corner Gorge or the Ikes Falls on the Klamath. The breathtaking forest drops of the California Salmon are at once beautiful and thrilling. On the other hand, you can float for days with nary a riffle on the lower Klamath and parts of the Trinity. New rafting programs put you in the seat of your own inflatable kayak, affectionately called "iks," for a personal encounter with the river.

Salmon and steelhead trout still spawn in these rivers, though not in the great numbers of a century ago. The Hoopa and Klamath tribes own ancestral fishing rights, still setting their traps and dipping their nets at the foot of Ishi Pishi Falls. If angling is your game, the fall run of salmon and steelhead is unparalleled in the state. Guides with grace-

Preceding pages, surveying the scenics at **Mokelumne Wilderness**. **Left**, sequoia forest at **Yosemite National Park**.

ful, swept-ended rowboats called "Mac-Kenzies" will lead you to the finest holding pools.

No matter the mission of the river trip, these streams often reward stealthy visitors with sightings of eagle, river otter, great blue heron, duck, fox, bobcat, and the occasional bear. Overnight campers are sometimes chilled by the howl of Sasquatch from just beyond the edge of the darkened woods.

Here, and all along the northern California coastal mountains, the heart of the woods is the redwoods. Some of these giants are a thousand years old or more, reaching 300 feet (90 meters) into the sky. They are the largest living things on earth (save a recently

discovered Wisconsin fungus) and their presence in every sense is majestic.

Sun filtering through the redwood canopy as if through leaded glass, the cool enveloping shade, and the imposing sense of age, often draws comparisons to the cathedrals of Europe. Many of California's redwood groves have fallen under the saw, but old-growth groves can still be found in state parks strung like pearls along the coast.

Forest-fringed beaches: The northwest coast is somberly beautiful: long, empty beaches scattered with driftwood, rugged sea cliffs, sawmills and fishing towns, and forests that come to the edge of the ocean cliffs. Swim-

ming is none-too inviting here – the sky is usually gray and the water is a constant 50°F (–17°C) – but you can enter the surf with a wetsuit. Surfing has a loyal following, particularly at the point breaks of river mouths and harbors. The waves here are powerful and dangerous and no place for the novice. Undertows and rip tides are also common, demanding caution.

Cold-water diving gear allows for abalone hunting. This giant mollusk is a delicacy, but prying them off the rocks at depth is not for the casual swimmer. Sometimes, at low tides, the intrepid wader will find a legal-sized "ab" in the tide pools.

Fishing is easy on the coast. You can cast from rocks or piers, or embark on a "party boat" to probe the depths. Unusual, chilling sport can be had pursuing surf smelt. The fisherman uses a big triangular net on a frame. Plunging the net into oncoming breaking waves, the fisherman is soaked completely. The nets are available for rent; the smelt, sometimes caught by the bucket full, are deep fried and eaten whole.

Northeast corner: By far California's remotest region, the northeast part of the state was home to its most recent volcanic eruption – Mount Lassen blew its lid in 1914 – and at Lassen National Park, you can view the bubbling mud pots of Bumpass Hell or hike to the rim and peer into the crater. Backpackers will find hot springs and geysers throughout the huge park.

Near the town of Redding, an ancient volcano stands solitary sentinel at the head of the Sacramento Valley. Mount Shasta is the southern point of the Cascade Range, a chain of volcanic mountains that extends all the way to Alaska. At 14,162 ft (4,317 meters), it is only a few yards shy of being the state's tallest mountain. The glacier-capped peak is a moderately difficult all-day climb in the summer, rating as one of California's premiere adventures with spectacular views. In the winter, the mountain is buried in snow and open to skiers.

Backpackers and cross-country skiers will revel in the wilderness of Lassen National Park and the surrounding National Forest. Many alpine lakes dot the area and children will spend long days paddling driftwood logs like surfboards and watching the big wary trout cruise below.

Fly fishermen in particular will find abundant game and frequent caddis and mayfly hatches in the McCloud, Pitt and Fall rivers, as well as within the winding banks of Hat Creek, Hot Creek, Battle Creek and the many other notorious streams of the area. Eagle Lake, an anomalous, highly-alkaline body of water straddling the Eastern Sierras on one side, sage desert on the other, is home to a splendid species of oversize Eagle Lake Rainbow Trout, found nowhere else. As the name of the lake implies, Osprey, Golden Eagle and Bald Eagle – the national bird – are often seen skimming this lake for hapless loafing fish.

Nearby Lake Almanor, a massive man-made reservoir, is a resort area with plentiful

wheels. Backpackers will find endless untrammeled trails.

The Central Coast: The coast begins, roughly, at Point Arena, 100 miles (160 km) north of San Francisco. It encompasses the huge natural harbor of San Francisco Bay, includes the coastal mountains that form – among other things – the hills of San Francisco, extends down through Half Moon Bay and Santa Cruz, includes the teeming marine environment of Monterey and Carmel, then follows the sheer, rugged cliffs of the coast through Big Sur. It then takes a sharp bend and heads turns east towards Santa Barbara and Los Angeles.

In that span, adventurers will find red-

waterskiing, sailing, lake trolling and sunbathing. The mountains of this region are notorious for their massive deer herds, stealthy cougar (aptly called "mountain lions," but smaller and much more solitary than their African cousins), black bear, and North America's only antelope, the pronghorn. From the foothills to the high Sierra ridges, this region is more wilderness than otherwise. Bicyclists (of both the road and mountain variety) will find abundant trails and out-of-the way roads to explore on two

Left, sign in the Sacramento River Valley. **Above**, whale-watchers along the coast have to be quick.

wood forests, lakes, rivers, estuaries, San Francisco Bay which contains many environments itself, rolling grass-covered hills and down-sized mountains, hundreds of miles of trails for hiking, horseback riding, biking and mountain biking. Travelers will find massive herds of marine mammals; kelp beds alive with fish, birds and sea otters; cypress gardens; underwater marine sanctuaries; salmon fishing fleets, sturgeon fishing fleets and crab fishing fleets.

San Francisco lured early arrivals with the shelter of the San Francisco Bay, a huge natural harbor that is home to myriad bird life, a noisy colony of sea lions that has taken residence at Fisherman's Wharf, island wild-life sanctuaries, and fascinating tidal marshes.

The parks and grassy hills near the city are oak and scrub on one side, redwood coastal forest on the side facing the sea. In the days of sail the Bay provided a much needed respite from the fierce prevailing winds that blow out of the Northwest virtually all summer long. Although a bane to old-time ships, it's a boon to modern sailors. Sailing craft of every description crowd the vast Bay on weekends. Surfers race the swells under the Golden Gate Bridge, and float like butterflies off the beach at Crissy Field, one of the world's greatest urban windsurfing spots.

Just north of the Golden Gate Bridge,

of the woodwork, and make their way to the stream beds where they spawn. Often in sight of vineyards and wineries, the Russian River and Cache Creek are popular rafting and canoeing streams.

To reach Monterey, travel south from San Francisco, using Highway 1 along the coast. All the way to Santa Cruz the coastline is a rough jumble of broken cliffs and long-misty beaches. Surf fishing is popular here, as is hang-gliding and surfing. Along this stretch you're likely to see hundreds of windsurfers braving the cracking swells and blowing sands. Waddell Creek is considered one of the best windsurfing spots in the country, and top sailors are often spotted jumping

opposite San Francisco, the Marin Head-lands and Mount Tamalpais are considered the birthplace of mountain biking. Miles of scenic trails are perfect for this bone-shaking form of cycling, and the bikes share the trails with hikers and equestrians.

Wine country: Some 30 miles (48 km) north of the Bay's northern-most tip lie the valleys of Napa and Sonoma, in the heart of California's wine country. Cyclists take long tours on the rolling hills that wind past scores of vineyards. In the forest slopes above Sonoma, rainy spring days are the occasion of one of California's strangest migrations: thousands of red-bellied salamanders come literally out

waves and pulling spectacular aerial maneuvers with names like "killer loop" and "cheese roll."

This despite the fact that Ano Nuevo State Park, a mile or two upwind, is a carefully protected nursery for the giant, billowing elephant seals, most noted for the male's ability to inflate its prodigious fleshy nose, and the fact that the male is often five times the size of the females in its harem.

While the seals themselves are of no bother to surfers, this is the one area in California that's truly a lunch counter for the great white shark. One attack per year is the norm, but few are fatal. Actually, the sharks are under far more predatorial pressure than the surfers and windsurfers; biologists fear that the prehistoric fish are being hunted to extinction out of misplaced fear and misunderstanding. This has disastrous consequences to the marine ecology.

A popular pastime in Monterey is to rent easily-paddled open-topped kayaks called "Scuppers," and to paddle out to the local kelp beds. The kelp, which ranges all along the coast, forms fantastic underwater forests. Scuba diving is extremely popular in Monterey and all along the coast to the south. The kelp is long and spindly at the base and stretches up to form thick mats at the surface. Divers swim through these forests for

lovers. The creatures are often seen floating on their backs with an infant sleeping on their belly, lolling about the water fastidiously cleaning their fur, or munching a shellfish, just as a sunbather might float on his back in a swimming pool.

Driving south, the road climbs away from the ocean to become a breathtaking drive along high seaside cliffs. There is little coastal access along this route, but along the way, travelers will eventually come to Big Sur, a huge wilderness in the coastal mountains.

The Sacramento Valley: If you leave San Francisco on a freighter traveling east, heading inland toward the source of the muddy water that flows into San Francisco Bay, you

sightings of California's territorial ocean goldfish, the Garibaldi, ling cod and many types of rockfish.

Where the divers and kayakers converge at the surface, both are likely to encounter one of California's most delightful wild animals, the sea otter. The otters were once hunted for their fur. But the animals, which survive on abalone and urchins plucked from the bottom, are too winsome and intelligent to have escaped the sympathy of animal

Left, a new, popular pastime is to bathe in seaweed. **Above**, cross-country skiing near Mammoth Mountains.

will enter a wide twisting delta formed by the confluence near sea level of the Sacramento and San Joaquin rivers. Like many huge river mouths, the Sacramento Delta has been turned into an agricultural bonanza. The river here is freshwater, but strongly affected by the tides. It winds through the delta in a thousand tiny threads, like lace. Each of the islands in this web has been walled off by levees and turned to farmland. Many farmers reach their homes by small bridges and roads; others are forced to ride ferries across one or more channels.

The entire delta was once an endless marsh. But, now that it is under more regular control, it is only the out-of-the-way corners that team with waterfowl. One of California's great adventures is a trip on the delta in a rented houseboat, for which the savvy visitor will bring or rent a waterski boat and every conceivable kind of watersports equipment he or she can muster.

The Sacramento River is by far California's largest. Its tributaries include most of the west slope of the Sierras and, while it travels through foothills, farmland, and, ultimately, into San Francisco Bay, its water is a hotly contested commodity. A major dam, Shasta, at the northern end of the state, is the first plug in the Sacramento's flow. Others block the progress of most of the other rivers that end up in the Sacramento, but along the way, this huge river is the source of all kinds of wild scenery.

Highest point: The Sierra Nevada range is 400 miles (640 km) long and up to 100 miles (160 km) wide. It peaks at the summit of Mt Whitney, 14,495 ft (4,420 meters), which is only a crow's fly away from the lowest point in the lower 48 states, Death Valley (150 ft/ 45 meters below sea level). This gives some idea of its severity; an imposing wall facing east. On the west slope, however, is a different story. This is the long, sloping Sierra of foothills, ponderosa, alpine meadows and granite domes. The sky here is clear and brilliant, the rivers steep and serious.

The pioneer conservationist John Muir, one of the co-founders of the Sierra Club, once wrote: "Well may the Sierra be named, not the Snowy Range, but the Range of Light." A wilderness trail of several hundred miles bears Muir's name, as do a vast wilderness and a college of the University of California. Any visitor to these mountains will find a deep spiritual connection in Muir's writing.

Yosemite, now a national park, was Muir's chief inspiration, a wondrous collection of granite domes and towers thousands of feet high, as sheer as if they had been lopped off with a knife. It was actually ancient glaciers that carved out the bowl of Yosemite, Touolumne (*Too-all-o-me*) and the other spectacular canyons of the region. The polished granite and the rarefied air of the area lend a feeling of crispness and clarity found in few other places.

In summer, the high season, be sure to avoid the crowds and buses of Yosemite Valley, however tempting. Opt instead for a visit to the remoter locations of the park, perhaps not as spectacular, but more scenic, without the bumper-to-bumper cars.

For Yosemite is, sadly, too crowded, and extreme care must be exercised. An original commissioner for the park, architect Frederick Law Olmsted, writing in 1865, was among the first to recognize in Yosemite "the value of the district...as a museum of natural science and the danger, indeed the certainty, that without care many of the species of plants now flourishing upon it will be lost and many interesting objects be defaced or obscured if not destroyed."

Sapphire of the Sierra: A good distance north of Yosemite, almost due east of San Francisco and Sacramento, is the sapphire of the Sierra, Lake Tahoe. This has the distinction of being the largest and most scenic lake in two states (it is split down the middle by the California/Nevada line), tucked in the bowl formed by high alpine peaks, redwood groves and pine forests. Tahoe is part outdoors playground, with some of the best sports in California, and part tourist park, with many boutiques, casinos (on the Nevada side) and cheap hotels.

Tahoe has two outdoors seasons: summer, when waterskiing on the lake is king; and winter (November through early May in good years) when the snow pack leads to cross-country and downhill skiing. Snowboarding is the sport of choice among youth, and telemark or back-country skiing, whereby you climb a mountain on skis and ski down, is also gaining favor.

The ski areas that attract the most tourists, Squaw Valley on the North Shore, and Heavenly Valley at the South Lake, are huge, full-featured resorts. Squaw has a giant hotel, an Olympic history, an ice skating rink on top of the mountain, a bungee jumping tower and a golf course. Heavenly is not to be outdone.

Many smaller areas, with names like Kirkwood, Homewood, Sugar Bowl, North Star and Donner Ridge, are friendlier spots to ski, though the sheer vertical drops are not as great. In the summer, adventurers can carry mountain bikes on the lifts of many ski areas, and explore the vast alpine network of trails, some with a soaring, bird's-eye view of Lake Tahoe.

Right, hang-gliding over the Pacific surf.

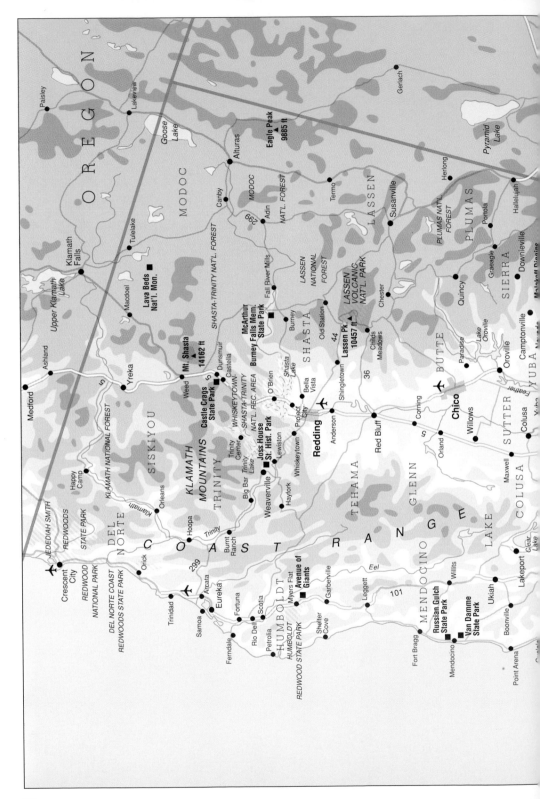

Northern California

40 miles / 64 km

PLACES

Unlike Paris or the Pyramids, Northern California isn't compact and easy to explore. It helps to make a little time; take a few chances. Visitors often fail to realize, for example, that there's almost as much of the state north of San Francisco as south of it, and in this probably least explored part of the state are some of the most attractive sights.

Within the arbitrary border assigned here to Northern California (state legislators have been discussing legal ones that would split California into two states) – an utterly imaginary line drawn northeast from San Luis Obispo over the mountains and through the Central Valley just south of Fresno, up to the Nevada border – lies more natural and social variety than in any similar-sized territory in the world.

The upper half of the state of California, in fact, harbors almost as many places of interest as Gallo has grapes; some charge that Southern Californians not only exploit Northern California's water, crops and lumber but that they add insult to injury by wanting to come and visit.

It's understandable, of course, because so do millions of tourists worldwide. The Golden Gate Bridge and Fisherman's Wharf are the stars of a thousand postcards. The austere glacial cirques around Desolation Valley, and the small peaceful tidepools on the Monterey Peninsula are perfect for personal explorations. The windswept meadows on the Mendocino coast and the hurried crush of San Francisco's Chinatown streets provide a visual essay of different environments.

There is rich bottomland and high desert plains, raging whitewater rivers and sweeping freeways, roller coasters and ski runs, lava caves and granite cliffs. And as if that wasn't enough, Northern California is also home to Yosemite, arguably the most beautiful national park to be found anywhere.

Visitors can follow the crowds, or be utterly alone. They can drink the best wines made in America, eat the best seafood on the West Coast, slither around in the best mud baths. They can play the best golf courses, climb the highest mountain, see the oldest tree, surf the biggest waves. Or, better yet, they can just take a map – and a walk – and discover a few other natural wonders most people don't even know about.

Certainly, this is a place for exploring, a place with secrets worth discovering by foot, bicycle, bus, car, train or plane. But be forewarned: one trip may be all it takes to turn another visitor (even someone from Southern California) into a life-long resident.

Preceding pages: the Big Sur coast; the Sierra Nevada, a Napa Valley vineyard. **Left**, Paul Bunyan statue, Trees of Mystery, Klamath.

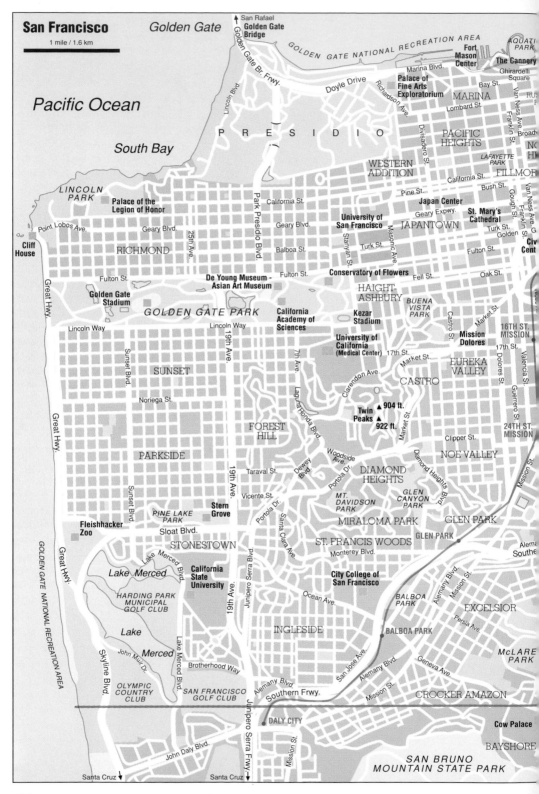

San Francisco

1 mile / 1.6 km

Golden Gate

San Rafael
**Golden Gate
Bridge**

Golden Gate Br. Frwy.

Golden Gate Br. Frwy.

GOLDEN GATE NATIONAL RECREATION AREA

AQUATIC PARK

**Fort
Mason
Center**

The Cannery

Ghirardelli Square

Doyle Drive

Marina Blvd.

**Palace of
Fine Arts
Exploratorium**

MARINA

Bay St.

Marina Blvd.

Lincoln Blvd.

Lombard St.

Van Ness

RU

Pacific Ocean

P R E S I D I O

Divisadero St.

PACIFIC
HEIGHTS

NO
H

South Bay

WESTERN
ADDITION

*LAFAYETTE
PARK*

California St.

FILLMOR

Pine St.

Bush St.

Van Ness St.

Franklin St.

Broad

**LINCOLN
PARK**

Park Presidio Blvd.

California St.

Japan Center

Geary Expwy.

**St. Mary's
Cathedral**

Turk St.

**Palace of the
Legion of Honor**

Geary Blvd.

**University of
San Francisco**

JAPANTOWN

Golden

Civ
Cent

Point Lobos Ave.

Geary Blvd.

25th Ave.

Masonic Ave.

Stanyan St.

Turk St.

Fulton St.

**Cliff
House**

RICHMOND

Balboa St.

Conservatory of Flowers

Oak St.

Fulton St.

Fulton St.

**De Young Museum -
Asian Art Museum**

HAIGHT
ASHBURY

*BUENA
VISTA
PARK*

Castro St.

Fell St.

16TH ST.
MISSION

**Golden Gate
Stadium**

GOLDEN GATE PARK

**California
Academy of
Sciences**

**Kezar
Stadium**

17th St.

**Mission
Dolores**

17th St.

Dolores St.

Market St.

Lincoln Way

Lincoln Way

**University of
California**
(Medical Center)

17th St.

Market St.

EUREKA
VALLEY

Valencia St.

19th Ave.

7th Ave.

CASTRO

Guerrero St.

SUNSET

Noriega St.

Laguna Honda Blvd.

**Twin
Peaks**

▲ 904 ft.

▲ 922 ft.

Market St.

Clipper St.

24TH ST.
MISSION

**FOREST
HILL**

Woodside Ave.

NOE VALLEY

PARKSIDE

Sunset Blvd.

Taraval St.

Dewey Blvd.

Portola Dr.

**DIAMOND
HEIGHTS**

Diamond Heights Blvd.

Vicente St.

Portola Dr.

*MT.
DAVIDSON
PARK*

*GLEN
CANYON
PARK*

GLEN PARK

Mission St.

19th Ave.

Santa Clara Ave.

**PINE LAKE
PARK**

**Stern
Grove**

MIRALOMA PARK

GLEN PARK

Alema
Southe

**Fleishhacker
Zoo**

Sloat Blvd.

ST. FRANCIS WOODS

STONESTOWN

Monterey Blvd.

Lake Merced

**California
State
University**

**City College of
San Francisco**

*BALBOA
PARK*

EXCELSIOR

Lake Merced Blvd.

*HARDING PARK
MUNICIPAL
GOLF CLUB*

Ocean Ave.

Alemany Blvd.

Mission St.

Persia Ave.

Lake

Juniper Serra Blvd.

BALBOA PARK

GOLDEN GATE NATIONAL RECREATION AREA

Great Hwy.

Skyline Blvd.

John Muir Dr.

Merced

Brotherhood Way

19th Ave.

San Jose Ave.

Alemany Blvd.

Geneva Ave.

*McLARE
PARK*

*OLYMPIC
COUNTRY
CLUB*

**SAN FRANCISCO
GOLF CLUB**

Alemany Blvd.

Southern Frwy.

Mission St.

CROCKER AMAZON

Junipero Serra Frwy.

Mission St.

DALY CITY

Cow Palace

BAYSHORE

John Daly Blvd.

Mission St.

*SAN BRUNO
MOUNTAIN STATE PARK*

Santa Cruz ↓

Santa Cruz ↓

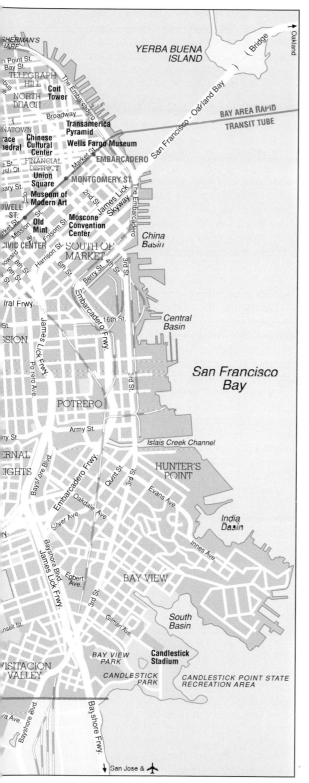

SAN FRANCISCO

San Francisco wins visitors' hearts, straightaway and effortlessly. It is a pastel city for lovers and pleasure seekers, soft and feminine and Mediterranean in mood. The city is comfortable with contradiction, jealously preserving the past and delighting in anachronism, yet always riding the latest wave of fashion, whether in *haute couture*, in gay and lesbian culture, or in computer chips. Haughty but humane, it may fleece the tourist and celebrate wealth, but it did maintain soup kitchens for the poor long before modern economics revived that custom elsewhere in the land.

San Francisco, or "Baghdad beside the Bay," as local columnist Herb Caen has tagged it, sits like a thumb at the end of a 32-mile (50-km) peninsular finger, surrounded by water on three sides and blessed by one of the world's great natural harbors. It is joined to the mainland by two of the acknowledged masterpieces of bridge design and construction, which blaze at night like strings of jewels. In the daylight, San Francisco's profile of towers and hills looks promisingly like a foreign land: it is a sleek courtesan among the cities of the world, beautiful, narcissistic and proud of it.

Everyone's favorite: Poll after poll acclaims San Francisco as the city Americans most like to visit, while 9 out of 10 people who come to the United States on foreign-exchange programs ask to be taken here. As a result, more than 3 million visitors a year pass through, leaving behind more than $1 billion annually and making tourism the city's most profitable industry.

Editor and essayist Lewis Lapoham has referred to "the dreaming narcisissism of San Francisco" while writing about the city's one-way rivalry with Los Angeles and the disillusionment that comes to Easterners when they discover that California doesn't offer them a solution to the problems they had back

Preceding pages: Transamerica Pyramid framed by the Golden Gate.

home. "More often than not," Lapham observes, "the person to whom one happens to be speaking turns out to be playing a part in his own movie. Given the high levels of disappointment in California, people retire to the screening rooms of their private fantasy."

It is a city of at least a dozen distinct and original neighborhoods. Social and economic diversity is embraced. The boundaries between social classes are less clearly drawn than elsewhere and the promise of social mobility at least *seems* more tangible.

Of course, the vast majority of San Franciscans are middle-class, ranging from the ambitious young professionals who have invaded the city's fashionable districts to the immigrant families who run neighborhood businesses. More than other people, all San Franciscans – from the richest to the poorest, from the hushed precincts of Presidio Terrace to the rundown projects of Hunters Point – are conscious of their stake in the city, the nation's 13th largest.

San Francisco's residents form a de-

mographic *bouillabaisse* not found elsewhere on the North American continent. Although the descendants of early Italian, German and Irish families are still found in snug neighborhood enclaves, their numbers have been greatly diminished by the lure of suburbia, with its cheaper and bigger houses. Their place has been filled by an influx of Asian and Hispanic people, and in recent years many Filipinos, the fastest growing minority; refugees from Southeast Asia; and both wealth and people from Hong Kong. The lively but small 23 square blocks of Chinatown haven't been able to absorb the new arrivals. So they have spread their cultures west through the avenues into the formerly all-white Richmond and Sunset districts.

San Francisco is to an extraordinary degree a city for young singles. In a single decade the number of single persons between 25 and 34 jumped an astonishing 40 percent to more than 150,000. The traditional family was, meanwhile, decamping. During the same decade, the number of children below 18 dropped by 27 percent.

Many of the new singles were homosexuals fleeing hometown disapproval for San Francisco's famed easy-going tolerance. The city's gays have emerged from a guilt-ridden existence to play a major role in its political, cultural and economic life. They have even been elected to the 11-member board of supervisors, which governs the city along with the mayor. The police department actively recruits gay men and women.

The quake next time: No one can predict when the next earthquake will come and lay waste to the city as it did in 1906 and 1989. This last quake caused billions of dollars of damage (although most of the downtown remained intact) and killed over 60 people.

Fun is easy to find, thanks to the happy accident of geography. Few cities reveal themselves as easily to the pedestrian. An unhurried 15-minute stroll will take you from the pinstriped heart of the Financial District into Chinatown. This contrast in cultures is so sharp, it feels as though you should have your passport stamped on arrival.

Left, sax appeal. Right, making tracks.

AROUND THE BAY

The massive earthquake of October 1989 left the Embarcadero Freeway – a main traffic artery into the city that once hugged the city's waterfront like a giant fence – severely damaged. But when the Embarcadero was closed down and demolished, it opened up previously obscured views of the northern waterfront – and restored one of the world's most famous ports to its stately grandeur. So the picture is now a pretty one down at the water's edge, San Francisco's historic northern waterfront, where the city and the Bay have their most dynamic meeting.

The heart of the Embarcadero is the **Ferry Building**. Built around the turn of the century, it survived the earthquake of 1906, which, incidentally, was the first time its clock ever stopped ticking. Before the construction of the Bay bridges, the Ferry Building was the second busiest passenger terminal in the world. Ferries still carry commuters to Tiburon and Sausalito and provide an idyllic and inexpensive way to spend an afternoon on the Bay. Today this area provides a pleasant respite from the hustle and bustle of Market Street. **Covarrubias' Mural**, preserved from the 1939 Golden Gate International Exposition, follows the ramp leading to the **World Trade Center**.

Water dashes against the seawall at the beginning of the 3½-mile (6-km) **Golden Gate Promenade**. Joggers and less energetic romantics favor this bracing walk which provides a panorama of San Francisco, Alcatraz, Angel Island, the Marin shoreline and the East Bay.

Part of the promenade goes through **Crissy Field**, an airfield belonging to the 1,400-acre (567-hectare) **Presidio**. Established by the Spanish in 1776 and owned by the United States Army, the Presidio is a very un-warlike military installation. Decommissioned in 1992, it is perceived as having some of the

Preceding pages: architectural contrast. **Left**, sailboats and Alcatraz Island.

most prized office space in the city. The Presidio's beautifully manicured grounds include stands of pine and eucalyptus, a museum, a hospital, a golf course, even a lake.

Further down the promenade is the **Marina Green**, beloved by kite flyers, joggers and sunbathers. The big yachts that are moored in the harbor belong to the wealthy members of the **San Francisco Yacht Club**, whose handsome Spanish-style clubhouse looks out on the Bay.

The Plaster Palace: Across Marina Boulevard to the south is the classic rococo rotunda of the **Palace of Fine Arts**. It stands before a reflecting pond where ducks and swans glide. Designed by Bernard Maybeck, the palace was originally built of plaster of paris for the Panama Pacific Exposition of 1915. It wasn't meant to last, but somehow it did. Not until 1967 was it strengthened and made permanent, thanks to the generosity of a millionaire who lived in the neighborhood.

The Palace houses the **Explor-**atorium, a museum with more than 500 exhibits to awaken even the most dormant interest in science. There is strong local opinion that this is the best science museum anywhere in the world.

The promenade continues past **Gas House Cove**, a middle-class yacht club, to **Fort Mason**, a former Army installation that has been turned over to the US Department of the Interior. The government administers the fort, part of the vast **Golden Gate National Recreation Area**, which extends north along the Marin County coast to include 20 miles (32 km) of beaches, timbered ridges and sylvan glades.

Fort Mason has many interesting little nooks and crannies, ranging from a fine vegetarian restaurant run by Zen Buddhists to museums, art galleries and the *SS Jeremiah O'Brien*, a lovingly restored World War II Liberty ship. It fires up its boilers once a year for a ceremonial tour of the Bay and can be visited most weekends.

Beyond Fort Mason is **Aquatic Park**, a terraced greensward that leads out to a

Left, Palace of Fine Arts. Below, Victorian view.

small beach and curving municipal pier usually crowded with local fishermen. It includes the **National Maritime Museum**, which has all kinds of natural displays and photographs, and is adjacent to the Hyde Street Pier, where the museum's floating displays are docked. These include a sidewheel ferry and three schooners that carried freight in the days of sailing.

Across the street is the fanciful **Ghirardelli Square**, a superb example of putting the past to work in the present. Ghirardelli Square was built as a wool mill during the Civil War era and later become a chocolate factory. When the chocolate business moved elsewhere, it could easily have been torn down to make way for something modern.

But William Matson Roth, a financier with a keen aesthetic sense, saw the possibilities for rebirth. Between 1962 and 1967, it was transformed into a brilliant showcase for retail shops, restaurants, bookstores and bars. There is usually some free entertainment going on somewhere in the square.

84 percent of visitors come to Fisherman's Wharf.

Down the street east of the square, across from a cable-car turnaround, is a durable attraction, the **Buena Vista Cafe**. The owners make so much selling Irish coffees to locals, who stand elbow-to-elbow with tourists at the bar, one wonders why they bother serving food.

Fisherman's Wharf: Tourism surveys claim **Fisherman's Wharf** – and, perhaps, its unruly but entertaining gang of resident sea lions – is what 84 percent of all San Francisco visitors have come to see. Although the fishing boats look like parts of a Walt Disney set, they are actual working vessels that put out before dawn to fish the abundant waters outside the Golden Gate.

The catch they bring back often determines the "special of the day" at the numerous restaurants clustered around the wharf. Italians historically skippered and manned the boats and also ran the restaurants. A glance at the names of the restaurants – Sabella's, Tarantino's, Alioto's – indicates that not all that much has changed.

Chances are Fisherman's Wharf will

be where visitors have their first encounter with one of the city's proudest legends, its crusty sourdough bread. It is quite unlike anything found elsewhere. Natives swear the secret ingredients roll in with the fog, working a mysterious influence on the bacteria in the sourdough starter. The best way to enjoy this bread is with sweet butter, Dungeness crab and a crisp Chablis.

The wharf has catered to generations of tourists and knows how to do it with skill. At sidewalk concessions, strollers can watch crabs being steamed and can buy shrimp or crab cocktails as takeaway treats. There are numerous shops selling low-budget souvenirs for friends and relatives who are not excessively encumbered by good taste. There is also an assortment of carnival midway-type attractions on Jefferson Street. **Ripley's Believe It or Not! Museum** and the **Guinness Museum** both display peculiar things, the latter specializing in the biggest, smallest, fastest, slowest and other such pacesetters from the pages of the Irish brewer's best-seller.

A short walk east, **Pier 39** is a popular tourist attraction. This 45-acre (18-hectare) collection of shops, arcades, fastfood restaurants and other diversions reproduces a cutesy but mythical past. Why, the critics asked, have they reproduced a turn-of-the-19th-century Cape Cod whaling village? The only thing authentic at Pier 39 is the **Eagle Cafe**, a waterfront fixture favored for decades by fishermen and longshoremen before it was moved intact from its original site a couple of blocks away.

Like the street artists in Ghirardelli Square, Pier 39 has a few ocean-going performers of its own. In recent years, the pier has become second home to a gang of more than 400 boisterous sea lions, drawn, apparently, by a bumper harvest of the Bay's spawning herring – a sea-lion favorite. Fifty or so sea lions took up residence on the boat docks next to Pier 39, from which they made nightly fishing forays into the Bay. The concept had legs – or fins. Within a year, the population grew to nearly 400.

While tourists lean over pier railings

Shopping for dinner.

and gawk and snap photos – some will do this for hours – the loudmouthed sea lions generally seem unimpressed by their celebrity status. All in a day's work, they sleep, swim, gargle, bark, and play around the boat ships and rafts that Pier 39 officials have kindly turned over to them.

If all this inspires an angling instinct, you can charter a fishing trip or can sign up at any of the boats that offer day trips for salmon fishing, or halibut, or other varieties, depending on the season. If you are a less active sailor, board a ferry headed across the Bay for a trip to Angel Island, Alcatraz or Tiburon. Departures are from the pier near Pier 43.

The tall masts and rigging at the water's edge belong to the graceful Scottish-built clipper *Balclutha*, a 265-ft (81-meter) beauty open to the public. It put to sea in 1886 and made many voyages around Cape Horn. Two piers away is another of the Wharf's draws, the *Pampanito*, a World War II submarine whose narrow passageways may awaken claustrophobia. Yellow helicopters take off at intervals near the *Balclutha*. The price is steep, but the ride they offer around Alcatraz is unforgettable.

Flying over the Bay is fun, but skimming across its waters is even better. For those with the time and money, chartering a sailboat is the best way to go. For those with less time and money, hopping aboard a big tour boat is nearly as good. Tour companies at Pier 41 and Pier 45 offer regular trips. They have snack and liquid bars on board. The usual route takes passengers out along the Marina Green and under the Golden Gate Bridge before heading back for a circuit that goes past Angel Island, Alcatraz and the Bay Bridge.

Awesome Alcatraz: Another tour boat outfit has headquarters at Pier 39, east of Fisherman's Wharf. There is a colorful rivalry between this company and another at Pier 41, which sometimes manifests itself in the maneuvering that goes on between the boats off Alcatraz. Each tries to sail close to the island to give its passengers the best view. The island's famous prison, however, is fall

Waterfront transportation.

ing apart. Its steel bars are being eaten away by salt air and its pastel buildings are slowly giving way to the ravages of time. What is it about ruins that make them so appealing?

In the case of Alcatraz, part of the explanation lies in its location. Just over a mile offshore of San Francisco, the island is windswept and scoured by swift tides. When first sighted in 1775 by Spanish Lieutenant Juan Manuel de Ayala, he named it Isla de los Alcatraces after its only occupants, the pelicans.

Because of its strategic location in the Bay it was garrisoned with soldiers in the 1850s and, since escape from the island was a remote possibility, renegade servicemen were incarcerated on Alcatraz. They were followed by Apaches who were taken prisoner in Arizona during the 1870s Indian wars and, later, by prisoners from the Spanish-American War.

Alcatraz evolved into a federal prison that housed such case-hardened criminals as Mafia leader Al Capone and the notorious Machine Gun Kelly. Those few desperate inmates who managed to "escape," perished in the frigid waters surrounding the island.

The prison was finally closed in 1963 when the costs of repairing the constant ravages of wind and weather grew too great. Since then, proposals have surfaced from time to time to put the island to some sort of use, but all have come to nothing. A band of Native Americans occupied the barren island for an 18-month period in the 1970s to highlight their differences with the Bureau of Indian Affairs, but eventually they were only too glad to leave.

So the prison buildings crumble away bit by bit as people increasingly think the best thing to do with Alcatraz is just to leave it as it is, a symbol of "man's inhumanity to man." Park rangers give one-hour guided tours including a peek at some of the cell blocks. Ferries leave from Pier 41, and warm clothing is essential.

The Golden Gate: Illuminated at night, often shrouded in a romantic fog by day, the **Golden Gate Bridge** is an unforget-

Sailing to Alcatraz.

table presence in San Francisco (*See page 153*). It's an image with worldwide recognition, the one that most people conjure up when they think about the city. But it was more than a decade – due to political squabbles and the onset of the Depression – before builder Joseph Strauss' 1922 plan could be implemented, and even then it was not his original ungainly structure that arose but a more elegant version modified by one of his staff.

When the bridge celebrated its 50th birthday in 1986 more than three quarters of a million people are said to have walked across its 3-mile span – a statistic to ponder upon when the entire population of San Francisco is scarely more than that figure. It does, however, indicate the affection felt for this famous landmark, long celebrated in story and song. "To pass through the portals of the Golden Gate" wrote Allan Dunn, "is to cross the threshhold of adventure."

In addition to the hundreds of thousands of cars that cross the bridge each day there are still hundreds who choose to walk – many of whom park their cars and then traverse the span both ways. Sadly, many hundreds over the years have also made it their last stop, plunging 220 ft (67 meters) into the frigid waters with a last look at the city that somehow failed them.

The **Richmond district**, foghound during much of the summer months, is an area of orderly streets, tidy homes and manicured lawns. These allow it to blend well into the neighboring **Sunset district**, which is equally middle class and conservative. One can easily become lost in this grid of streets, so the best thing drivers can do is to follow the frequent signs that guide them along the city's fascinating 49-mile (79-km) **Scenic Drive**.

The drive snakes past the **Cliff House**, which overlooks the Pacific Ocean and peers down upon barking seals clinging wetly to the rocks below. This is worth a stop, as generations of San Franciscans have testified since 1863. The present Cliff House is the fifth to have been built here. Its predecessors have all burned

Alcatraz and Marin County from Fort Point.

down or suffered some other calamity.

North of Cliff House is verdant **Lincoln Park**, whose 270 acres (109 hectares) include an 18-hole municipal golf course and the handsome French-style **California Palace of the Legion of Honor**. At the entrance is one of five existing bronze casts of Rodin's famous statue, *The Thinker*. The museum also has 18th-century paintings and tapestries as well as works by Impressionists like Monet, Renoir and Degas. Also within the palace is the **Achenbach Foundation for Graphic Arts**, the largest collection of prints and drawings in western America.

Golden Gate Park: South from the Cliff House, the Scenic Drive leads past the pounding surf of **Ocean Beach** (too dangerous for swimming) into **Golden Gate Park**, one of the great urban parks in the world. It is 3 miles (5 km) long and a half mile (1 km) wide, and consists of groves of redwoods, eucalyptus, pine and countless varieties of other trees from all over the world. It is dotted with lakes, grassy meadows and sunlit dells.

There can be thousands of people within its borders, but Golden Gate Park is so large that one can easily find solitary tranquility in a misty forest grove or by a peaceful pond.

More than a century ago, the park was painstakingly reclaimed from sand dunes through the herculean efforts of a crusty Scottish landscape architect named John McLaren. Park superintendent for 55 years, McLaren so disliked statuary that he shrouded all human likeness in dense vegetation. Most park statues remain "lost" today.

The park has many varied attractions. There are baseball and soccer fields, horseback-riding trails, tennis courts, bowling and horseshoe pitching areas, flycasting ponds, even a polo field. Visitors can rent bicycles to tour the park from any of a number of adjacent shops, as well as roller skates from vendors who keep their stock in the back of trucks. Part of John F. Kennedy Drive, which runs through the park, is closed off on Sundays so that skaters can strut their stuff. Some

Left, Conservatory of Flowers. Below, park pleasures.

of their routines are quite spectacular.

The park has feasts for the mind as well as the eyes. The **California Academy of Sciences** comprises three museums in one. The natural history section incorporates displays of anthropology and ethnology with dioramas of North American and African animals. The **Morrison Planetarium** has a whiz-bang laser light show about our tiny, undistinguished corner of the universe under its 65-ft (20-meter) dome.

The **Steinhart Aquarium** has nearly 16,000 specimens of marine and shore life on display in its 190 tanks. In addition to a gang of appealing warm-water penguins, the aquarium also features a simulated swamp and doughnut-shaped "fish roundabout." The Steinhart's attractions include a first-hand look at the intricate pattern of sea life around a living coral reef, and the fierce anatomy of a frozen great white shark.

Past the Music Concourse, where Sunday afternoon concerts are given, is the **M.H. De Young Memorial Museum**. Blockbuster traveling exhibits are pre-sented here but, even without these shows, the De Young – which opened in 1921 – is one of the city's best museums. Its collection includes Renaissance and Medieval paintings and tapestries, sculpture and suits of armor, and African and Polynesian galleries.

An adjunct of the De Young is the **Asian Art Museum**, donated to the city by the late Avery Brundage, the iron-willed millionaire who dominated the international Olympic movement for half a century. The Brundage collection has some 10,000 items, making it the largest of its kind outside the Orient. It includes precious jades, ceramics, sculptures, bronzes, vases, figurines and a host of other examples of Chinese and other Asian art, some dating back 3,500 years. Brundage bought his pieces during his global travels, paying top dollar at a time when there was little Western interest in Asian art. Near the end of this century, the museum will move downtown into the beautiful premises vacated by the city's Main Library.

South of the museums is **Stow Lake**,

Below, hippie heaven. **Right**, Haight shopping.

a pleasant body of water where sporty types can rent rowboats or pedal boats and work up a sweat before quenching their thirst with a beer at the snack bar. The island in the middle of the lake is called Strawberry Hill. Summer concerts are held in the dell beside the lake.

The **Conservatory of Flowers**, half a mile (1 km) east of Stow Lake, was built in 1878, modeled after the Palm House at London's Kew Gardens. It was shipped piece by piece around Cape Horn from Dublin. It has permanent displays of many plants and features spectacular seasonal displays of blooms.

The **Japanese Tea Garden**, built in 1894, is a harmonious blend of architecture, landscaping and pools where here, many years ago, fortune cookies were invented. The custom spread to Chinatown, then traveled throughout the Chinese food industry in the Western world. The garden was disassembled during World War II, then restored to its former grace when the threat of wartime vandalism had passed.

Stanyan Street borders the eastern edge of the park and intersects with **Haight Street**, which became one of the world's most famous thoroughfares in the 1960s. That was when long hair, tie-dyed fabrics, hallucinogens and a belief in the power of love and peace persuaded a generation of alienated young people that they could create an alternative lifestyle.

These "hippies" openly smoked marijuana, took up forms of Eastern mysticism, declined to be sent overseas to fight in foreign conflicts such as the Vietnam War, and otherwise were a thorn in the sides of their elders, who sometimes sent police in riot gear to the middle of the **Haight-Ashbury** district to clean it up.

Haight Street was once so gaudy and bizarre that tour buses ran up and down it with their windows full of goggle-eyed tourists. Like most such radical departures from the social norm, the hippie experiment fell victim to time and fashion. Haight-Ashbury itself has returned to a quiet existence as a faintly down-at-the-heel neighborhood.

Ghirardelli Square.

GOLDEN GATE BRIDGE

When sailing under the Golden Gate Bridge, it is interesting to consider that at one time many engineers felt that it would be impossible to build a span at this point because of the depth of the water (318 ft/97 meters, at the deepest point) and the powerful tidal rush. The city authorized studies in 1918, but not until 1933 was the first shovelful of earth turned under the gaze of master engineer Joseph B. Strauss (no relation to the Waltz King). Four years later, it was finished at a cost of $35 million and the lives of 11 construction workers. Today it serves 114,000 motorists a day driving between the city and regions to the north.

San Franciscans think of it as their own, of course, but the unwieldy board that runs it consists of 19 members, some from as far away as Mendocino or Humboldt counties, 350 miles (560 km) to the north. It is argued that, short of taking a lengthy detour across the Bay, the bridge connects the only direct route to these regions but there is a more mundane reason for the association.

These two counties, as well as the other four with seats on the board (San Francisco, Marin, Sonoma and Napa), helped to pay for the bridge's construction by backing the bond issue. They must have recouped their investment many times over: Marin and Sonoma alone receive $27 million a year as their share of bridge tolls, now a stiff $3 a car. More than 17 million southbound cars cross the bridge each year. Nobody counts the northbound cars, however, because no toll is collected from them.

Nevertheless, the Golden Gate Bridge Highway and Transportation District justifies its unilateral decisions by pointing to the responsibilities it has accrued over the past half-century. These include operating an extensive transit system which includes four luxurious ferries and 281 diesel buses between the city and northern counties; the $6.2 million purchase of a high-speed catamaran to operate between San Francisco and Larkspur; and such one-off expenditures as a $165 million earthquake retrofit for the bridge itself. Board members are well compensated for their efforts: the general manager's salary of around $116,000 a year is 20 percent more than that of

California's director of transportation who supervises nine bridges and thousands more employees.

The district's independent – and virtually unaccountable – status has raised the ire of critics, especially since the prediction of federal officials that it will be running in the red by 1998.

The Golden Gate's statistics always fascinate. Including its freeway approaches, the bridge is 7 miles (11 km) long, with the suspension section stretching for 6,450 ft (2,320 meters). The towers stand 746 ft (228 meters) above the water, and the span is 220 ft (67 meters) above the water at low tide. The bigger of the two supporting piers extends 100 ft (30 meters) below the water. The builders poured 693,000 cubic yards (520,000 cubic meters) of concrete and used more than 100,000 tons of steel in its construction: 80,000 miles (128,700 km) of cable help to support it.

The bridge was built so sturdily that it has been closed only three times due to high winds. Crews, continually sandblasting rust off the bridge and repainting it, use 10,000 gallons (38,000 liters) of orange paint a year. ∎

Fourth of July fireworks.

AROUND DOWNTOWN

Though San Francisco is anything but an old-fashioned village, **Union Square** still fulfils to some extent the role that plazas and public squares once played in small towns. All walks of life have gathered in and around here: socialites seeking gowns for debutante balls, business-minded people plotting corporation growth, tourists boarding cable cars for a ride over Nob Hill, and residents visiting theaters and shops. A considerable homeless population congregates alongside street musicians and evangelists. As has been the case with the downtown plazas of many American cities, the square's steady deterioration over the years has sparked a contentious debate in the local papers about what must be done to restore it to some of its former glory.

The square itself offers performances that can't be matched. It's not a bad idea to grab a box lunch and take a seat on one of the park benches. From this vantage, you'll notice the bronze nude atop the memorial to President William McKinley (who died in San Francisco in 1901), by sculptor Robert Aitken. Aitken used as his model teenaged Alma de Bretteville, who became famous for marrying, at 22, Adolph Spreckels, the much older and well-to-do president of the San Francisco Parks Commission. Alma became the richest woman in the West, lived in a vast mansion at 2080 Washington Street and donated $14 million to various charities while becoming a generous patron of the arts, noted for her "unorthodox behavior and uninhibited remarks."

In the heart of the shopping and hotel district, the square's west side is fronted by the **Westin St Francis Hotel** with a 90-year record of housing dignitaries and celebrities. The plaza of the more modern **Hyatt on Union Square** is adorned with a Ruth Asawa fountain that literally embodies San Francisco. The bronze friezes of typical city scenes were cast in molds made from bread dough by some 250 schoolchildren and

Preceding pages: parade in the Mission district. **Left**, the Sheraton Palace Hotel. **Right**, St Mary's Cathedral, Western Addition.

other local residents. Also surrounding the perimeter of the square are the city's major "big" department stores – **Macy's**, **Saks Fifth Avenue**, and **Neiman-Marcus**, the last-mentioned roofed by an exquisite stained glass rotunda preserved from the City of Paris, the city's first department store and original occupant of the site.

Though the area is now primarily a commercial center, the flavor of "Old San Francisco" still prevails. San Francisco's **Montgomery Street**, for example, is paved with city lore. Sam Brannan ran down Montgomery when he announced the discovery of gold in 1848. Mark Twain found inspiration here in a local fireman named Tom Sawyer. Outlaws, actresses and authors have all found inspiration, opportunity or solace of a sort around these old city blocks. And during the Gold Rush, the area was soon overrun by the '49ers, a rugged lot who came in search of gold the year after Brannan's news spread throughout the world. (The city's beloved National Football League team, the '49ers,

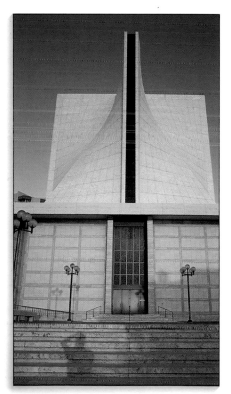

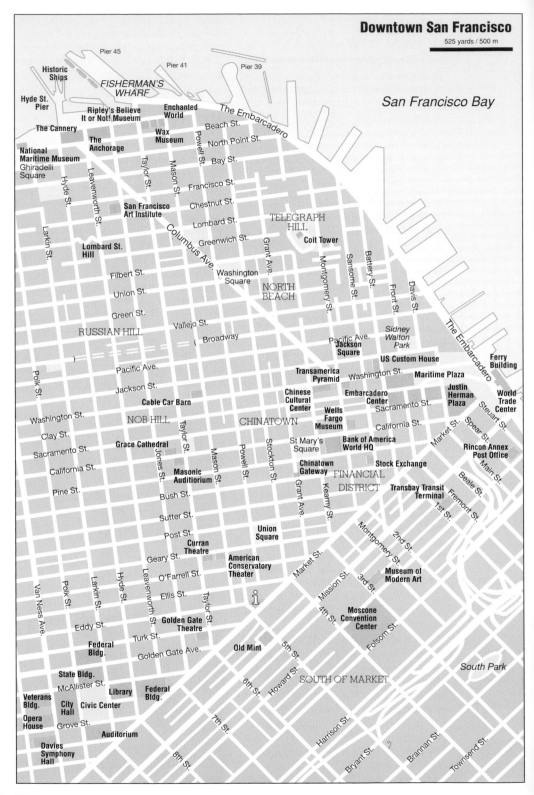

Downtown San Francisco

525 yards / 500 m

San Francisco Bay

Pier 45

Pier 41

Pier 39

Historic Ships

FISHERMAN'S WHARF

Hyde St. Pier

Ripley's Believe It or Not! Museum

Enchanted World

The Embarcadero

The Cannery

Wax Museum

Beach St.

North Point St.

The Anchorage

National Maritime Museum

Ghiradelli Square

Bay St.

Powell St.

Mason St.

Taylor St.

Francisco St.

Hyde St.

Leavenworth St.

Larkin St.

Chestnut St.

San Francisco Art Institute

Lombard St.

Columbus Ave.

Greenwich St.

TELEGRAPH HILL

Coit Tower

Lombard St. Hill

Filbert St.

Union St.

Green St.

Washington Square

Grant Ave.

NORTH BEACH

Montgomery St.

Sansome St.

Battery St.

Front St.

Davis St.

RUSSIAN HILL

Vallejo St.

Broadway

Pacific Ave.

Jackson St.

Pacific Ave.

Jackson Square

Sidney Walton Park

US Custom House

Ferry Building

Polk St.

Cable Car Barn

NOB HILL

CHINATOWN

Transamerica Pyramid

Washington St.

Maritime Plaza

The Embarcadero

Washington St.

Clay St.

Chinese Cultural Center

Embarcadero Center

Justin Herman Plaza

World Trade Center

Sacramento St.

Wells Fargo Museum

Sacramento St.

Grace Cathedral

California St.

California St.

Taylor St.

Jones St.

Mason St.

Powell St.

Stockton St.

St Mary's Square

Bank of America World HQ

Rincon Annex Post Office

Pine St.

Masonic Auditorium

Chinatown Gateway

Stock Exchange

Market St.

Spear St.

Main St.

Bush St.

Grant Ave.

Kearny St.

FINANCIAL DISTRICT

Transbay Transit Terminal

Beale St.

Sutter St.

Post St.

Union Square

Fremont St.

1st St.

Curran Theatre

Geary St.

Montgomery St.

2nd St.

American Conservatory Theater

Market St.

3rd St.

Museum of Modern Art

O'Farrell St.

Ellis St.

Van Ness Ave.

Polk St.

Larkin St.

Hyde St.

Leavenworth St.

Taylor St.

Mission St.

4th St.

Moscone Convention Center

Folsom St.

Eddy St.

Golden Gate Theatre

5th St.

South Park

Turk St.

Federal Bldg.

Golden Gate Ave.

Old Mint

Howard St.

State Bldg.

McAllister St.

Library

Federal Bldg.

6th St.

SOUTH OF MARKET

Veterans Bldg.

City Hall

Civic Center

7th St.

Opera House

Grove St.

Auditorium

Harrison St.

Bryant St.

Brannan St.

Townsend St.

Davies Symphony Hall

8th St.

takes its name from this crew of roughnecks.)

The original '49ers sailed into the San Francisco Bay, dropped anchor and often abandoned ship to pursue their dream of striking gold. It wasn't long before the city's original shoreline began to burgeon, contributing to the birth of today's **Financial District**. Brokers, bankers and insurance agents now pursue wealth on several acres of landfill on and around Montgomery Street, nicknamed Wall Street West.

Fun with finance: The intellectual challenge of the financial world can be explored at the **Federal Reserve Bank** (101 Market Street). Its World of Economics gallery explains finance principles through hands-on computer games, videotapes, murals and even cartoons. Visitors can try their skill at being board chairperson turning even stock market crashes and federal deficits into fun.

The aesthetic and historic value of filthy lucre is dealt with in the Museum of American Money from the West (400 California Street). Housed in the **Bank of California** – the oldest banking hall in the district – this cache includes historic coins, currency and gold and silver ingots. The exhibit's value exceeds one million dollars.

In a similar vein, the gold nuggets on display in the History Room of the **Wells Fargo Bank** (420 Montgomery Street) offer insights into San Francisco's turbulent and often-prosperous past. There are banking articles, miner's equipment, and dioramas from the Gold Rush era. One of those colorful 19th-century Wells Fargo Overland Stages, once used on the coach trails of the West and now seen on the bank's logo, provides the museum's centerpiece.

Many other historic buildings have been preserved in the downtown area with Art Deco, Romanesque and Chicago School styles just a few of those on view. Notice the Gothic styling of the **Hallidie Building**'s glass wall curtain (130 Sutter Street); the terracotta carvings of ox-heads, eagles and young nymphs on the **Hunter-Dulin Building** (111 Sutter Street); the 21-ft (6.5-meter) high modern sculptures – *Mother Earth*

and *Man and His Inventions* – that flank the **Pacific Stock Exchange** (Pine and Sansome); the geometric designs of the **Shell Building** (100 Bush Street); and the winged gargoyles adorning the portico of the **Kohl Building** (400 Montgomery Street).

The **Transamerica Pyramid** (600 Montgomery Street) commands attention because of its great size and unusual shape. The city's tallest building, it pierces the sky at 853 ft (260 meters) and, while some find its unique shape aesthetically appealing, others denounce it as "The Great Alien Ring Toss." There's no debate, however, about its most surprising feature: flanking the building is one of the world's few urban redwood groves.

The best bird's eye view of San Francisco can be gained from the 52nd floor of the **Bank of America**'s world headquarters building, where a cocktail lounge/restaurant opens daily to the public from 3pm. The building's exterior is faced with red carnelian granite and a slyly named sculpture adorns the

The Transamerica Pyramid and Columbus Tower on Columbus Avenue.

outdoor plaza: *Banker's Heart*, which is a huge stone of polished granite.

Ancient and opulent: The interiors of many of these buildings are just as remarkable as their facades, and are open for public viewing. The Garden Court of the **Sheraton Palace Hotel,** at New Montgomery and Market streets, is turn-of-the-century opulent, a magnificent dining room surrounded by 16 marble columns. An intricate iron framework supports a leaded glass skylight 48 ft (15 meters) above the floor and 10 crystal chandeliers.

The Garden Court's modern counterpart is the **Hyatt Regency Hotel**, whose indoor atrium is 20 stories high, housing over 100 trees and thousands of strands of hanging ivy. Birds flit about the overhead skylight, while 170 ft (50 meters) below, visitors sink into the plush conversation pits that line the lobby. Even Charles Perry's geometric sculpture – rising just four stories above the reflecting pool – seems huge and impressive.

The Hyatt Regency is just part of the "city within a city" that John Portman

envisioned when he designed the **Embarcadero Center**. This 8½-acre (3.5-hectare) development consists of four high-rise office towers, the **Justin Hermann Plaza**, and an interwoven complex of 45 restaurants and 130 retail stores, all linked by pedestrian bridges and outdoor courtyards filled with displays of sculpture.

The Embarcadero Center's only rival for this kind of variety in the Financial District is the **Crocker Galleria** shopping arcade between Post and Sutter streets (off Montgomery). But truly serious shoppers will venture west, back to Union Square, at the center of one of the country's most compact and varied retail cores.

Art and Eats: The Circle Gallery (140 Maiden Lane), just one of many private showrooms that art lovers will want to visit, is a spiral-ramped showroom, designed by Frank Lloyd Wright before he undertook the larger task of designing New York City's Guggenheim Museum. Further along Maiden Lane, Sergio Old Prints, is the city's only dealer in pre-

Climbing the walls of color.

1880 prints and art exhibition posters, while the Lone Wolf Gallery on Sutter Street and the Rorick Gallery on Mason present almost exclusively the art of Bay Area and California residents.

Here too are some of the city's best restaurants: Masa's on Bush Street, Campton Place on Stockton, Kinokawa on Grant and China Moon on Post. Original Joe's on Taylor Street has the city's best burgers.

Just across Market Street, the ambitious renewal project **Yerba Buena Gardens** is set on 87 acres (35 hectares) behind the **Moscone Convention Center**. Extending over 12 full blocks, it includes a garden big enough to have a redwood grove and a waterfall, theaters, pleasant restaurants, and a shimmering glass memorial to Martin Luther King Jr. The **Ansel Adams Center for Photography** and the **California Historical Society** are also here.

Adjacent to Yerba Buena Gardens is **San Francisco**'s **Museum of Modern Art**. SFMOMA's state-of-the-art building, designed by Swiss architect Mario

Botta, has a stepped-back brick-and stone facade with a soaring, cylindrical skylight, and serves as the West Coast's most comprehensive resource center of 20th-century art. Over 15,000 exhibits are on permanent display in these impressive surroundings, including paintings by Salvador Dalí, Jackson Pollock, Francis Bacon, Willem de Kooning, Roy Lichtenstein, Andy Warhol and Diego Rivera. The museum's undeniable masterpiece is the haunting *Femme au Chapeau,* one of several works in the museum by Matisse.

SFMOMA is also distinguished as one of the first US museums to have recognized photography as an art form, and now has a collection of over 9,000 works. There are also a number of major video installations, the focus being on the role of media in 20th-century art. Technology-minded visitors can walk around the galleries in a choice of routes listening to interactive audio tours. These include recordings by artists, historians and curators using CD-quality sound.

It is eight blocks from Union Square

Below, the city's Museum of Modern Art. **Right**, *Femme au Chapeau* by Matisse.

west to **Van Ness Avenue**, a broad thoroughfare running from north to south with a planter strip in the middle. This is one of the city's main arteries, serving as the gateway (via Lombard Street) to all points north across the Golden Gate Bridge.

Abutting Van Ness at McAllister Street is **City Hall**, one of the most beautiful public buildings in the United States. It was designed by Arthur Brown, an architect so young and so unknown that he figured he might as well shoot for the moon in the early 20th-century competition to select the building design. To his surprise, Brown and his partner, John Bakewell, won with a design that called for the lavish use of costly marble, and an immense dome that was patterned after St Peter's Cathedral in Rome.

Built in 1914, City Hall is honeycombed with municipal offices and both civil and criminal courts. The full effect of the building is best felt from its **Polk Street** entrance, which faces a plaza. The magnificent stairway inside leads to the second-floor Board of Supervisors chambers.

This is the building in which Supervisor Dan White shot Mayor George Moscone in 1978 for refusing to reappoint him to the seat White had resigned. White then shot gay Supervisor Harvey Milk for smirking at him. After White was convicted of manslaughter and given a wrist-slapping sentence, howling mobs descended on City Hall and were only narrowly prevented from breaking in.

Across the plaza from City Hall is the stately main branch of the **Public Library**, built in 1916. The library plans to move to nearby premises in late 1996. The building will then be refurbished in anticipation of housing the Asian Art Museum, sometime near the turn of the century. The south end of the plaza is occupied by the **Civic Auditorium** (1913) and the north side by a **State Office Building** (1926). Together, they present an appearance of order and harmony. This comprises San Francisco's **Civic Center**. The brutal federal build- **City Hall**.

ing standing behind the state building on Golden Gate Avenue is a reminder of just how badly the Civic Center could have turned out had it been planned less carefully.

Opposite City Hall on Van Ness Avenue is a series of distinguished buildings. The Veterans Auditorium Building (1932) at the corner of Van Ness and McAllister streets houses the 915-seat **Herbst Auditorium.**

Next to it is the 3,535-seat **Opera House**, one of the country's greatest, and built the same year as the **Veterans Auditorium**. It has a summer opera festival and a regular season running from September–December. The opera company, which draws the foremost artists of the day to its stage, shares quarters with the highly regarded San Francisco Ballet. Across the street from the Opera House is the lavish 2,958-seat **Louise M. Davies Symphony Hall**.

Davies Hall has triggered quite a boom in the Civic Center area. Expensive condominium buildings are rising to the north, hotels are being smartened up, and excellent restaurants like the Hayes Street Grill have opened. The **Opera Plaza** complex, where apartments begin at around $240,000, is a good example of the quality. It has a street-level bar with a European flavor. Its Modesto Lanzone cafe, like its sister restaurant in Ghirardelli Square, draws raves over its lighter-than-air pasta.

West from the Civic Center is an area known as the **Western Addition**, a neighborhood of public housing and derelict Victorian buildings feeling the touches of restoration. Increasingly popular with the gay community, the district is full of theaters and interesting bars and cafes. There is a great deal of streetlife but, having said that, anyone visiting should take care when walking around, even during the daylight hours.

Market Street is a thoroughfare of variety. In the Financial District, it's comfortably interesting. But it turns seedy down toward 5th Street, and stays that way for four blocks before beginning to revive. It finally ends at the multi-intersection that includes 24th

Candlestick Park.

Street and **Castro Street**, one of the busy hubs of gay action. Broad, tree-lined and well-lit at night, it has all the elements needed to become one of the world's great avenues. The city even spent millions of dollars building a tunnel beneath Market Street in order to eliminate the clutter of streetcars. But somehow the street has never achieved its full potential.

South of Union Square, Powell Street passes near the eastern fringe of the **Tenderloin district**, a neighborhood of sleazy bars, porn parlors and residential hotels where the poor are ruthlessly exploited by the owners and their agents. Drag queens traipse coquettishly, drug dealers sell their stepped-on cocaine and sugared heroin, hookers beckon, and street-wise Vietnamese children offer bags of garlic to passersby. It's a good area to avoid after dark.

When people talk about South of Market (**SoMa**), they refer to the hodge-podge of businesses and run-down residences that once ran to China Basin and the waterfront. Once an exclusively in-dustrial neighborhood, Market or SoMa, home of the **Old Mint**, built in 1874 and a survivor of the 1906 earthquake, has become one of the hottest nightlife areas of the city.

Mission Street heads due south into the heart of the Mission district, San Francisco's great melting pot of Latin American cultures. **Mission Dolores** (Dolores Avenue near 16th Street) was founded less than a week before the American Declaration of Independence was signed in 1776, and its 4-ft (1.5 km) adobe walls still form what is the oldest building in San Francisco. The graves of many of the city's earliest pioneers, and thousands of native Costonoan Indians, can be found in the mission cemetery.

The Mission district oozes Hispanic culture. Red-tile roofs predominate on public buildings, palms and utilitarian shops line the streets, and restaurants offer the gamut of Latin-American cuisine – from Mexican to Chilean, Cuban to Salvadorean. The macho Latino culture sometimes clashes with the neighboring gay culture of **Noe Valley**. The busy promiscuity that once characterized the gay scene in San Francisco has been chilled by the onset of Aids. But the restaurants are still crowded, the bars are still hopping, and the sidewalks are still filled with shoppers.

Much the same can be said for nearby **Union Street**. By day, Union Street is a chic stretch of boutiques, antique stores, gourmet shops, delicatessens and classy restaurants. At night, the singles bars are the main attraction where the young and beautiful go in search of each other's images.

Sports fans flock to famed **Candlestick Park** on a rocky promontory at the southeast corner of the city. The San Francisco '49ers football team and the San Francisco Giants baseball team have both made their homes in this windy, 60,000-capacity stadium.

Not far to the west, amidst the look-alike suburban homes of **Daly City**, the **Cow Palace** with its seating capacity of 14,300 has hosted everything from rock concerts and basketball games to livestock shows.

Left, grave of California's first governor at Mission Dolores. **Right**, hats off to San Francisco.

NORTH BEACH TO CHINATOWN

The heart of San Francisco's nightclub district is **Broadway**, a stretch tawdry enough for the most jaded tastes. On weekend nights, the streets are thronged with people who come to ogle the hookers and to be lured into dark joints by cold-eyed barkers with smiles as dazzling as zircons.

Despite the sleaze, there is an undeniable excitement to Broadway. The neon lights are bright, and live music blares from inside many clubs. There are also some good restaurants and a variety of wonderful coffee shops where midnight snackers can sip espresso or *caffe latte*, feast on fresh pastry, and eavesdrop on some first-rate conversation at neighboring tables.

This area, known as **North Beach**, has always been congenial to writers, artists and other deep thinkers. At the same time, it has retained the flavor of an old-fashioned Italian neighborhood whose dual anchors are the **Church of Saints Peter and Paul** on grassy **Washington Square**, and the little workingmen's bars where elderly Italians sip red wine and consider the affairs of the day. A word of warning – parking is near impossible in North Beach at night, and police are very strict in dealing with illegally parked vehicles. It is best to walk or take a taxi.

The outside tables at **Enrico's** on Broadway are a good place from which to study the passing scene. Many interesting local characters and homegrown celebrities drop by at night, including entertainers from up and down the street who are taking their breaks between shows. The man in the beret is the excitable owner, Enrico Banducci, and no prudent man would dream of giving the sizable bartender any trouble.

Most people find a visit to **Finocchio's** fun – it's one of the world's best drag shows. There are four shows a night and busloads of tourists from all over the world troop in to gape and rub their eyes in disbelief.

A few steps away is the **Condor Club**, where a waitress named Carol Doda peeled to the waist one night in 1964 and ushered in the topless boom. The venerable Doda used to descend nightly from the ceiling atop a piano. She was clad only in a G-string, showing her debt to silicone technology.

The **Washington Square Bar and Grill** is a hangout for lawyers, politicians, writers and others who make their living from words. Rugby experience is helpful in getting a drink from the small crowded bar. Another favorite North Beach haunt of wordsmiths is the **City Lights** bookstore in Columbus Street.

For some 30 years City Lights has been operated by poet Lawrence Ferlinghetti, one of the literary lights of the 1950s Beat era. Across the alley is **Vesuvio's**, a wonderfully atmospheric bar where intellectuals in rimless glasses sip aperitifs and think long thoughts. And nearby, on Columbus, is the **Tosca Cafe**, where off duty cops and society swells play pool and listen to opera records that play on the jukebox.

Above North Beach, at the end of

Lombard Street, is **Telegraph Hill**. Originally called *Loma Alta* by the Spaniards, the hill has gone through a number of names over the years, including Goat Hill, Windmill Hill, Tin Can Hill and Signal Hill. The *moderne* tiara crowning Telegraph Hill is **Coit Tower**, built in 1934 by Mrs Lillie Coit in memory of the city's heroic corps of firefighters.

As a teenager, Lillie became the official mascot of Knickerbocker Engine Company No. 5, and spent long hours playing cards and roaming around in the company's uniform – much to the consternation of San Francisco's society ladies. In order to show her admiration for the firefighters, Lillie left enough funds to the city to build a splendid commemorative tower. Many people have noted the tower's resemblance to a firehouse nozzle, but historians insist that this was never the intention.

The best-known of the city's hills, just to the west above Chinatown, is **Nob Hill**, celebrated mostly for the size and elegance of the mansions that were built there a century ago. Writer Robert Louis Stevenson called it the "hill of palaces." The **cable car** lines cross at **California and Powell** streets. From here there is a magnificent view of the Bay crossed by the Oakland Bay Bridge and framed by the pagodas of Chinatown and the pyramidal spire of the Transamerica Pyramid. In a fevered rush to outdo each other in opulence, the robber barons of the last century built their palatial homes on Nob Hill. Many of the houses that remain have now been converted into condos or multi-dwelling apartment buildings.

The best-known landmark on the hill today is the **Mark Hopkins Hotel** which occupies the site of the former Mark Hopkins mansion. The mansion's original stables boasted rosewood stalls with silver trimmings and mosaic floors covered with Belgian carpets. Much of this luxury vanished in the Great Fire that raged for five days and nights following the earthquake of 1906. The **Pacific Union Club**, built for silver magnate James Flood in 1855, is the only survivor of the fire. Today the sturdy

Left, Fairmont Hotel. Below, view towards Russian Hill.

brownstone structure with its pine-framed entrance is a private club.

The **Stanford Court**, Mark Hopkins and **Huntington** hotels were built on the ashes of the great mansions and retain an aura of the original splendor, especially the **Fairmont Hotel** with its gilded lobby and faux-marble pillars. The Big Four bar at the Huntington celebrates Messrs Crocker, Hopkins, Huntington and Stanford, the tycoons who built the transcontinental railroad, and evokes the robber baron era through a woody, masculine interior. During the Christmas season, the Nob Hill hotels host free choral concerts in festively decorated lobbies.

America's most famously curving thoroughfare, **Lombard Street**, is on nearby **Russian Hill**. For some inexplicable reason visiting motorists like to make their way to the top and then drive down this unique slalom course, all the while watched by spectators who line the adjoining sidewalks.

Asian imports.

Chinatown: Standing on the corner of Broadway and Columbus Avenue, surrounded by the glitter and sleaze of North Beach, one is near enough to the **Grant Avenue** entrance of exotic Chinatown to hear the clacking of *mahjong* tiles. If Chinatown were the only attraction San Francisco had to offer visitors, it would still be worth making the trip just to visit it.

San Francisco's Chinatown is the biggest Chinatown outside of Asia, and the steady influx of immigrants keeps it growing. Its streets are narrow, crowded and alive with color and movement. It extends for eight blocks, far enough to make visitors feel after a time that they might be walking the teeming, traffic-choked streets of Hong Kong or Shanghai. Mysterious alleys abound. Tiny cluttered herb shops offer powders and poultices which promise everything from rheumatism relief to the restoration of sexual powers.

In Chinatown's dozens of hole-in-the-wall shops, it's possible to buy anything from cheap trinkets to exquisite screens and massive hand-carved furniture costing thousands of dollars. Silken

clothing, hand-painted vases, paper lanterns, rattan furniture, and many other Asian articles are for sale.

Some of the world's finest Chinese restaurants can be found in this quarter, and it would be supreme folly for visitors not to take advantage and have at least one meal here. **Johnny Kan's** and the **Empress of China** are the best known of the fancy restaurants, but there are any number of obscure restaurants and tiny cafes where diners can sit down with the Chinese locals and eat well and very cheaply.

Veteran gastronomes have been known to cry out in ecstasy after a meal of *dim sum*. These delicious pastries, filled with meat, chicken, shrimp or vegetables, are a favorite Chinatown lunch. Waitresses push them from table to table on carts like peddlers. Diners select the dishes they want; the number of empty dishes on the table at the end of a meal determines the cost.

Stockton Street: Intriguing though it is, Grant Avenue should not be the sole focus of Chinatown exploration. Grant is the face Chinatown wears for tourists. One block over is **Stockton Street**, where the real business of life is carried on, and the atmosphere here is unquestionably authentic. Tiny Chinese women, ancient enough to have had their feet bound many decades ago, totter on shopping errands. Old men smoke cigarettes and read Chinese-language newspapers. Bright-eyed children chatter on their way to or from school. Crates of fresh produce and raw meat are unloaded from double-parked trucks as staccato bursts of Chinese dialect are exchanged.

The **Chinese Cultural Center** in the Holiday Inn on Kearny Street is worth a visit. It offers art shows, entertainment and guided tours.

Built in 1968 as part of San Francisco's redevelopment project known as the Western Addition (*see page 163*), the **Japan Center** is a complex with restaurants, bookstores, and gift shops that is the heart of the city's Japanese community.

The Center has become a locus for **Japantown**'s community both eco-nomically and culturally, especially during the last two weeks of April. Every year the Cherry Blossom Festival is celebrated here. Roughly 12,000 Japanese live in San Francisco, many of them between Geary Boulevard and California Street to the north and south, and between Octavia and Fillmore streets to the east and west.

On Laguna Street, at Sutter, is the **Soto Zen Mission**'s *Sokoji*. (*Soko* is San Francisco's Japanese name), its austere interior in stark contrast to the remarkably upbeat nature of the ceremonies held here, distinguished by chanting, drums and bells. Public sittings are usually scheduled for Wednesdays and Sundays. Meditation services are offered in both Japanese and English.

Further along Sutter Street the **Nichi Bei Kai Cultural Center** is the home of the Ura Senke Foundation (the Japanese-American Tea Society), and the site of a *chashitsu* – a specially designed room for tea ceremonies. The interior and the simple ceremony performed within tell volumes about the aesthetic and ethical principles that are inherent to Japanese thinking. *Chanoyu* is a tea cult of Japan that incorporates the study of etiquette, interior design, ceramics, calligraphy, flower arrangement, and gardening.

This *chashitsu* was designed in Japan according to some 250 precise prescriptions established in the 16th century. Only natural materials, often unfinished or asymmetrical, are allowed. The rooms are purposefully small for intimacy; light is controlled by the careful placement of windows and doors; ornamentation is kept simple and seasonable. The fundamental philosophy of *chanoyu* promotes four principles: harmony, respect, purity, and tranquility.

Crossing the intersection from the nearby Super Koyama Market leads to the *torii* gate. The gate is the entrance to **Nihonmachi Mall**, a block-long cobblestone pedestrian shopping and eating area. The mall was designed by Ruth Asawa and is meant to resemble a small Japanese village with a meandering stream (this one made of a serpentine pattern of cobblestones).

Right, Japanese fan dancers at the Aki Matsuri Festival.

CABLE CARS

Only about one out of every 10 riders was a local when the city decided to retire its fleet of cable cars in 1947, but the news galvanized San Francisco. A Citizens' Committee to Save the Cable Cars was promptly set up, its chairman, Frieda Klussman, a doctor's wife, declaring that "any present monetary loss was more than compensated for by the wide publicity they give San Francisco," and, indeed, appeals and protests began to flood in from all over the world.

Landmark: Seven years later the battle was won when an amendment was written into the City Charter perpetuating the system. A decade after that, the cable cars were designated a National Landmark. Although 50 percent of the system had been lost during the lengthy struggle (and 95 other cities had abandoned cable cars as obsolete) three San Francisco lines remained – **Mason-Taylor**, which goes through Chinatown and North Beach to Fisherman's Wharf; **Powell-Hyde**, over Nob Hill and Russian Hill to Aquatic Park; and **California**, which runs from the Financial District to Van Ness Avenue.

Today they carry 12 million passengers a year, more than half of them local residents. In 1972, the Post Office issued a postcard (6¢ domestic, 15¢ foreign air mail) depicting a cable car.

Perhaps the most glorious day in the cable cars' history was June 3, 1981, when, after being removed for a $65 million renovation of the system that lasted almost two years, a citywide party celebrated their return. During the cars' absence, the number of visitors to the Fisherman's Wharf area dropped by 15 percent. "They're Back" read the inscription on thousands of colored balloons, and employees of MUNI, the city-owned transit system that operates above-ground transportation, served free coffee, brownies and wontons to lines of customers who had waited since dawn

<u>Right</u>, San Francisco's cable cars carry around 12 million passengers a year.

to be among the first passengers to board.

Three weeks later, the singer Tony Bennett turned up for the official party, and the Chinese Chamber of Commerce organized a 120-ft (36-meter) long golden dragon to cavort outside restaurants that were serving sidewalk food. A joyful Frieda Klussman, 30 years after her initial triumph, commented, "They're better than ever."

In a special 28-page supplement, the *San Francisco Examiner* warned freeloaders that it was tacky to try and avoid paying the fare, and ran a feature on cable car etiquette ("If you choose to ride on the running board, it's imperative you face the traffic... don't lean out"), surrounded by ads for engraved knives ($29.95), belt buckles ($18.95), and the usual clutch of coins, posters and T-shirts, all bearing pictures of the famous cable cars.

During the 20-month absence of the cars, San Franciscans had been part-consoled by a substitute Trolley Festival in which were paraded the city's formidable array of ancient vintage streetcars from St Louis, Los Angeles, Australia, Germany, Great Britain and Mexico. And, of course, the Citizens' Committee had been busy raising money, offering, in return for hefty donations, genuine cable car bells and handcrafted walnut music boxes programmed to play *I Left My Heart in San Francisco*. The fund-raising was necessary because only 80 percent of the $65 million for renovations was provided by the federal government.

The renovations were completed on time and under budget, partly because the euphoria spread into the ranks of the workers on the project who donated 5,000 hours of overtime. This kind of sentiment about cable cars has been prevalent since the earliest days of the system, when one family living at Washington and Gough streets used to leave milk and hot apple pie on the stoop of their home for the benefit of crews taking a midday break.

In similar fashion, the cable car crews would be indulgent at some stops about waiting for regular passengers to finish

Fire truck covers the tracks.

their coffee before boarding. And hundreds of San Franciscans have memories of being pulled up the steep hills on their roller skates, as they hung onto the back of ascending cars.

Not everybody was delighted by the the refurbished cable car system in the mid-1980s. One family living at Hyde and Chestnut streets initiated a suit against the noise – "like a dial tone with a sore throat," one columnist wrote – which was measured at 85 decibels at street level.

Despite their claim that the sound had made their house almost uninhabitable, the couple lost when a judge ruled that the city was not (in this case) subject to its own noise ordinances.

Back in 1970, in another case, the city was not so fortunate. At that time, 29-year-old Gloria Sykes, described by some newspapers as a buxom, blonde data processor, sued for $500,000 after an accident on a car left her with what she described as "an insatiable desire for affection." The press called it nymphomania – but Ms Sykes won her case

and was awarded a cut-price $50,000.

Some critics say that the cable cars, which are of course on a fixed track and thus have no ability to duck potential collisions, are inherently unsafe. Columnist Dick Nolan called the braking system "unimprovable" and "blacksmith shop crudity at its worst." In a typical year, about 12 percent of the injuries sustained by passengers who sue the city's transit system are sustained on or through cable cars.

Some exuberant riders lean out too far. Many accidents are due to the unthinking behavior of passing motorists, few of whom are as adept or lucky as Barbra Streisand in the famous scene in the 1972 comedy *What's Up Doc?* where she maneuvered a Volkswagen between two cable cars that were traveling in opposite directions.

Actually, the cars' braking system is unusually elaborate, based on the timely skill of a "gripman" who applies pressure on the endless wire rope running beneath the track's entire route, passing through the winding machinery in the

Market and Powell Street turnaround.

cable car barn at Mason and Washington streets. The rope has a hemp center braced by steel wire, six strands of 19 wires each in the original version devised by Andrew Hallidie, the English-born inventor usually credited with creating the system in 1876.

Seven years before, it's said, he saw a horse slip, causing the chain to break on the overloaded streetcar it was pulling uphill. He was determined to devise a system to eliminate such accidents.

Although Andrew Hallidie and his friends put up the $20,000 to get the cable cars operating, he was anticipated in 1870 by Benjamin Brooks, son of a local lawyer, who had been awarded a franchise to operate a similar system, but had failed to raise the necessary financing. Skepticism was the order of the day.

"I'd like to see it happen," said realtor L.C. Carlson, "but I don't know who is going to want to ride the dang thing." By 1906, the date of the San Francisco earthquake, 600 cars rolled over 115 miles (185 km) of track. But overhead wires strung up to power more modern electric trolleys hastened the cable cars' demise. Today, the system has 30 cars and a mere 10 miles (16 km) of track.

Butterscotch: From the earliest days, visitors have been impressed. "They turn corners almost at right angles, cross over other lines and for aught I know run up the sides of houses," wrote Rudyard Kipling, who stopped off in the city for a few days in 1889 on his way to India. President Lyndon Johnson's daughter, Lynda Bird, was less impressed a century later when she was ejected from a cable car by the gripman for eating a butterscotch ice cream cone. (To make amends, the city later made Lynda Bird an "honorary conductor.")

It is the gripmen – there are, as yet, no gripwomen – who have become the stars of the system. With their gentle exhortations to "climb aboard my magic cable car," they have attracted their own brand of groupies who offer them gifts – and sometimes more. Dealing with wedding parties – ceremonies are sometimes conducted while aboard – exhibitionists who suddenly fling off raincoats to pose nude for photographers, and passengers who try to operate the bells, they have become deft at handling almost any situation.

"You've got a much closer relationship here with people than on a bus or a streetcar," explains veteran senior grip Sam McDaniel. "They're happy people... the cable car's a fun thing. The men who work them still have a lot of little boy in them."

And a colleague adds: "The job requires a certain amount of diplomacy. If somebody's blocking the door, I'll say, 'Why don't you step inside, there's a TV in there,' or if they're smoking, 'You got to put that joint out or pass it to the driver first'."

Anyone fascinated by cable cars should head for the **Cable Car Museum** at Mason and Washington streets. Open daily all year round, this free, working museum houses the winding machinery used for turnaround, as well as exhibits, photographs and a viewing gallery called the Sheave Room that looks out over the cars on the street.

Left and **right**, 30 cable cars are now running.

OAKLAND, BERKELEY AND THE PENINSULA

Despite all the hard knocks – especially Gertrude Stein's infamous quip that "there is no *there* there" – Oakland, California, the state's eighth largest city, is doing all it can to emerge from the long shadow cast by its older sister, San Francisco, to the west. Oakland and the rest of the East Bay – which exists, says *San Francisco Chronicle* columnist Herb Caen, only because "the Bay Bridge had to end somewhere" – seems to thrive on such adversity.

And diversity. Socially, Oakland may be one of the most diverse cities in the country; block by block, it is among the best integrated. Its population is 47 percent black, 38 percent white, most of the rest Asian and Hispanic. Urban redevelopment has brightened up a once-shabby downtown facade, thanks to black community leaders who have been the heart of the city's political life in recent years.

Livable city: Although gang violence and crime are still prevalent in the city's poorer neighborhoods, Oakland recently ranked as the 15th most livable urban area in the country. Tucked into the hillside communities behind Oakland are some of the Bay Area's most expensive (and expensive) homes, many now rebuilt following the 1991 fire that swept through the Oakland hills, destroying over 3,000 structures and killing 25 people. Cheaper rents and a slightly slower urban pace have attracted would-be San Franciscans, much like Brooklyn can draw frustrated Manhattanites away from New York City.

At second glance, Oakland seems to offer much of what San Francisco has – even its own Chinatown and thriving waterfront – without the fog, the crowds, and the stop-and-go traffic. Nearly 60 years after Stein passed through town, visitors might reconsider: There is a *there* here. It's just a little harder to find.

Oakland's version of Fisherman's Wharf is the tediously pedestrian **Jack London Square** and Jack London Village. The author of *The Sea Wolf* and *The Call of the Wild* might not be im-

pressed were he alive to see the over-priced restaurants and T-shirt shops here, but he'd be able to munch crab, listen to live music and watch the sailboats pass by without elbowing his way through crowds to the pier.

The **First and Last Chance Saloon**, which London himself (an Oakland native) frequented, is here, as is the writer's sod-roofed Yukon cabin, which was moved from Alaska to the Oakland waterfront in tribute to the city's native son. On Sundays, there's a large farmers' market, open until early afternoon.

Oakland's most obvious landmarks are the distinctive tower of the **Tribune Building**; **City Hall**, with its wedding cake cupola; and, in the hills above the city, the five-towered, white granite **Mormon Temple**. Also visible from the Nimitz Freeway, if you're driving toward the airport, is the Oakland-Alameda County **Coliseum** complex, home of the Oakland A's baseball team, and the National Basketball Association's Golden State Warriors.

There's also a natural landmark, **Lake**

Preceding pages:
Pigeon Point Lighthouse; wildlife on Mount Tamalpais.
Left, the Campanile, Berkeley.
Right, sculpture at Berkeley's Lawrence Hall of Science.

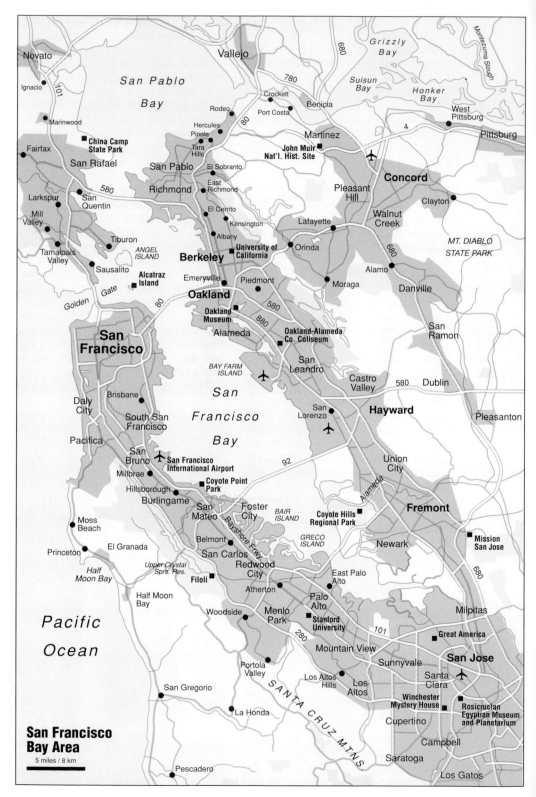

San Francisco Bay Area

5 miles / 8 km

Merritt, a large salt-water lake and wildlife refuge, edged by Victorian homes and a necklace of lights, which is home to **Children's Fairyland**, touted as the country's first "3-D" theme park. Visitors can board a pirate ship reminiscent of Peter Pan, or step into the mouth of the whale that "swallowed Pinocchio." The lake is also good for sailing or picnicking year-round. At the **Oakland Zoo**, visitors can ride in the sky in gondolas overlooking some of the zoo's 330 animals.

Within walking distance of the lake are two wonderfully contrasting architectural delights – the **Oakland Museum** on Oak Street, and the **Paramount Theater** on Broadway. The museum, built on three levels, is considered the finest museum of California art, history and natural science. (Tip: take the museum's simulated walk across the state.) The Paramount, a renovated Art Deco theater, is home of the Oakland Ballet and the Paramount Organ Pops, and shows old movies, complete with newsreels.

Among Oakland's newer attractions are the **City Center**, a pedestrian mall with quaint restaurants, jazz concerts and changing art exhibits, and **Preservation Park**, a restored Victorian village complete with 19th-century street lamps and lush gardens.

Berkeley: Just north of Oakland is Berkeley, another East Bay rival of San Francisco. A city famous for social experimentation and the birth of the Free Speech movement, Beserkely (its slang name), has become slightly less flamboyant, and slightly more commercial.

The city grew up around the **University of California**, considered one of the country's finest public universities, outranking all other American universities in its number of Nobel laureates. It began as a humble prep school operating out of a former fandango house in Oakland, and grew into the nine-campus University of California system.

In 1866 the new college town was named for Bishop George Berkeley, an 18th-century Irish philosopher who had written a poem about a new golden age of learning in America. In 1878,

Berkeley had a population of only 2,000, but the town grew along with the university; also when thousands of San Franciscans moved to the East Bay after the earthquake and fire of 1906.

Unrest to rest: It was the Free Speech movement of 1964 that put Berkeley on the map. At issue was a **University of California** at Berkeley administration order limiting political activities on campus. This touched off massive student protests and, in turn, similar protests on campuses throughout America. For several years thereafter the campus was a smoldering center of protest and politics.

In 1969, students once more took to the streets to stop the university's expansion in an area they wanted to preserve as **People's Park**. They prevailed ultimately, despite the intervention of 2,000 National Guard troops and violence that led to the death of an onlooker. Years later, People's Park began to draw more drug dealers and homeless people than students. Today, the student unrest here has turned to rest

and recreation: the city later added basketball and volleyball courts.

Where the city's political leaders once dabbled in foreign policy and social experimentation, now they seem more occupied by practical matters, like fixing potholes and promoting business. The city is still a carnival of demonstrative politics, but the dust of the 1960s has settled. (City merchants recently "protested" students' prolonged use of the city's coffeehouses for study halls.)

On the approach to Berkeley, two buildings can clearly been seen. On a hillside toward the south is a fairy-tale white palace. That's the **Claremont Resort Hotel**, which, like San Francisco's Palace of Fine Arts, was finished just before the Panama Pacific Exposition of 1915. The other landmark is a tall, thin, pointed structure, the university's bell tower. Its official name is **Sather Tower**, but it's known to all simply as the "Campanile" because it's modeled after St Mark's Campanile in Venice, Italy. Up **Strawberry Canyon** is the university's **Botanical Gardens**,

filled with over 25,000 species of South American, South African, European and Australian plants. Further along **Centennial Drive** is the university's **Lawrence Science Hall** where weekend visitors conduct biology experiments or operate computer terminals.

Over the Berkeley ridge and past Walnut Creek is **Mount Diablo**, a central landmark in California. Meaning "mountain of the devil," its name stems from a phenomenon which occurred when the United States government tried to usurp the mountain from the local tribes. A strange spirit was reported to have intervened on behalf of the Indians, scaring off the soliders. Hence the name: Mount Devil.

To get the feel of Berkeley at its liveliest, walk down **Telegraph Avenue** from Dwight Way to the university. Here students, townspeople and "street people" pick their way past interesting cafes, excellent bookstores and street vendors offering jewelry, pottery, plants and tie-dyed everything.

Like Oakland, Berkeley offers res-

Jazz on the lake, Oakland.

pite for those who run screaming from San Francisco's weather and traffic, but who still yearn for a lively, cosmopolitan community that represents urban life – on a slighter smaller scale. Among the lovely hillside homes are several by Julia Morgan, the architect who designed San Simeon (*see page 203*) for William Randolph Hearst.

The Peninsula: The San Francisco **Peninsula**, roughly a 55-mile (89-km) swath of high hills, tall trees and beautiful estates, is wedged between the Pacific Ocean and San Francisco Bay. To its north is San Francisco. At its southern end lies the sprawl of the **Silicon Valley** – or what used to be known as Santa Clara Valley when apples and pears, not computers and silicon chips, were harvested here. In the valley, the highlands of the peninsula glide head-on into the affluent, high-tech communities of Palo Alto, Los Altos, Sunnyvale, Santa Clara and San Jose.

As the drive south from San Francisco on **El Camino Real** – the main thoroughfare that runs through all these cities down to San Jose – will prove, the only true borders between cities on the peninsula seem to be stoplights. Where the commercial and spartan-finish industrial strips end, the high-rent suburban homes spread like a heat rash across the ample flatlands.

The style of the peninsula is sophisticated, shamelessly commercial, and contemporary. Six thousand residents have doctorate degrees, and Stanford University is the hub of much academic and cultural activity. Mixed with the high-mindedness, however, is a great deal of new money (new millionaires are as common here as tennis courts) and old money (San Mateo is one of the four wealthiest counties in California).

Stanford University is the academic lifeblood of the peninsula, located in the northwestern corner of **Palo Alto**, a comely city of 57,000 known for its strict environmental policies and praised as one of the best "model little cities of the world." A little over a century ago, when Leland Stanford and photographer Eadweard Muybridge began their

Below, Silicon Valley architecture. Right, Filoli Estate, Woodside.

experiments with moving images (which were to lead to the creation of motion pictures), the land on which the university stands was little more than a blue-blooded horse farm.

Stanford first proposed his plan for a private university in the 1880s. The response ranged from curious surprise to outright criticism, with one East Coast academician claiming that there was as much need for a new university in the West as there was for "an asylum for decayed sea captains in Switzerland." But a Yale of the West it became. Today, it is an acclaimed center for the study of science, engineering and medicine. More than 10 Nobel laureates are among its 1,200 faculty members, as well as 75 members of the National Academy of Science, and three Pulitzer Prize winners.

Stanford's handsome, rough-hewn sandstone buildings are Romanesque in style, though the red-tiled roofs, the burnt adobe color of the stone, and the wide arches give the university a Spanish mission look. The exception to the university's prosaic quality is **Memorial Church**, which dominates the **Inner Quad**, also known as the central courtyard. The church is resplendent in stained glass and richly colored murals, and has a domed ceiling.

Seaside: The most scenic route in the peninsula is State Highway 1, winding from **Pacifica**, a San Francisco suburb, to Santa Cruz in the south. Though less dramatic than the cliffside reaches of the Monterey Peninsula, this leg of Highway 1 is an enchanting day's drive, boasting two vintage lighthouses: **Pigeon Point** near Pescadero (west of San Jose), the second tallest lighthouse in the US; and **Montara** in the north, where there is a youth hostel nearby.

A special coastal spot is **Año Nuevo State Park**, 20 miles (32 km) north of Santa Cruz near the San Mateo-Santa Cruz county line. Here, whiskered and roly-poly elephant seal pups are born during January, when entire seal families are visible from lookout points along the beachfront. The seal families are so popular with sightseers that the beach

Rosicrucian Egyptian Museum, San Jose.

often gets crowded. Call Año Nuevo State Reserve after October 1 for information and reservations.

South peninsula: San Jose was the first pueblo to be founded in Northern California by the Spanish, in 1777. Until 1956, the San Jose area was providing America with half its supply of prunes, but the orchards of three decades ago have now sprouted condominiums and industrial parks. Today, San Jose is the fourth largest city in California with a population approaching 700,000.

It is a busy, fast-paced place, with several major hotels, nightclubs and no fewer than 100 shopping centers. Sightseeing is minimal in metropolitan San Jose, although three major wineries are located within the city limits – **Almaden, Mirassou**, and **Turgeon and Lohr**. All offer free tours and tastings

For entertainment of a more eccentric bent there is the sprawling, touristy but nonetheless fascinating **Winchester Mystery House** in downtown San Jose. It was built in convoluted stages by Sara L. Winchester, who inherited the fortune of her father-in-law, the famed gun manufacturer. Sarah was a spiritualist who believed that she would live as long as she kept adding to her house. Sixteen carpenters worked on the mansion for 36 years, adding stairways that lead to nowhere and doors without rooms.

The spiritual realm is also the basis for the **Rosicrucian Egyptian Museum** and planetarium. A recreated walk-in tomb of 2000 BC and the West Coast's largest collection of Egyptian, Babylonian and Assyrian artifacts draw 500,000 visitors a year.

For youngsters, in particular, the most exciting attraction in the San Jose area is **Marriott's Great America**, located off the Bayshore Freeway near **Sunnyvale**. An amusement park drawing on five themes of old America (Hometown Square, Orleans Place, Yankee Harbor, Yukon Territory, and Midwest Livestock Exposition and County Fair), it has live stage shows, arcades, snack bars and gift shops. But it is perhaps best known for its wild rides that leave your lunch far behind.

Winchester Mystery House, San Jose.

BIG SUR AND MONTEREY

The coastal drive south of San Francisco is a series of visual delights and literary associations: the gorgeous Monterey Peninsula and Big Sur associated first with author John Steinbeck's *Cannery Row* and then for almost half a century with Henry Miller; Carmel, whose most famous resident Clint Eastwood served for a term as mayor; and the splendid hilltop "castle" built by Julia Morgan for the newspaper tycoon William Randolph Hearst.

First though, a mere 25 miles (40 km) south of the Bay Area comes the delightful town of **Half Moon Bay** with its stately **Pigeon Point Lighthouse** and a youth hostel that boasts a clifftop hot tub. (More famous for its hot tub culture, of course, is the Esalen Institute, the "human potential" center 100 miles (160 km) to the south, so popular with the 1960s searchers-after-self).

When the garlic is harvested in July, the little town of **Gilroy** on US Highway 101 welcomes as many as 150,000 visitors to the annual Garlic Festival to exchange recipes, compete in cook-offs and races and admire the arts and crafts. But the so-called Garlic Capital of the World sees tourists all year around, both lovers of "the stinking rose" and others just plain curious. There's a tiny museum in town and various restaurants specializing in heavily flavored scampi and calimari, but it is hardly necessary to go into town at all: in addition to a pair of enormous "factory outlet" centers near the junction of Highway 101 and Highway 152 offering cut-price, name-brand clothing, there's also on Highway 101 itself an amazing/amusing store called Garlic World. Here you'll find garlic in braids, wreaths, boxes and as the major flavoring in everything from mayonnaise to cooking wine.

Back inland on Highway 101, **King City** should really be called King Smalltown because there's not an awful lot going on. Still, it is a major center for the fertile Salinas Valley which is sometimes called "the nation's salad bowl."

Every May King City springs to life as host of the Salinas Valley Fair and in September it stages a Mexican fiesta. There is access to the **Pinnacles National Monument**, a spectacularly craggy park whose peaks tower as much as 1,200 ft (360 meters) above the canyon floor, but access is more direct via Highway 146 from **Soledad** from which a visit might also be made to the **Mission Nuestra Señora de la Soledad**, 5 miles (8 km) west of town. Another mission, the impressive **Mission San Juan Bautista**, lies about 20 miles (32 km) north of the town of **Salinas**.

Cruisin' Santa Cruz: At the northern end of Monterey Bay – 28 miles (45 km) from Monterey via State Highway 1 – is **Santa Cruz**, a cool, green, redwood-shingled beach town with excellent restaurants, cafes, pastry shops, bookstores and a multitude of shops selling everything from 10-speed bicycles to Japanese kites. The **University of California** opened its Santa Cruz campus on remote hills high above the city in 1965 intending to create an Oxford-style uni-

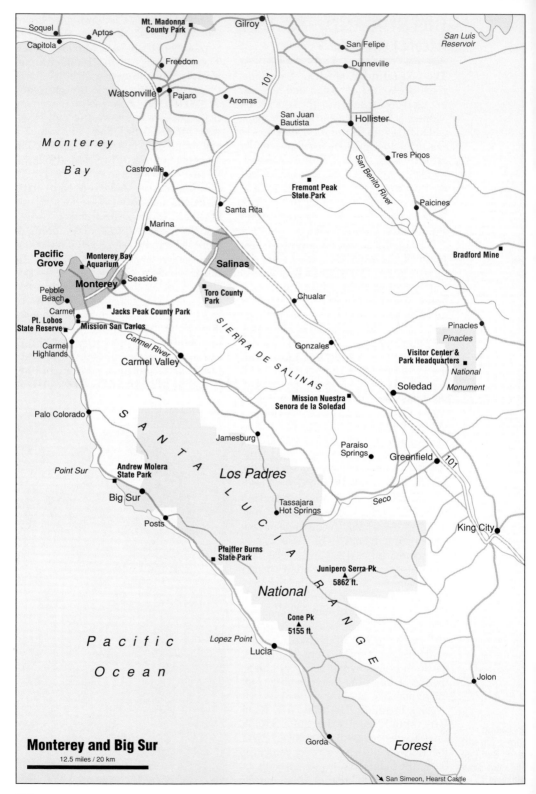

Soquel
Capitola
Aptos
Mt. Madonna
County Park
Gilroy
San Felipe
San Luis
Reservoir
Freedom
Dunneville
Watsonville
Pajaro
Aromas
101
San Juan
Bautista
Hollister
Monterey
Castroville
Tres Pinos
Bay
San Benito River
Fremont Peak
State Park
Paicines
Santa Rita
Marina
Bradford Mine
Pacific
Grove
Monterey Bay
Aquarium
Salinas
Pebble
Beach
Monterey
Seaside
Toro County
Park
Chualar
Pinacles
Pinacles
Carmel
Jacks Peak County Park
Pt. Lobos
State Reserve
Mission San Carlos
S I E R R A   D E   S A L I N A S
Gonzales
Visitor Center &
Park Headquarters
National
Carmel
Highlands
Carmel River
Carmel Valley
Soledad
Monument
Palo Colorado
S
A
N
T
A
Mission Nuestra
Senora de la Soledad
Jamesburg
Paraiso
Springs
Greenfield
101
Point Sur
Andrew Molera
State Park
Los Padres
L
U
C
Seco
Big Sur
I
Tassajara
Hot Springs
King City
Posts
A
Pfeiffer Burns
State Park
Junipero Serra Pk
5862 ft.
National
R
Cone Pk
5155 ft.
P a c i f i c
Lopez Point
A
N
Jolon
O c e a n
Lucia
G
E
Monterey and Big Sur
Gorda
Forest
12.5 miles / 20 km
San Simeon, Hearst Castle

versity where students could devote themselves to four years of intense semi-cloistered study, uninterrupted by the hue and cry of the outside world.

But what students craved in the 1960s was "relevance," not ivory-tower scholarship, and within a few years their energy and sense of mission transformed what had previously been a quiet backwater town into an activist community.

In the process, they restored and rejuvenated downtown Santa Cruz, retaining the oak on the turn-of-the-century buildings, polishing the brass, installing stained glass, replacing cement block and aluminum with natural redwood and hanging ferns. Santa Cruz has sparkling clean air in the summer; its only drawback is the torrential winter rain that turns canyons into rivers.

The Santa Cruz **municipal pier** features restaurants, fish markets and fishing facilities. Next to it is a wide white sandy beach. On the other side is the **Boardwalk Amusement Park**, a throwback to an earlier era with its carousel, Ferris wheel, thrilling roller coaster and old-fashioned arcade containing shooting galleries, as well as an unwelcome invasion of video games.

Charming Carmel: A couple of chance factors molded **Carmel**: starving writers and unwanted painters fleeing the devastation of the 1906 San Francisco earthquake, and canny developers who, to reduce their real-estate taxes, covered the previously treeless site with a thick carpet of Monterey pines. The result is one of the most endearing little seaside towns on the West Coast. When the evening fog rolls in from the Bay, the lights inside the cozy houses, plus the faint whiff of wood smoke, give Carmel the peaceful feeling of an 18th-century European village.

The street, plazas and little malls attract pedestrians to wine shops and booksellers, antique stores, art galleries and numerous boutiques. The local market offers freshly picked artichokes (from fields barely a mile away), sweet basil, French cheeses, German sausages, liver pâté, and floor-to-ceiling racks of imported and domestic wines.

At night, on the side streets, a dozen couples might be dining quietly by candlelight behind dark restaurant windows. In the residential parts of town, the streets meander casually through the forest, sometimes even splitting in two to accommodate an especially praiseworthy specimen of pine.

Carmel has firmly resisted any temptation to yield to used-car lots, fast-food franchises, high-rise buildings and neon signs, but the charms of the **Monterey Peninsula** lure up to four million people each year and more remote (and equally picturesque communities) shudder and print bumper stickers reading: "Don't Carmelize California." Aside from the town itself, Carmel's main attraction is Father Junípero Serra's **Mission San Carlos Borromeo del Rio Carmelo**, better known as the Carmel Mission. Established in 1770, it was Serra's headquarters until his death in 1784. Today it is his tomb; he is buried beneath the basilica floor, in front of the altar.

Scenic journey: Just north of the foot of Ocean Avenue is the Carmel Gate entrance to the **17 Mile Drive**, which

The Lone Pine Cypress on the 17 Mile Drive.

meanders around the Monterey Peninsula, via the **Del Monte Forest**, to Pacific Grove. Because all the roads in the Del Monte Forest are privately owned, travelers on the 17 Mile Drive must pay a fee to the Pebble Beach Company. The trip is worth it, if for no other reason than to see, close to the **Ghost Tree** cypress, a big stone mansion looking like something seen in a lightning flash which cleaves the midnight darkness of the Scottish moors.

Still, the elitist attitude of the Pebble Beach Company toward tourists seems more than a little condescending. Along their exclusive golf courses are signs every few feet warning visitors that trespassing on the course is a misdemeanor punishable by a fine and imprisonment. At the famous **Lone Pine Cypress**, a single gnarled and windswept tree near the top of a huge wave-battered rock, the sign on the protective fence reads "No Trespassing Beyond This Point," as if merely being in the forest were a trespass in itself.

Steinbeck by the sea: The history of the people who passed through **Monterey** is the history of California itself. First there were the native Indians, then the Spanish explorers, the Mexican ranchers, the American settlers, the Sicilian fishermen and finally the most ubiquitous and persistent invader of all, the modern tourist.

Thanks to John Steinbeck, the most famous attraction in town is the former Ocean View Avenue, now known as **Cannery Row**. During World War II, Monterey was the sardine capital of the Western Hemisphere, processing some 200,000 tons of the fish a year. As Steinbeck described it then, the street was "a poem, a stink, a grating noise, a quality of light, a tone, a habit, a nostalgia, a dream." (The century-old adobe in which Steinbeck wrote the novel of the same name is on Pierce Street at Franklin.)

When the fishing boats came in, heavy with their catch, the canneries blew their whistles and the residents of Monterey came streaming down the hill to take their places amid the rumbling, rattling,

Mission San Juan Bautista.

squealing machinery of the canning plants. When finally the last sardine was cleaned, cut, cooked and canned, the whistle blew again, and the workers trudged back up the hill, dripping, wet and smelly.

After the war, whether due to over-fishing or changing currents, the sardines suddenly disappeared from Monterey Bay and all the canneries went broke. An unplanned side effect was that the sickening stench that had covered the town for decades was finally gone, along with the sardines.

Today the beaches are bright and clean, and the air is sparkling fresh. In the town's historic center is a **Sensory Garden** with waist-high beds of bold colored, strong-smelling flowers. Cannery Row, located along the waterfront on the northwest side of town just beyond the **Presidio**, has become an impressive tourist attraction. Its old buildings are filled with lusty bars, gaudy restaurants, a wax museum, dozens of shops, a carousel, an arcade and peddlers selling hot pretzels and caramel

Cannery Row, Monterey.

corn. The Presidio, founded in 1770 by Gaspar de Portolá, now serves as the US Army Language School and in the grounds of its chapel – in constant use since 1794 – US President Herbert Hoover was married.

A trip to Cannery Row these days usually means a visit to one of the world's premier aquariums, the **Monterey Bay Aquarium**, which stands on the site of what was Cannery Row's largest cannery, the Hovden Cannery. More than 100 galleries and underwater exhibits include over 6,500 specimens, from California sea otters, leopard sharks, bat rays and giant octopuses, to towering underwater kelp forests. Since the aquarium opened in 1984, over 15 million visitors have passed through. Ocean fish on display in an enormous three-story glass tank are just one of the things to ponder.

The main downtown visitor attraction **Fisherman's Wharf**, two blocks east of the working wharf, is lined with restaurants, shops, fish markets and noisy sea lions which swim among the

pilings. An organ grinder is likely to entertain with his monkey.

The town's most interesting sites lie along a 3-mile (5-km) walking tour called **The Path of History** which includes the **Customs House**, the oldest public building in California, now a museum; and **Pacific House**, a two-story, balconied adobe containing various historical artifacts. Other attractions include **Colton Hall**, a two-story building with a classical portico which was the site of the state's first (1849) constitutional convention, and **Stevenson House**, a smaller former hotel where the romantic (and sickly) Robert Louis Stevenson lived for a few months while courting his wife.

Other points of interest in Monterey are the **Monterey Peninsula Museum** of regional art, and the **Allen Knight Maritime Museum**, featuring relics of the era of sailing ships and whaling. In mid-September each year, the acclaimed Monterey Jazz Festival attracts major contemporary music stars to the Monterey Fairgrounds.

Kayaking on Monterey Bay is growing in popularity, too, offering a delightful opportunity to get out among the otters and sea lions. A local company adjoining the state beach operates tours out to see the gray whales on their regular migrations past here between Alaska and Baja.

The next few years will see some major changes in what for generations has been the military base of Fort Ord. The 28,000 acres (11,300 hectares) of prime coastal land is now destined to become a new campus of California State Univerity.

Spectacular Big Sur: Between the two great world wars, convict labor built a narrow, twisting road over the virgin California coastline from the Hearst Castle at San Simeon 93 miles (150 km) north to the Monterey Peninsula. Except for the road itself, it's not much different today than it was then – there are no billboards or streetlights, only occasional scattered mailboxes and, with the possible exception of the village of **Big Sur** itself, nothing even resembling a town.

In some parts, State Highway 1 rises 1,000 ft (300 meters) above sea level in a matter of a few miles. One minute, travelers are shivering in a cold gray mist, sharp with the smell of salt water and kelp. Five minutes later, they are standing atop a sunny hillside looking over a billowy white blanket of ocean fog as far as the eye can see. On really hot days in the inland valleys, air currents pull the fog up the mountainside, turning Highway 1 into an endless gray tunnel with fog skimming overhead like an upward flowing waterfall.

Because the blasting needed to build the road weakened the underlying rock, the highway is prone to damage. During heavy winter rains, huge chunks of roadway sometimes slide into the ocean, cutting off local residents for days or weeks at a time. There are a number of inns, lodges, motels and campgrounds scattered along Highway 1. There are also places out of sight of the road where persistent wayfarers can make camp, sip their wine and listen to the barking of sea lions high above the crashing surf.

The Carmel Valley.

Until the end of World War II, Big Sur was mainly populated by ranchers, loggers and miners. But following the war, literary people began turning up to live cheaply, grow marijuana in remote canyons, and commune with what long-time resident Henry Miller called "the face of the earth as the creator intended it to look." Miller died in 1989 but the **Henry Miller Memorial Library** (just south of the Nepenthe Inn) welcomes visitors most days from May through October. Opened by Miller's longtime friend Emil White in 1981, it contains an extensive collection of the author's books and memorabilia.

By the end of the 1960s, Big Sur had become a cultural fad where neo-agrarian hippies lived off the land (and welfare stamps), made non-negotiable demands on behalf of the environment and, every dry season, inadvertently set fire to sections of the hills. At the same time, affluent San Franciscans, having discovered that there's nothing like an ocean view to bring out the subtle taste of brie and Chablis, began arriving by Porsche and BMW in an ever-increasing stream.

Notable among the handful of Big Sur's upmarket "romantic country inns" is **Ventana**, a hot-tub-and fireplace-dotted hideaway that has caused innumerable travel writers to trot out such superlatives as "hedonistic hideaway" and "sensuous, sumptuous and serene."

High on a hill above the village of **San Simeon** is what has come to be known as **Hearst Castle** *(see box on page 203)* which is second only to Disneyland as California's top tourist attraction. It is actually the vast mansion built by publishing tycoon William Randolph Hearst who, at his death in 1951, owned the country's largest newspaper chain and was the subject of Orson Welles's 1941 movie *Citizen Kane*. Hearst lived at Simeon periodically until 1947 when ill health caused him to move.

Hearst's biographer W. A. Swanberg wrote in *Citizen Hearst*: "It was almost as if Hearst subconsciously realized that his newspapers were trashy, his political life a failure, even his motion pic-

Big Sur near Andrew Molera State Park.

tures not entirely successful and he was determined that in San Simeon, if nothing else, he would leave an enduring monument to his greatness."

La Cuesta Encantada, as Hearst's father George, a multi-millionaire from his gold, silver and copper mines, called his hilltop ranch, covered 275,000 acres (111,000 hectares). After his parents died, the younger Hearst hired architect Julia Morgan to design the twin-towered main house with its 38 bedrooms, Gothic dining room and indoor mosaic pool, as well as three sumptuous guest houses and marble Neptune Pool flanked by Roman statuary.

Then he proceeded to stock the grounds with animals from all over the world, and to fill the buildings with carvings, furnishings and works of art from European castles and cathedrals. The total effect is quite remarkable – which is why the four daily tours of the castle are booked solid, sometimes weeks in advance.

In spring and fall there is also a tour most evenings. Then, the terraces, gardens and walkways are illuminated, and 1930s music plays indoors where attendants dressed as staff and guests go about their languid activities, and a period Hearst newsreel plays in the theater. Construction work continued at the site for a time after 1947 but the only visitors were those attending occasional Hearst Corporation meetings or the sons bringing their wives for a holiday weekend. The pear orchards continued to produce for canning under the Hearst label. W.R. died in 1951, aged 88, and was buried in the family mausoleum at Colma, California.

Northwest of **San Luis Obispo**, with its historic mission founded by Father Junípero Serra in 1772, Highway 1 branches off to hug the coast passing close to **Morro Bay**, dominated by a 576-ft (176-meter) rock just offshore. Along the town's waterfront, from which "clam taxis" ferry hopeful diggers to sand dunes across the bay, are numerous seafood restaurants. **Pismo Beach** has 23 miles (37 km) of fine beaches and a famous namesake clam.

San Simeon's main dining room.

HEARST'S CASTLE

William Randolph Hearst is said to have acquired his taste for collecting at 10 years old while visiting European castles and museums with his mother. Certainly, by the time he and architect Julia Morgan began to create the San Simeon "castle" he had the means to satisfy his hobby and provide a suitably grand home for his acquisitions. The task that Hearst and Ms Morgan embarked upon was hardly a conventional building project.

All supplies had to be brought up the coast by steamer, then hauled 5 miles (8 km) up the hill. Tons of topsoil were brought up to create flower beds for the 127 acres (50 hectares) of gardens. Half-grown, 3-ton cypresses were also replanted during landscaping. Five greenhouses went up to supply plants for year-round color. To hide a water tank on the adjoining hill, 6,000 Monterey pines were planted, plus an additional 4,000 trees planted each year on the estate.

White marble statues flanked the 104-feet (32-meter) outdoor Neptune Pool. A pair of tennis courts was sited atop the indoor Roman pool. The 85-ft (26-meter) long assembly hall in the main house was constructed around a 400-year-old carved wooden ceiling from Italy.

By the time W.R. was advised by his doctors to move to Beverly Hills in 1947, the "ranch" had 165 rooms filled with mostly Spanish and Italian art and antiques spread over Casa Grande and three guesthouses.

Hearst moved into San Simeon when the last of his five sons went off to school. Instead of his wife Millicent – whom he had married when he was 39 and she 21 – he installed his longtime mistress, Marion Davies, who had been a teenaged chorus girl when he first wooed her with diamonds.

Almost every weekend San Simeon welcomed moviedom's élite. "The society people always wanted to meet the movie stars so I mixed them together," wrote Marion Davies. "Jean Harlow came up quite frequently. She was very nice and I liked her. She didn't have an awful lot to say... all the men used to flock around her. She was very attractive in an evening dress because she never wore anything under it."

Clark Gable was another regular guest.

"Women were always running after him but he'd just give them a look as if to say, 'How crazy these people are,' and he stayed pretty much to himself."

A special train with a jazz band and open bar from Glendale station brought the weekend party guests 210 miles (338 km) from Hollywood to San Luis Obispo, where limousines transported them through the estate's grounds filled with lions, bears, ostriches, elephants, pumas and leopards. On arrival at the floodlit mansion, each was allocated a personal maid or valet and was free to wander – except for a mandatory attendance at the late-night dinner over which W.R. would preside in the Great Hall, at the head of the 16th-century monastery table. Paper napkins, catsup from bottles and the absence of tablecloths preserved the illusion of "camping out." After dinner Hearst showed a movie, often one as yet unreleased; *Gone With the Wind*, for example, was screened six months before its December 1939 premiere.

In 1957, six years after William Randolph Hearst's death, the Hearst Corporation deeded the San Simeon property to the state of California. ∎

San Simeon.

203

minute, and no mercy is afforded anyone who is stopped for drunken driving.

The best way to arrive in Sausalito, and to meet the local people, is to sail into port aboard a large boat. Alternately, a ferry departs regularly from the foot of Market Street in San Francisco. Operated by the Golden Gate Transit District, these plush, stable and well-maintained boats carry a loyal traffic of commuters from Sausalito and Larkspur (near San Rafael). On the return runs on weekday afternoons, the bars on board are opened and it often turns into a party boat.

On weekends, the ferries sail for the benefit of the tourist trade. They are great fun and are relatively cheap. Another ferry company operates a weekend run between Tiburon, Angel Island State Park and Fisherman's Wharf.

Larkspur and Tiburon: The Larkspur ferry terminal is easily recognized from afar as a strange triangular egg crate that provides a dubious shelter for 2,000 daily commuters. Around the terminal are shops and restaurants housed in modern buildings painted to look weathered and salty. The high point of the complex is an excellent bookstore – known in all humility as **A Clean Well-Lighted Place for Books**.

Right around the corner from the Larkspur terminal, on a little peninsula, is the infamous **San Quentin State Prison**, its grounds surrounded by chain fence topped by barbed wire. The buff-colored prison has been the scene of more than 400 state-sanctioned executions, plus numerous informal ones practiced by the inmates on each other. The prison is grossly overcrowded, seethes with the potential for violence, and is widely regarded as a national disgrace. Thus, there are no public tours. There is, however, a gift shop at the main gate.

Tiburon is a pleasant enough ferry destination – touristy, but also home to the leisured and the well-to-do. The deck of **Sam's Anchor Cafe** is the place to sip a gin fizz while waiting for the return ferry.

Probably the *ne plus ultra* for ferryboat fans is a trip to **Angel Island**, a

Sausalito houseboats.

state park which can be reached only by boat. In the summer, open-air trams oblige sightseers; year-round there are several good hikes. Of particular interest is the trek up **North Ridge Trail** to the top of the island, where there is a wonderful panoramic view. Another walk winds around to **Camp Reynolds**, which includes the remains of a military garrison, an old schoolhouse and several pre-Civil War officers' homes. A third walk goes to **Point Blunt**, once a dueling ground and site of a famous brothel.

If you plan to tour Marin County by car, the thing to remember is that US Highway 101, which is connected by the Golden Gate Bridge, is the north–south spinal cord which ties all communities together. With rare exceptions, off-ramps and feeder roads are well marked, and most destinations are easy to find.

Heading north from Sausalito, on the left is **Marin City**. The well-kept barracks like buildings were raised in World War II as housing for shipyard workers.

Point Bonita Lighthouse.

Today they have been renovated as low-income public housing. Close to Marin City is a giant open-air **flea market** where many small-change entrepreneurs haggle with passers-by over what they claim is the best deal the buyers will ever make. The market, open every weekend in good weather, offers merchandise ranging from out-right junk to the occasional bargain.

Clinging to the southeastern slope of Mount Tamalpais, just a few miles north of Sausalito, is the charming town of **Mill Valley**. This community is frequently cited for its Old World charm, secreted just beyond the supermarkets and shopping centers. **Throckmorton Street** comprises the heart of town, and a couple of blocks are all that casual visitors will really want to see, save for those who enjoy peering at the rustic homes hidden among serpentine lanes.

Mill Valley is an ideal base for day excursions to the mountain. Many visitors head first to Mill Valley's **Book Depot**, a renovated railroad station, where they study Freese maps (bound in distinctive orange covers) of the mountain while sipping cups of expresso. Later, returning footsore and weary from the mountain, they may check into the **Physical Therapy Center** on Throckmorton Street for a hot-tub, sauna and hour-long massage treatment. The masseuse accommodates desires for Swedish or Esalen-style massages, but reservations must be made.

For relaxing after the massage, the town boasts several outstanding restaurants. Alternatively, the **Mill Valley Market**, despite its unpretentious name, features a full line of gourmet food, bakery goods and excellent wines. On a balmy evening, a visit to the market and a picnic at **Old Mill Park** might be in order.

Most of Mill Valley's commuters are, of course, commuters up and down Highway 101 which gave the excellent local paper, the *Pacific Sun*, an idea. Not long ago the paper promoted a Freeway Fiction contest with stories restricted to 101 words. A lady from Petaluma carved out a slice of her life within the word limits ("Met him. Met me. Liked him.

Liked me. Moved in. Loved him passionately. Loved me indifferently. Wanted marriage. Wanted space. Tried to accommodate. Gave him space. Betrayed me" etc.); a man from Sausalito daydreamed a bank heist and his subsequent life in Rio – until the bus arrived and reality returned.

Mount Tamalpais: In recent years, Mount "Tam" has become a weekend traffic jam of hikers, mountain bikers, and runners. Still, there seems to be enough beauty to go around. Over 30 miles (48 km) of trails wind their way through 6,000 acres (2,430 hectares), as well as many more miles of hiking in the contiguous watershed lands. (Biker-hiker relations have soured in the last couple years. If you're walking, watch your step. If you're riding, beware: bike cops now issue speeding tickets on the mountain.)

On Mount Tam's lower elevations, often shrouded in fog, are stands of virgin redwood. Above, the mountain's chaparral-covered high slopes jut proudly into the sunshine, overlooking San Francisco Bay and the Pacific. At the base of Mount Tam is the **Muir Woods** National Monument.

At the turn of the 20th century, the Marin water district planned to condemn a property called Redwood Canyon, cut the timber on it, and with the profits build a dam and reservoir. The scheme so appalled one wealthy Marinite, William Kent, that he bought the land outright, then deeded the redwood stand to the government as a national monument. Kent modestly declined to have the monument named after him, out of deference to his old friend, naturalist John Muir.

About 1 million visitors a year visit the giant sequoia trees here, which grow to 200 ft (60 meters) in height, 16 ft (5 meters) in diameter, live up to 1,000 years, and are spread out through Muir Woods' 300-plus acres (120 hectares). Energetic walkers would be well advised to leave the rows of parked cars behind and head up the steep slope of Mount Tam on the **Ben Johnson Trail** through deeply shaded glens rife with

Mount Tamalpais.

ferns and mushrooms, past ever-changing groves of bay, tan oaks, madrona and nutmeg.

Beyond Mount Tam, Marin County's green belt extends some 50 miles (80 km) to the distant tip of Point Reyes National Seashore. The coastal country, known as the **Marin Headlands** (easily accessible off Highway 1 just north of the Golden Gate Bridge), has miles of coastal and beach-bound trails.

Muir and **Stinson beaches**, at the foot of Mount Tamalpais, are popular among anglers hoping to hook surf perch and rockfish, and among bird watchers who want to spy such out-of-the-way creatures as the sooty shearwater, brown pelican, Western grebe, killdeer and millet. When the fog pulls back, the beaches also attract sunbathers.

Past Stinson Beach, which gets overcrowded most sunny weekends, and tiny nudist-lovers Red Rock Beach, a lagoon cuts off Highway 1 from the village of **Bolinas** whose residents like it that way, discouraging visitors to the extent of constantly removing the high-

Muir Woods.

way signs. When San Francisco was growing during the gold fever of 1849, Bolinas stripped 13 million board feet of timber off the ridge and shipped it across the Bay.

A few miles further north, it's worth stopping for lunch or a drink on the outdoor deck of the lovely Gray Whale at **Inverness.** Three doors away Vladimir's Czech restaurant is operated by the colorful Vladimir Nevi who escaped from the communists in his homeland by skiing over the Alps to freedom.

Point Reyes Station, created in 1875 as a narrow gauge railroad stop, became the market town for the ranches of the area. When the trains left in 1933, the depot became a post office and the engine house was turned into the town's community center. Check out the Station House Cafe with its garden patio. The town is surrounded by ranches on all sides and a tape-recorded "moo" instead of a train whistle is played at noon and 6pm most days.

The **Point Reyes National Seashore** is on a triangular peninsula separated

WINE COUNTRY

Standing on the summit of Mount St Helena, you can see the vast expanse and emerald vineyards of Napa, Sonoma, Mendocino and Lake counties stretching for miles below your feet. From the redwood groves surrounding the Russian River to the burgundy-hued Mendocino ridges, the Northern California vineyards are renowned for producing some of the world's finest wines. The area owes its premier grapes to the excellent growing conditions: temperate climate and rich, drainable soil.

In fact, there is no individual California wine county. Wine grapes are grown in 45 of California's 54 counties, and the northern wineries produce just over one-sixth of the state's total output. Most of the remaining grapes come from the hot, arid San Joaquin Valley, several hundred miles south, and are often used to make modestly-priced "jug" wines. Nevertheless, when most people hear the phrase "California Wine Country" they think of the high-profile Napa and Sonoma valleys.

The first winemakers in California were 18th-century Spanish missionaries who used wine in religious ceremonies. Father Junípero Serra, who founded the state's earliest missions, had no taste for California's indigenous wild grapes and instead imported quality vines from his native Spain. Large-scale vineyards were established around the Los Angeles area in the 1830s by Jean Louis Vignes, a French vintner. Vignes' wine operation lasted until 1862; after that, California's first commercial vineyards closed and were swallowed by LA's expanding suburbs.

Family grants: In the north, it was two men – Father Jose Altimira, the founder of the Mission San Francisco de Solano at Sonoma, and General Vallejo, who colonized Sonoma and Napa counties with land grants to his relatives and friends – who dabbled in early California winemaking. But it was Count Agoston Haraszthy who pushed the Sonoma region into wine stardom.

Haraszthy, a flamboyant Hungarian political refugee, began **Buena Vista,** Northern California's oldest winery, in 1857. He trekked across Europe to cull wine-grape cuttings for California's growers. Ever restless, Haraszthy migrated to Nicaragua, but his efforts were short-lived; he was eaten by alligators.

He wasn't forgotten, however. One of Haraszthy's protégés, Charles Krug, a German political exile, opened Napa Valley's first commercial winery in 1861. By the 1880s, valley wines were winning medals in Europe, although Prohibition nearly wiped out this blossoming industry. Following its repeal in 1933, **Beaulieu Vineyard**'s Georges de Latour, the Mondavi family and others began resurrecting the industry.

Vintners mutiply: In the 1960s, a wine boom began as large corporations marketed vintage-dated varietal wines at reasonable prices, and small, privately owned wineries produced more expensive estate-bottled wines at higher costs. Old-time winemaking families were joined by oil barons, engineers, doctors

and actors who revitalized old wineries and opened new ones. Many vintners began exploring the regions beyond the Napa-Sonoma valleys and established premier wineries in central and southern California. By 1976, California wines were beating French vintages in some European tastings.

A recent phenomenon in wine country is the discovery of oil – not the viscous underground stuff but olive oil, which of course, is the product of thousands of trees. It happened almost accidentally when vintners Bill and Lila Jaeger at Napa's **Rutherford Hill Winery** realized that a deserted hillside was covered with a suddenly re-invigorated century-old olive plantation.

The 150-member Northern California Olive Oil Council ambitiously hopes to revive the state's once-prosperous industry. (Up until about half a century ago California had almost 100 olive oil producers, most of whom went out of business with the importation of cheaper oil from the Mediterranean.)

Today dozens of other vintners are producing olive oil as a secondary crop, many of them having their harvest pressed by the Tra Vigue restaurant in St Helena.

A wine primer: Wines begin at the crusher, where the juice is freed from the grapes. Red wines are created when the grape skin and pulp go into the fermenting tank, where yeast is added to convert sugar to alcohol and carbon dioxide. Grape skins are pressed to extract more juice, then the reds are aged in stainless steel or wooden tanks. The wine is clarified, then aged further before bottling.

White wines are made from the fermentation of the juice alone, drawn off from the grapes immediately after crushing. Yeast is added, and fermentation occurs in stainless steel tanks. Leaving the yeast creates dry wines; stopping yeast action makes sweeter wines. Champagne or sparkling wine begins the same way, then undergoes a second fermentation. The carbon dioxide is trapped in the bottle, hence the bubbles.

Vintages mean less in California than

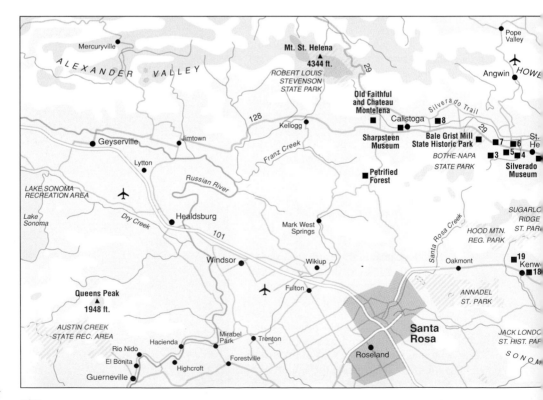

in Europe, thanks to the state's relatively benign climate, although to purists some years are definitely better than others. Most wineries are open between 10am and 4pm daily, some by appointment only. The tour (usually 1½ hours) ends up in the combination shop and tasting room, so you might want to think twice before driving home.

Napa County: Wineries, delicatessens, restaurants and country inns lie close together in compact **Napa Valley** (*napa* meaning "plenty" in the local Indian dialect). Although rural, the area's mix of San Francisco socialites, titled Europeans, semi-retired Hollywood screenwriters and producers gives Napa County a genteel, wealthy, if sometimes slick, aura.

A 30-mile (48-km) thrust of flatland between the pine-forested Mayacamas Mountains and the buff-colored Howell Mountains, the Napa Valley is pinched off in the north by Mount St Helena. The valley's expanses of vineyards are broken up by farmhouses, stone wineries and a series of towns stretched along

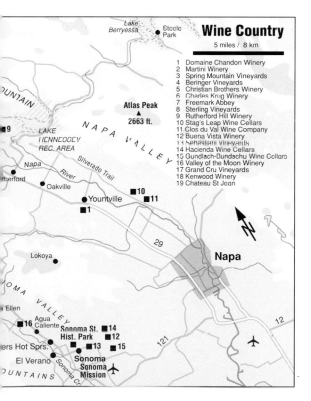

Wine Country

5 miles / 8 km

1 Domaine Chandon Winery
2 Martini Winery
3 Spring Mountain Vineyards
4 Beringer Vineyards
5 Christian Brothers Winery
6 Charles Krug Winery
7 Freemark Abbey
8 Sterling Vineyards
9 Rutherford Hill Winery
10 Stag's Leap Wine Cellars
11 Clos du Val Wine Company
12 Buena Vista Winery
13 Sebastiani Vineyards
14 Hacienda Wine Cellars
15 Gundlach-Dundschu Wine Cellars
16 Valley of the Moon Winery
17 Grand Cru Vineyards
18 Kenwood Winery
19 Chateau St Jean

State Highway 29, "The Great Wine Way." Strict land-control measures have confined valley development to the towns and the freeway south of Yountville, but have also escalated land prices.

Napa wine country begins in earnest at **Yountville** (population 3,300), where the vineyards abut the village's historic, renovated brick and stone buildings. Yountville's city-park picnic stop is across from George Yount's grave at the pioneer cemetery. One of General Vallejo's beneficiaries, Yount received his 11,000-acre (4,450-hectare) land grant for roofing Vallejo's Petaluma adobe – surely one of history's most lucrative contracting deals.

Domaine Chandon Winery, next to the California Veterans Home, is French throughout; in deference to Gallic sensibilities, the champagne is called sparkling wine. The winery, owned by Moët and Chandon, makes sparkling wine in the *méthode champenoise*; that is, it is fermented in the same bottle from which it is poured.

Adventurers can take an early morning hot-air balloon sweep above the vineyards, followed by a champagne picnic. Most flights leave from Yountville. Several balloon companies operate in the valley, and there are bicycle and moped rentals, too.

Four of the stateliest wineries in Napa were the work of one man, Hamden W. McIntyre, who although the most sought-after winery architect in the boom of the 1880s is almost forgotten today. His sturdy constructions still stand however in the buildngs of **Inglenook**, **Far Niente**, **Trefethen** and **Greystone**.

St Helena, the wine country's capital, is noted for its 40 wineries, historic stone buildings, picnic parks, chic shops, pricey restaurants and country inns. The **Silverado Museum** is stuffed with Robert Louis Stevenson memorabilia – first editions of his work and souvenirs of his global jaunts.

South of town, the **Martini Winery**, run by one of the valley's oldest winemaking clans, offers reasonably priced wines (Cabernet Sauvignon to sherry) in an unpretentious setting. Wine and soap mix at **Spring Mountain Vine-**

yards, planted in the hill country west of St Helena. Television's *Falcon Crest* soap opera was filmed at the winery's **Miravalle** mansion, which was built in 1885 by playboy Tiburcio Parrott.

A trinity of giant wineries – **Beringer, Christian Brothers** and **Charles Krug** – lie north of St Helena. Jacob and Frederick Beringer started their winery in 1876, modeling the **Rhine House** (1883) after their ancestral estate in Mainz, Germany. They dug limestone caves for aging wine. Today's winery, owned by Nestlé (yes, the chocolate people) features Fumé Blanc and Cabernet Sauvignon in the mansion tasting room. Outside, spacious lawns and a regal row of elms fronts the winery.

Christian Brothers' Greystone building was the world's largest stone winery when erected in 1889 by mining magnate William Bourn. This white-elephant winery changed hands often until the Christian Brothers, a Catholic educational order, bought it in 1950. The tour is informal, the tasting room elegant.

Founding father Charles Krug's winery building dates from 1874. There is an informative, traditional tour, with tastings of Krug and C.K. Mondavi label wines, including Cabernet Sauvignon and Chenin Blanc.

Two miles north of St Helena is **Freemark Abbey**, a winery, restaurant and shopping place. There's no abbey here; the name is an amalgamation of the owners' names. The once-a-day tours are small, a welcome change from larger wineries. A mile further north is the **Bale Grist Mill State Historic Park**.

Sterling Vineyards – part-Greek monastery, part-fantasy – reign over the upper valley atop a knoll. For a fee, a tram whisks visitors 300 ft (90 meters) up for a self-guided tour. The tram fee is deductible toward the purchase of Cabernet Sauvignon, Sauvignon Blanc and other wines.

The Silverado Trail: Running alongside State Highway 29 between Napa and Calistoga, the Silverado Trail joins with the highway as the route into Lake County's resort and wine region. Built as the road from Mount St Helena's cinnabar

The Rhine House, Beringer Brothers Winery.

mines to Napa's river docks, it is an elevated, two-lane road above the valley floor offering panoramic views, uncrowded wineries (most with picnic areas) and hidden valleys in the Howell Mountains.

At the head of the valley, **Calistoga** (population 4,500) is famous for its hot springs, bottled mineral water and mud baths (*see page 109*). Just west of town is the Old Faithful Geyser which erupts every 40 minutes, sending 350°F (177°C) superheated boiling water 60 ft (18 meters) into the air. It is said to be able to forecast pending earthquakes in advance by increasing its eruption rate.

Amidst all the big companies sits the **Wermuth Winery,** the mom-and-pop vineyard of Ralph Wermuth and his wife in Calistoga. At the Wermuth Winery on Silverado Trail, a sign reads: "If I'm not here honk horn; I am around."

Wermuth, a true individualist, was a doctor when they began the winery in 1982. His artist wife designs the labels and they autograph bottles for visitors. The winery uses old Italian-made bas-ket presses which in most places are museum pieces and Wermuth claims to be the only one in the valley making a dry Colombard. "History shows us that winemaking is one of the oldest professions known to man," he says. "It is as old as the hills around us. Wine should be smooth and gentle like our lives and most of all there is nothing new but to keep on mowing the weeds."

A popular stop is the Jaeger's previously mentioned **Rutherford Hill Winery**, an ark-like structure with picnic grounds and Chardonnay, Cabernet Sauvignon and Zinfandel wines. **Stag's Leap**, a rocky promontory where a 16-point Roosevelt elk once plunged to its death, overlooks the award-winning **Stag's Leap Wine Cellars** and **Clos du Val Wine Company**.

The tragedy-ridden Berryessa family lost sons and soil in the Mexican War; today their Napa county land grant is a warm-water paradise. **Lake Berryessa** can be reached via State Highway 128 from St Helena or State Highway 121 from Napa. Fishermen pull in trout,

Acres of grapes.

bass and catfish while sailors, water-skiers and swimmers have a choice of seven resorts around this lake, which has more shoreline than Lake Tahoe.

Bold and friendly, **Lake County**'s visitor-seeking wineries are scattered along State Highway 29 as it wraps around **Clear Lake**, California's largest natural lake. (Lake Tahoe lies partly in Nevada.) Besides producing Cabernet Sauvignon, Zinfandel and Sauvignon Blanc grapes, Lake County is famous for Bartlett pears and walnuts.

The first stop for travelers northbound from Napa County is **Guenoc Winery**, on Butts Canyon Road near **Middletown**. This winery was once owned by British actress Lillie Langtry, companion to the Prince of Wales, later King Edward VII.

Kelseyville's orchard country surrounds **Konocti Winery**. Every October, you can drink Cabernet Sauvignon or Johannisberg Riesling while toe-tapping to bluegrass music during Konocti's Fall Harvest Festival. Clear Lake's alpine, sun-warmed waters attract bass and catfish fishermen, waterskiers, boaters and swimmers. Resorts ring the lake; or campers can pitch a tent in **Clear Lake State Park** at the foot of conical **Mount Konocti**, an extinct volcano.

Sonoma County: A patchwork of country roads, towns, orchards and hills is an apt description of Sonoma. US Highway 101, the wine country's only freeway, traverses the north–south length of Sonoma County, entering the county near **Petaluma**. The freeway continues through Santa Rosa, Healdsburg (gateway to the Alexander, Dry Creek and Russian River valleys), and Cloverdale on the Mendocino County border.

The **Sonoma Valley** is steeped in wine, literary and political history. (*Sonoma* is a Patwin Indian word meaning "land of Chief Nose," after an Indian leader with a prominent proboscis.) Vallejo romanticized it as the "Valley of the Moon," and author Jack London took up the call with a book of the same title about frazzled urbanites rejuvenated by clean country living. State Highway 12 runs the length of the val-

The Silverado Trail.

ley, passing through Sonoma and Kenwood. **Glen Ellen**, Jack London's old haunt, is just off the highway.

Father Altimira founded California's last mission, **San Francisco de Solano**, in 1823. Vallejo set up the town in 1835, making **Sonoma** the northernmost outpost of a Catholic, Spanish-speaking realm that, at its peak, extended all the way to the tip of South America.

It briefly became a republic after the Bear Flag Revolt in 1846, when Americans stormed Vallejo's home. Haraszthy's winemaking innovations at Buena Vista Winery a decade later forced residents to recognize the region's vinicultural potential.

The **Sonoma Plaza**, largest in California, today dominates the town. Several restored adobes and the **Sonoma State Historic Park** – Mission San Francisco de Solano, the **Sonoma Barracks** and Vallejo's home – ring the plaza and nearby streets.

Two blocks from the plaza stand **Sebastiani Vineyards**, some dating from mission days; Sam Sebastiani is the third generation to run them. East of Sonoma, **Hacienda Wine Cellars** and Buena Vista Winery both have old-style connections with Haraszthy. During the summer months, Buena Vista hosts classical concerts.

The Gundlach and Bundschu families have been involved in winemaking for over 125 years; **Gundlach-Bundschu Wine Cellars'** Zinfandel, Cabernet Sauvignon and Merlot are especially good and are exported around the globe. Nearby, the super-expensive, beautifully decorated **Sonoma Mission Inn and Spa** offers complete health and fitness facilities and tasty meals.

The **Valley of the Moon Winery** occupies part of California politician George Hearst's 19th-century vineyards. Today those vineyards produce a fine Zinfandel. **Grand Cru Vineyards**, a secluded winery born during the wine boom of the 1960s and 70s, has picnic sites plus fine Gewurztraminer and Chenin Blanc.

North on Highway 12, visitors come to two wineries in Kenwood. **Kenwood**

Below, United Church of Cloverdale, Sonoma County. **Right**, Sterling Winery, Calistoga.

Winery features Zinfandel, Cabernet Sauvignon and Chenin Blanc. Chardonnay lovers head for **Chateau St Jean** with its medieval-style tower and fine Johannisberg Riesling.

Famed botanist Luther Burbank picked **Santa Rosa** as "the chosen spot of all the earth" to conduct his plant experiments. He developed more than 800 new plants, including many fruits, vegetables and flowers, yet relished few of them except asparagus. Visitors can tour his home (in summer) and gardens (all year) in the heart of Santa Rosa.

Santa Rosa's trinity of adjoining parks form a 5,000-acre (2,000-hectare) urban oasis with a children's amusement park and lake in **Howarth Park**; camping, picnicking and boating in **Spring Lake Park**, and hiking and equestrian trails in **Annadel State Park**.

Monterey County: Driving south on Highway 101, you won't see anything like the miles of grape vines that border Napa and Sonoma's highways. Although there are 30,000 acres (12,000 hectares) of grapes here, the vineyards are tucked into the foothills of the Gavilan Mountains to the east and the Santa Lucia coastal range off to the west, both offering good drainage and protection from the cool winds of the Salinas Valley.

This region is where the author John Steinbeck set many of his novels. The first vintners to discover this area came from the South Bay in the 1960s, when suburban subdivisions began to crowd out their wineries.

Many winemakers have tasting rooms in the popular coastal towns of Monterey and Carmel, a good option for travelers who don't have the time for a leisurely tour. Along Monterey's **Cannery Row**, the bustling waterfront stretch of restaurants and tourist shops, the **Paul Masson, Bargetto**, and **Roudon-Smith** wineries have tasting rooms within a few blocks of one another. On the second floor of an old cannery, Paul Masson offers the best view of Monterey Bay. You can sample Sauvignon Blanc, Pinot Noir and Zinfandel while watching the view.

South of Monterey along Highway

Winemaking in the 19th century.

224

101, outside of **Gonzales**, the **Monterey Vineyard** is an attractive Mediterranean-style building housing ultra-modern facilities. It produces an excellent Chardonnay and Chenin Blanc. Inside the winery is a gallery featuring a permanent exhibit of Ansel Adams's 1960 black and white photo essay, "The Story of a Winery." The winery in Adams's photos is Paul Masson's, which is not open to the public; the series was commissioned by Seagrams Classic Wine Company, which owns both Monterey Vineyard and Masson.

Two other wineries in the area are off the beaten path. South of Carmel, on Carmel Valley Road, is the fanciful castle-like **Chateau Julien Winery**. Its tasting room features an Arthurian round tasting-table. Tours are available but you must make an advance reservation. **Smith and Hook** Vineyards in Soledad is a rustic winery cradled in the Santa Lucia foothills. It offers a good selection of red wines.

The South Central Coast: Almost overnight (by vintners' standards, where wineries often date back a century), the south central coastal region has become a vital participant in California's wine production. Since the 1970s, more than 40 wineries have opened, centered around Paso Robles, the Edna Valley, and further south, the Santa Ynez Valley. Major players from Napa-Sonoma like Robert Mondavi have invested in vineyards here. The wineries are conveniently clustered together in three distinct regions amid scenic hillsides of oak and chaparral, making for excellent touring by car.

About 25 wineries are scattered along Vineyard Drive and State Highway 46 to the east and west of **Paso Robles**. Unlike Edna and Santa Ynez valleys, this area's winemaking history is fairly extensive. **York Mountain Winery**, on York Mountain Road (an offshoot of the eastern arm of Highway 46), could be the oldest commercial winery in Southern California, established by Andrew York in 1882.

Another old-timer, **Pesenti Winery**, on Vineyard Drive, dates back to the

just post-Prohibition days of 1934. Still run by the Pesenti family, it produces an intriguing hard cider in addition to their award-winning Cabernet Sauvignon and Riesling. Tastings are, alas, served in small shot glasses.

Opened in 1984, **Arciero Winery**, also outside of Paso Robles, is an example of the newer breed of wineries. It features state-of-the-art facilities, an elegant Spanish tile-roofed chateau, and landscaped grounds for picnicking. The winery offers a well-designed self-guided tour.

Of the eight wineries in the Edna Valley area, the oldest dates back to 1981. **Edna Valley Vineyard**, on Biddle Ranch Road outside of San Luis Obispo, offers Pinot Noir and sparkling wine in an austere setting. The nearby, handsome **Corbett Canyon Vineyards**, built in 1984, has won awards despite its young age.

Further south, outside Arroyo Grande, **Maison Deutz**, a joint venture between Wine World Inc. and the 150-year-old Champagne Deutz of France, produces sparkling wines. You can see the Pacific Ocean from its stylish, high-ceilinged tasting room.

After the repeal of Prohibition in 1933, the **Santa Ynez Valley**'s many wineries were mostly left abandoned. Vintners didn't return to harvesting grapes here until 1971, when Richard Sanford opened his **Sanford Winery** outside of Buellton. Other notable wineries include the **Gainey Vineyard** on State Highway 246, just south of the town of Santa Ynez, and **Firestone Vineyard**, north of Santa Ynez on Zacca Station Road. The latter was opened by tire magnate Leonard Firestone's son Brooks.

The Santa Ynez Valley is also known for the Danish town of **Solvang**. The town was established by a group of Danes who first arrived in 1910. Remarkably consistent Scandinavian architecture has made this a tourist attraction. Danish windmills churn, but they generate nothing but the self-consciously quaint atmosphere. In the summer, Solvang (which translates as "Sunny Field") hosts an outdoor theater festival.

In northern Mendocino County the wineries are mostly clustered north of **Boonville** on Highway 128 to the east of US Highway 101 or close to 101 itself between **Hopland** and **Willits.** Early settlers as long as a century ago discovered that the coastal valleys and well-drained rocky ridges provided ideal conditions for varietal grapes. Warm summer afternoons are followed by cool nights which grapes enjoy as much as visitors. The county's first vineyard was established in Hopland in 1879 and by 1900 almost 3,000 acres (1,200 hectares) of grapes were under cultivation.

Tiny Hopland derives its name from what used to be its most plentiful crop which flourished in the damp soils of the nearby Russian River. Prohibition ended this phase but the village was revived in 1977 with the arrival of Fetzer Vineyards.

Two years later **McDowell Valley Vineyards** built the country's first solar-integrated winery and in 1983 the Mendocino Brewing company opened California's first brew on the highway at Center Street. It is an area rich in excellent micro breweries, among them being the **Anderson Valley Brewing Company** with its handsome Buckhorn Saloon in Boonville, and Fort Bragg's **North Coast Brewing Company**, one of whose brews, Old No. 38 Stout, is named after an engine of the famous Skunk Train.

Boonville is at the southeastern (and warmer) end of the 25-mile (40-km) long Anderson Valley which follows the path of the Navarro River. It was in this valley that the French champagne-maker Louis Roederer began planting vines in 1983.

Another of the valley's winemakers, Greenwood Ridge Vineyards at **Philo,** holds Wine Tasting Championships every July at which winners can earn free stays at local inns or cases of wine.

The **Ukiah Valley** to the north was where some of the region's oldest vineyards established themselves half a century ago and most of these – **Hidden Cellars, Parducci, Whaler Vineyards, Dunnewood Vineyards** and **Weibel Cellars** – offer tours, tastings and well-stocked giftshops.

Right, cheers!

SACRAMENTO

Although it is the state's capital city, Sacramento (population 385,000) has always lived in the long shadows of prominence and popularity cast by San Francisco, 90 miles (145 km) to the southwest. Nestled in the middle of California's 500-mile (800-km) long Central Valley at the intersection of US highways 5, 80 and 50, this once hot and dusty cow town has endured scathing putdowns from many who found themselves here without advance warning.

The town grew up where the Sacramento and American rivers join, where steamers from San Francisco disgorged passengers who continued overland to the gold fields. Sacramento was the western terminus of the Pony Express, then of the Transcontinental Railroad. It remains a transportation hub today.

There was at least gold here, and it was that which first put Sacramento on the map, the community starting out as

John Sutter's New Helvetia Colony until 1848, when James Marshall discovered gold in the nearby Sierra foothills. From the ensuing Gold Rush emerged Sacramento, which by 1845 had been named the state capital.

Today, the city is home to more than a million people, countless industrial parks, spacious, tree-lined parks, expansive shopping malls, suburban tracts, and a tangle of multi-lane highways that joins it all together. But even when the locals speak about going to "the city," they often mean San Francisco. Until comparatively recently in fact, Sacramento was the ultimate cow town, a nice, big, prosperous, comfortable, tree-shaded cow town. There are something like 100,000 trees – one-quarter of them elms which arch over countless streets – although now even many of those are in jeopardy with the city's municipal arborist trying hard to prevent on onslaught of Dutch elm disease.

Necessary shade: The trees are indispensable because in contrast to its glamorous coastal neighbor, Sacramento is a blazing furnace in midsummer, with temperatures often passing 100°F (41°C) for days at a time. In the winter, the city, which lays low in the 150-mile (240-km) long Sacramento Valley, is a resting bed for thick tule fog, which, like the summer sun, can last for weeks. The city's location – just north of the upper reaches of the maze of waterways and low-lying islands called the Delta was the southernmost site that could be expected to stay relatively dry during the winter floods.

In recent years Sacramento has joined the ranks of progressive, major-league US cities, becoming a serious player in Pacific Rim trade, as well as the smallest American city to build a light-rail commuter transit line. Sacramento also added a National Basketball Association franchise, the Kings, to its entertainment line-up, and, in 1989, became the first American city to close a nuclear power plant by a vote of the people.

Beneath the imposing facade of Sacramento's mirrored-glass office buildings lies a distinct image of the old West. Tucked just below the fork of the

Preceding pages: Sacramento's Railroad Museum. Left, the State Capitol.

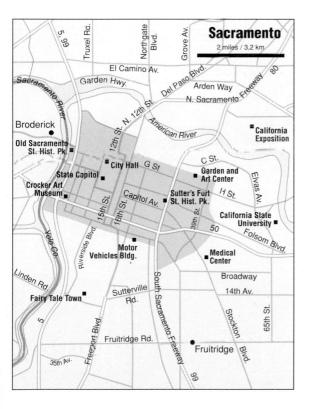

Sacramento and Americans rivers is **Old Sacramento**, where the old Pony Express and Transcontinental Railroad stations have been fully restored.

An afternoon's stroll in what the city likes to call **Museum Mile** (it's actually a square mile bordered roughly by the river, the freeway and 16th Street) will take you to the **California State Railroad Museum,** where over 50 restored engines bring alive the history of railroading in California; the **Sacramento History Center,** a reproduction of the 1854 City Hall and Water Works building; and the **Crocker Art Museum,** the oldest art museum west of the Mississippi River.

On Front Street, a few blocks from Old Town, is the **Towe Ford Museum**, housing the largest collection of a single make of car in the world. Across the river is Broderick, site of the world's first salmon cannery a century ago.

Downtown: At the northeast corner of Museum Mile are the restored **California State Capitol,** where daily tours are offered on the hour; the old **Governor's Mansion**, an 1877 Victorian mansion where 13 California governors lived between 1903 and 1967; and the restored **Sutter's Fort**. Half a dozen blocks north, at 1701 C Street is the **Blue Diamond Visitors Center**, home of the Del Monte Corporation's Packing Plant #11, the city's last operating cannery. On the free daily tours (by appointment, call (916) 446-8409), visitors can see a film and sample the tasty almonds of the kind they used to be served on most airline flights. Regrettably, the airlines have discovered that peanuts and mini pretzels are a cheaper alternative.

Seasonal events in Sacramento have also lent it big-city prominence. The Dixieland Jazz Jubilee, held each May in Old Sacramento, is the world's largest celebration of dixieland jazz, featuring more than 120 bands from around the world. Highlight of the summer is the California State Fair, which runs the 18 days before Labor Day at **California State Exposition,** the city's outdoor exposition facility. During the fall, the **Old Sacramento** Blues Festival draws the **Old Sacramento.**

biggest names in the business, while a drive up Highway 50 to the east brings you to the Apple Hill Growers Festival in the town of **Camino**, where 43 apple ranches offer their finest fruits, pies, and other goodies.

Folsom, an old gold rush town, has an interestingly historic feel to it and the eponymously named lake is a major recreation area.

Placerville (population 8,500) on US 49, where it crosses State Highway 49, is the biggest town around here and during the Gold Rush era was known as Hangtown, for obvious reasons. John Studebaker, inventor of the automobile that bears his name, worked here in a blacksmith shop early this century.

The Delta Country: In the Gold Rush era, Sacramento's waterfront was crowded with bars, brothels and gambling halls but today it is popular with houseboaters, waterskiers, anglers and sailors, for its access by boat to the **Sacramento River Delta**, hundreds of miles of interconnected river channels which percolate slowly toward San Fran-

Delta houseboats.

cisco Bay and the Pacific Ocean. Standing in for the Deep South, the region has been the backdrop for such movies as *Huckleberry Finn* and *Porgy and Bess.*

Formerly an immense swampland, much of the Delta was reclaimed for agriculture – tomatoes, asparagus, pears and sugar beet are major crops – by thousands of Chinese laborers who handbuilt the levees literally with shovel and wheelbarrow.

State Highway 160 runs along the levees, crossing and recrossing the river where thousands of pleasure boats are moored. and fishing boats search for the ubiquitous white catfish. This river country contains hundreds of islands and such charming olde-worlde towns as **Walnut Grove,** once a hangout for river pirates, and **Locke,** a town built by the Chinese laborers who had poured into the Delta after the completion of the Central Pacific railroad in 1870. Locke's main street retains some of the aura of the Old West.

The deepwater port of **Stockton,** known as the "Gateway to the Delta" has more the atmosphere of a river port than its larger upriver neighbor because the river penetrates the heart of the city. The older part of town was demolished in the 1960s but still has some century-old homes, the interesting Haggin Museum (local history) and several wineries offering free tastings.

Although most of the paddlewheel steamers were phased out as the rivers gradually silted up, one still runs: the 110-foot (34-meter) *Spirit of Sacramento* departs from the city's L Street Landing on one-hour sightseeing cruises both during the day and at dinner time but not every day. One or two-day cruises to the Delta depart regularly from the port, it being possible to go one way by boat and back by bus.

The Delta is a labyrinth of waterways – 1,000 miles (1,609 km) of navigable channels – formed by the confluence of the Sacramento, Mokelumne and San Joaquin rivers as they flow into San Francisco Bay.

Industrious valley: Surrounding the city of Sacramento is the Sacramento Valley. Drained by the Sacramento River, it is the northern third of California's great Central Valley. Agriculture is the Number 1 industry in California, and the bulk of it is carried out in this vast valley. Roadside fruit stands offer an opportunity to sample these riches. Life holds few experiences to equal the sensations that go with consuming an almost-liquid, tree-ripened, softball-sized Fay Elberta peach on a hot August afternoon near **Marysville**. The small stands that offer produce only from the owner's fields have fresher products at lower prices, since they are exempted from a state law requiring all farm products to go through a licensed packing shed.

Heading up State 70 is Marysville, an old gold camp and river-steamer port on the Feather and Yuba rivers. At the toe of the Yuba levee downtown is the **Bok Kai Temple**, maintained by a full-time caretaker employed by the local Chinese societies (*tongs*). The shrine's central deity is Bok Kai, whose province is spring rain and fruitful agriculture. Every March, Marysville conducts a Bok Kai Festival and parade.

Further north on Highway 99, about one hour from Sacramento is a mountain range jutting from the center of the valley. These are the **Sutter Buttes**, a beautiful place to hike in spring and fall. Landowners won't let visitors in without a guide: contact Allan Sartain in Davis (tel: 916-756-6283), for information about tours.

North and west of the range is the **Buttes Sink**, a low-lying area where an amazing collection of waterfowl gathers in winter. It is not uncommon to see a flock of 100,000 snow geese all take to the air at once. Best viewing is at **Gray Lodge**, west of **Live Oak** and **Gridley**.

Oak-shaded park: About two hours' drive north of Sacramento is **Chico**, a pleasant farming and college town founded by General John Bidwell about the time Sutter was founding Sacramento. Bidwell's greatest legacy is **Bidwell Park**, 2,000 acres (800 hectares) of magnificent oak woodland along Big Chico Creek right in town, with hiking trails, swimming holes and picnic spots among the oaks.

Chico.

DIDION'S SACRAMENTO

Joan Didion, the journalist and novelist (Play It as It Lays, A Book of Common Prayer), *is one of California's best-known writers. Here, she recalls her childhood in Sacramento.*

I was born in Mercy Hospital on J Street. For a time we lived in town, on U Street, and then, after World War II, we moved to the country — it was the country then, it's not any more — out toward Carmichael. We lived in a surplus mess hall that we turned into a house. It was mostly one room, but a very large room. We had 10 acres (4 hectares) with a lot of oak trees.

There were a lot of farms and ranches then. Just across the American River from town was the Horst Ranch, where they grew hops. Now that ranch is a subdivision; the 10 acres on which we lived is a subdivision, too. Later, we moved to a house further in, off Fair Oaks Boulevard.

Sacramento was hotter when I was growing up than it is now. I know that sounds like something a very old person might say, but it's actually true. When the big dams went on the river, it got cooler in Sacramento. In the summer, we tried to go swimming in the afternoons; we didn't have a pool but we knew a few people who did. Or we swam in the rivers. The trick was to stay wet all afternoon, then jump in an open car — we had a Jeep — and get home before your bathing suit dried, or almost, just as the sun was going down.

People didn't have air-conditioning in those days, so all the houses were dark, the curtains closed, the windows closed. When the sun went down, we opened up the house. I remember the summer evenings in Sacramento. It was as if the whole world opened up. There was a sense of infinite possibilities.

I had no sense of Sacramento as a political town. Once a year we'd go down to the State Capitol to see the legislature in action, if we couldn't get out of it. My best friend's father was a lobbyist, and once a year her mother would have a tea for all the legislators' wives, and we'd serve at it.

I have been in Old Town (the tourist-oriented reconstruction of Old Sacramento) a few times. I remember once going down with my mother and daughter, Quintana, on a very hot Saturday afternoon. Quintana was wearing a big hat of my mother's to keep the sun off, and a little dress, and there was nothing open. It was very quiet. She walked ahead of us on these wooden sidewalks. I remember thinking about my father's great-grandfather, who operated a saloon down there when it wasn't "Old Sacramento" but "Sacramento City," the real thing, a frontier river town. And there was my daughter, walking down this back-lot Western street. It was a peculiar collision of generations. Or cultures. Or something.

I can't even find my way [around] anymore, there are so many streets that don't go where they used to, so many highways with numbers instead of names.

In *Slouching Towards Bethlehem*, I wrote an essay about Sacramento ("Notes From a Native Daughter"), and there's a line in there: "All that is constant about the California of my childhood is the rate at which it disappears." That was written almost 20 years ago. I must have had a sense then that there was something there to disappear. Now, it's just gone. ∎

SAN JOAQUIN VALLEY

Stuck between the brash, self-indulgent coast and the awe-inspiring Sierras, the San Joaquin Valley suffers the kind of image problem more associated with the American Midwest than the Golden State. That's because in many ways, it *is* the Midwest. Up to 500,000 so-called "Okies" – the Dust Bowl victims of the Great Depression that gave life to John Steinbeck's *The Grapes of Wrath* – migrated here. Like ants on a honey trail, they piled into overloaded caravans and streamed west on old Route 66, through the chalk-dry Mojave Desert, past "bum barricades," and the abuse heaped on them by native Californians.

What became of them? Nearly one-eighth of the current California population – or around 4 million residents – claim Okie ancestry, and the core of that gritty family-based community is still here in the heart of the San Joaquin. Stop by any town in San Joaquin Valley and, as one Dust Bowl survivor said: "You might as well be in Tulsa or Little Rock or Amarillo… Same music, same values, same churches, same politics."

Agriculture is California's biggest industry, and more than half of its $14 billion a year in farm goods is produced in the San Joaquin. Fresno County alone accounts for $2 billion of that, making it America's Number 1 farming county. The valley's alluvial soil, covering more than a million irrigated acres (400,000 hectares), supports some of the most productive farming in the world.

Recently, as population has grown, valley cities have experienced a boom as commercial and manufacturing centers. But it's still the fields, orchards, canneries and processing plants that sustain the area. Employment in the valley is more closely tied to rainfall than to the vagaries of the economy.

It is the abundance of that most precious of the state's resources – water – that keeps things going and makes the San Joaquin Valley a recreational as well as an agriculture heartland. Aside from the Sacramento River Delta and the mammoth irrigation project it supports, several of California's great rivers flow through the area – the **San Joaquin**, the **Stanislaus**, the **Tuolumne**, the **Merced**, the **Kings**, and the **Kern**. Most are renowned for outstanding, and occasionally terrifying, stretches of whitewater rafting.

The San Joaquin is also wine country. It can't match the trendiness, or maybe even the quality, of Napa Valley, but it's got the quantity. San Joaquin Valley is home to dozens of wineries, many of them offering tours and picnic grounds. And all those roadside attractions that have fallen to boutiques, theme stores and amusement parks elsewhere in the state still exist here – canneries, chocolate factories, nut trees, not to mention parks, ranchlands and wildflowers.

The Valley: Though its name is often mistakenly applied to California's entire Central Valley, the San Joaquin comprises just the southern two-thirds of that 450-mile (720-km) long, 50-mile (80-km) wide basin. It follows the course of the **San Joaquin River**, flow-

Preceding pages, left and right: San Joaquin's Fresno County is America's Number 1 farming community.

ing south to north, to the Sacramento–San Joaquin Delta, where both rivers empty into San Francisco Bay.

It doesn't take long to see that the San Joaquin Valley is the lifeline of California. An hour out of San Francisco going eastward, Interstate 580 crosses **Altamont Pass**, one of the windiest spots on the coast. It is marked by an exquisitely rural sight – a windmill farm, overhead power lines and dairy cows peacefully coexisting. As the descent begins, the highway crosses a branch of the **California Aqueduct**. Almost immediately the freeway is full of trucks hauling double trailers of bottled tomato catsup, or canned peaches or pears. Welcome to the valley.

Mostly flat and treeless, the valley doesn't at first appear to offer much to an outsider. There are two ways to travel its length: Interstate 5 is the main link between Los Angeles and the Bay Area, getting you from San Francisco to Los Angeles in barely six hours. It guarantees uninterrupted and uninteresting highway driving. The east–west routes to Lake Tahoe and the Sierras all cross the valley.

One slight detour southwest of Fresno, leads 12 miles (19 km) to one of the valley's most celebrated sights. The oil fields north of **Coalinga** – the little town that survived a devastating series of earthquakes in the summer of 1983 – are an unexpected delight in an otherwise dreary landscape, with oil pumps festively decorated as Native Americans, animals and mythical creatures.

State Highway 99, the other north–south route, is the valley's main business artery. It is much slower than the interstate, but reveals more of San Joaquin's secrets, passing through the valley's most populated areas and some of the best roadside produce stands.

Caswell State Park, reached after a drive through miles of almond orchards, is just off Highway 99 near the town of **Ripon**. More than 250 acres (100 hectares) of oak-shaded trails, campgrounds and beaches along the Stanislaus spell relief from the heat of summer, when temperatures can reach 100°F (38°C).

Harvesting corn, Madera County.

240

Though it has more to do with outpourings from the **Melones Reservoir** than from the melting icepack, even in the dog days of summer the Stanislaus runs cold and deep. The last wild stretch of whitewater, several miles upstream, has been lost to the dam, but the river still delivers fine swimming and fishing. **McConnell State Recreation Area**, 8 miles (13 km) south of Modesto on the Merced River, also offers swimming and fishing, camping and picnicking.

Seventy-eight miles (125 km) east of San Francisco, between Interstate 5 and Highway 99, is **Stockton**, queen city of the Delta, where the valley is crisscrossed by sloughs and mudflats. A rambling old river city and mining settlement still showing traces of 1910 grandeur, Stockton is the state's oldest and largest inland riverport. The city's most prestigious institution is the **University of the Pacific**, the first chartered university in California. Local eateries reflect the area's diverse population – Chinese, Mexican and American family style. Stockton is a good place to find all kinds of tasty, inexpensive food.

Ten miles (16 km) north, on the **Mokelumne River**, **Lodi** is home to the county's **Micke Grove Park and Zoo**, with its gardens, swimming pool, kiddie rides and picnic facilities. **Guild Wineries** on Highway 12 have a tasting room open year-round. Between Stockton and the **Modesto** area are several major wineries, including **E & J Gallo**, the world's largest independent winery.

Rail town: Like much of California, **Modesto** is the creation of Leland Stanford's Central Pacific Railroad. The Tuolumne River runs almost unnoticed through the southern fringes of town. A turn-of-the-century steel arch along the main thoroughfare promotes the town's virtues: "Water, Wealth, Contentment, Health." It was the site for the 1973 film *American Graffiti* whose producer, George Lucas, grew up here.

As in most of the valley, food is king – not food eating but food producing. A "Gourmet Taste Tour" includes stops at an almond exchange, a mushroom farm,

Melon farmer.

a cheese processor, a Hershey chocolate plant and local wineries.

Halfway between Modesto and Fresno, **Merced** is a major access point to Yosemite. A major attraction is the **Castle Air Museum's** three dozen restored vintage fighters.

Fresno (population 515,000) is the sleeping giant of central California. From a train station by a wheatfield, it has grown to a city with 11 freeway exits, rows of highrises and a symphony orchestra as well as the excellent **Metropolitan Museum of Art, Science and History**. Fresno is the financial and cultural as well as the service and commercial center of the San Joaquin Valley. Two wineries offer tours – **Cribari Winery** and **A. Nonini Winery**.

Roeding Park, right off Highway 99 in west Fresno, features a number of family amusements – a zoo with more than 1,000 animals, a Playland with rides, and Storyland, a cute walk-through village where plaster fairytale figures tell their story.

Woodward Park in central Fresno

has a Japanese Garden and a bird sanctuary. But the most bizarre attraction in town is **Forestiere Underground Gardens**, 5021 Shaw Avenue. The gardens were once the domicile of sculptor-horticulturist Baldasare Forestiere, who single-handedly carved out the maze of 100 rooms, passageways and courtyards over 40 years.

But despite its increasing importance to the cultural and economic life of the valley, Fresno retains the flavor of small-town America. Weekends are likely to be spent watering the lawn, washing the car, and almost certainly watching football on television or at local schools. At night, young people gather in bookstores and theaters as well as on the streets, cruising the city's wide boulevards in classic 1950s style.

Fresno boasts of being the only community in the US within little more than an hour's drive of three national parks. There are 90-minute flights over Yosemite from its local little airport.

The annual rodeo in nearby **Clovis** brings buckeroos together for two days of roping, riding and bronco-busting the last weekend in April. Buffalo roam year-round 40 miles (64 km) northwest at **Safari World** in **Coarsegold**.

A few miles to the south is **Selma**, home of a famous but now defunct TV commercial for California's "Dancing Raisins." Nearby **Kingsburg**, settled by Swedish immigrants in 1886, is the HQ for the Sunmaid Raisin Company.

The San Joaquin *is* known for some unpleasant natural phenomena. Valley fever – a little-known respiratory illness – is spread when strong winds stir up the spores of a fungus indigenous to the arid soil in parts of the valley. And in December and January, dense "tule fog" blankets the area for days at a time, making driving hazardous.

But its second-class status bothers San Joaquin Valley residents very little. The business of the valley is farming, and it succeeds at that like few other spots on earth. The nearby Gold Country mining claims were abandoned long ago, but the valley is still enjoying general prosperity. It has become one of the fastest growing areas in the state.

Left, virgin ketchup. **Right**, California farmers supply $14 billion worth of produce a year.

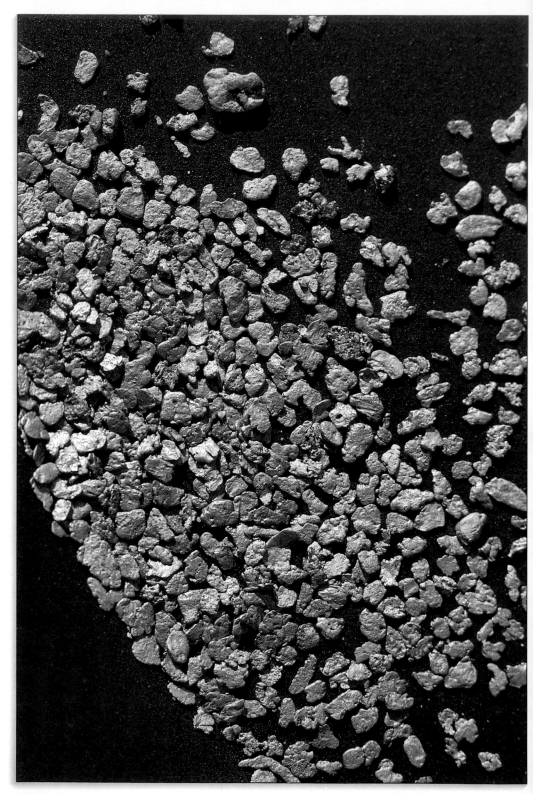

GOLD COUNTRY

The Gold Rush didn't end because they ran out of gold. They simply ran out of the gold that was lying near the top of the ground. As the holes got deeper and more dangerous, the work got harder, slower and more expensive, until it was no longer cost-efficient to dig.

Geologists say there is at least as much gold in the Mother Lode today as was taken out in the previous century, that the 7 million pounds (3 million kilograms) extracted was only 10 percent of the resources contained in the ground. Obviously there is a good deal left – and these days quite a few people are looking for it. Today, modern mining operations dig deeper and deeper into the Sierra with automated machinery, but there are still the rough-hewn old-timers who crouch by mountain streams, squinting for the glimmer of gold flakes in shallow tin pans.

There's another 20th-century rush going in the gold country foothills from Mariposa to Nevada City, but this time it's real estate, not just valuable minerals, that is at stake. Travelers on State Highway 49, Gold Country's main highway, are likely to see more real-estate signs than ghost towns. The modern miner now competes with housing developers – not claim jumpers – for land.

Gold mining was always a hard way to make a living but what is not so hard is making a living off those who themselves are looking for gold. The names of rich men history remembers from the great California Gold Rush tend to be those of retail merchants. Levi Strauss made the trousers that stood up to the rigors of panning; Philip Armour sold meat. Mark Twain and Bret Harte wrote about the miners, while John Marshall, who found the first flakes of gold, died impoverished.

Hidden treasures: The placid Gold Country landscape hides its treasures well. In the lowest of the Gold Country foothills, where spring begins in March, the roadsides from the Central Valley towns of Sacramento, Stockton and Fresno are crowded with wild mustard, an edible plant that adds tang to a salad and covers the beef-cattle grazing land with miles of yellow blossoms.

During spring a succession of wild-flowers moves up the hills and turns entire mountainsides blue and purple with lupine and brodiaea. There are larkspur and popcorn flowers, purple vetch and baby blue eyes, and the maroon of the red bud, a flowering bush. In the canyon of the Merced around Metzler's, there are a few weeks in spring when fresh, new, unnamed waterfalls appear every few hundred yards. The waterfalls last until native California poppies bloom, usually in June.

Mariposa, the southernmost of the old gold towns, is a good place to begin a tour. Mariposa is cattle and timber country now, as is much of the Mother Lode. It enjoys a substantial business as a recreation area for city folks and can be reached by car or via Amtrak trains from San Francisco and Oakland. These are met in Merced by a bus that takes tourists to Yosemite, with a stop in

Preceding pages: Fiddletown, Mother Lode. Left and below, nuggets for all.

Mariposa in which can be found the state's oldest functioning **courthouse** as well as a large mineral collection gathered from all over California.

The country around here was home to Murieta, the Mexican bandit with a Robin Hood reputation who was said to have been wrongly abused and beaten by Anglo miners and afterwards revenged himself by devoting his career to robbing them. Historians, an unromatic lot, say it may only be a legend. There is no such argument about John Charles Frémont, who lived in the mid-19th century just north of Mariposa in **Bear Valley** and owned virtually the entire place, including the gold beneath the ground. It was Frémont, with a great deal of help from Kit Carson, who scouted and marked many of the important routes into California through the mountains. Frémont was the first senator from the new state of California in 1850 and the first Republican candidate for US President.

From his Bear Valley home, Frémont watched the substantial profits of his mine eaten up by lawyers and overheads. Today in Bear Valley, there are the ruins of his house, a store, the Odd Fellows Hall and a couple of pleasant places to eat.

The drive to **Coulterville** involves a tortuous hairpin descent from the rocky, scrub-covered country where the Bear Valley mines are to the Merced River and back up the other side. It is precisely the kind of road highway engineers dislike, so enjoy it while it's still around. Many other such stretches of Highway 49 have been bypassed or bridged but between Bear Valley and Coulterville there is a chance to see what the country was like when the miners worked it – tough, demanding and beautiful. There are many mines along the road, few of them now operating. Both open and closed mines are dangerous, for different reasons; a gold mine should never be visited without an invitation.

At the bottom of the Coulterville grade is another creation of engineers – **Lake McClure**, located on the former site of the Merced River, the town of Bagby, a

Panning for gold near Mariposa.

railroad to Yosemite and some mines. The lake can be fished for rainbow and brown trout, bluegill, bass and catfish.

Coulterville itself is so picturesque that it seems as though it might have been built on a Hollywood backlot and shipped up piece by piece. It is not scarred by a freeway like some Gold Rush towns and it is still a bit dusty. The 25 bars of the old days are gone but travelers can still get a cold beer at the **Jeffrey Hotel**, whose original adobe walls are 3 ft (1 meter) thick.

As the road north of Coulterville dips into the valley of the **Tuolumne River**, travelers can't miss seeing the **Moccasin** plant of San Francisco's Hetch Hetchy hydroelectric system on the right. It provides water and some power to San Francisco, but the cost is high. A dam above Moccasin has destroyed the beautiful Hetch Hetchy Valley, thought by many early explorers to be second in beauty only to the Yosemite Valley.

Further along Highway 49 is the near-ghost town of **Chinese Camp**, which actually has a post office, a few hardy

El Dorado.

residents, and a little life yet. There were Chinese miners by the thousands here during the first Gold Rush – and enough some years later to make for a second gold rush when the great labor gangs that built the transcontinental railroads were disbanded. The second time around, many of the old surface deposits were painstakingly reworked.

Of the ghost towns already abandoned when he visited the Gold Country in 1864, Mark Twain wrote: "You will find it hard to believe that here stood at one time a fiercely flourishing little city of 2,000 or 3,000 souls… In no other land, in modern times, have towns so absolutely died and disappeared, as in the old mining regions of California." In Chinese Camp there were 5,000 miners at the height of the Gold Rush.

Sonora, named for the Mexican state from which many of its first '49ers came, is a city that may be losing a struggle with the real-estate hustlers. Shopping centers now border the edges of town. Beyond are the homes on small lots that burden the community's water

and sewage facilities and pack its streets until traffic stops. But all this development has happened because Sonora is as beautiful as it was during the Gold Rush – and its quaint downtown has remained true to the miner spirit.

The Mother Lode: In the 1870s there was a pocket mine at the north end of Sonora where the operators found a vein of nearly pure gold. They claim to have recovered $160,000 worth of gold in one day. This was part of *La Veta Madre*, "The Mother Lode," from which legends sprang and which keeps miners at work today in the dark tunnels.

The real treasure of Tuolumne County these days is **Columbia**, a few minutes north of Sonora just off Highway 49, an old town that has been restored as a state park. It bears some resemblance to Williamsburg, Virginia, another restored historic town.

Columbia, its population once 15,000, and with 50 saloons, competing daily newspapers and at least one church, produced almost $90 million worth of gold in one 20-year period. Most of its restored streets are now closed to automobiles, but the quiet majesty of the town makes it worthwhile parking and walking around. Among the shops, theaters and a museum is the splendid **Columbia City Hotel** which is operated as a training ground for students of hotel management.

Back on Highway 49, still headed north, a sign indicates the summit of **Jackass Hill,** named for the animals so central to gold prospecting, and where Mark Twain lived in 1864. It was in Jackass that Twain heard what is possibly his most famous yarn, "The Celebrated Jumping Frog of Calaveras County." The actual jumping frogs were supposed to have been a bit north in **Angels Camp** – and they still are.

The Twain cabin has been reconstructed around the original hearth, and the **Angels Hotel** (where the author is said to have heard the story about the contestant who surreptitiously filled his rival's frog with leadshot) is still there. Each May the community holds a frog-jumping contest that attracts so many **Columbia.**

people to the area that the only way to actually see a jumping frog is to enter your own. Any frog more than 4 inches (10 cm) in length is eligible.

From the Angels Camp area, a detour leads up into the mountains to **Murphys**, a Gold Rush period town that is enough off the track to be a natural museum. The **Mercer Caverns**, well worth a visit, are in this area. Farther up State Highway 4 is **Calaveras Big Trees State Park**, a magnificent stand of sequoias.

San Andreas is another town whose past echoes with romance. Black Bart, a stagecoach bandit originally from San Francisco, was tried here in 1883 for some of the 28 polite and bloodless robberies he committed. When he held up the gold-laden stages his shotgun was always unloaded and no one was ever hurt. Nevertheless, he served six years in San Quentin prison, and was not heard from after his release.

In good weather, it's a beautiful drive on the Mountain Ranch and Railroad Flat roads from San Andreas to **West Point**, so named because it marked the end of Kit Carson's attempt to cross the Sierras. It has just a few hundred people, and a marker to remind us of the past.

Same methods: Attempts have been made to reopen some of the hundreds of old mine shafts; a few now crush ore and even welcome visitors. Modern techniques of deep-rock mining differ little from those used by the '49ers, with the gold pan and sluice boxes used by weekend miners today essentially the same tools used 100 years ago.

From West Point, travelers can loop back west to **Mokelumne Hill**, a town once so rich in gold that its claims were limited to 16 sq. ft (1.5 sq. meters). According to legend, the lust for wealth ran so high that for more than four months there was a murder a week here.

From Sutter Creek to Grass Valley, about 75 miles (120 km), the countryside surrounding Highway 49 is mostly a commuter suburb of Sacramento with big supermarkets, rush-hour traffic and cable television. In fact, in the Auburn area and again around Grass Valley, the highway suddenly and inexplicably be

Gold rush.

comes a freeway. But there are many things to do and see along the way.

El Dorado, a town just south of Placerville, is a good place to eat barbecued ribs and chicken. **Apple Hill,** just above Placerville on US Highway 50, has made a cooperative business of marketing apples. In fall, the whole countryside smells of cider and bushels of fruit are exceptionally cheap.

Placerville itself was once called Hangtown because of the chosen method of execution. Being the nexus of wagon, mail, Pony Express and telegraph routes, it was always an exciting place. The **Gold Bug Mine**, north of town, is in a public park and is open for inspection.

North of Placerville on Highway 49 is **Coloma**, birthplace of the Gold Rush. A state historic park now covers the site where, in 1848, James Marshall discovered gold while building a waterway for John Sutter's lumber mill. The state has reconstructed the mill, though not exactly at the same place, since the **American River** has changed its course in the past century. Marshall's cabin still stands, as does the Chinese Wah Hop Store. **Monument Trail** leads to a huge statue of Marshall holding an imitation gold nugget, and the four-mile (6 km) **Monroe Ridge Trail** loops through the hills back to the riverside town. Raft trips of one day or longer are offered on the river by a number of companies.

Auburn, at the junction of Highway 49 and Interstate 80, is so much a part of the Sacramento economy today that there is a proposal to link the communities with a light rail commuter service. The town's **Placer County Museum** has an admirable collection of Native American materials as well as gold-mining paraphernalia. Nearby is the colorful and unusual **firehouse**.

Auburn is a good place to jump off for a visit to Lake Tahoe (up I-80) with a return via State Highway 20 near **Emigrant Gap**. Highway 20, the old Tahoe-Pacific Highway, is one of California's great drives. It rejoins Highway 49 in the Nevada City-Grass Valley area.

Grass Valley was the center of the deep mines, some of which, including the **North Star**, have shafts that go hundreds of feet below sea level. The shafts are now closed and flooded. The **Empire Mine State Park**, east of town, is the site of a mine that produced $100 million worth of gold before it closed in the mid-20th century. Restored buildings surround a visitor center where films are shown daily and there are miles of hiking trails.

Grass Valley is now the center of high-technology industry, most notably the manufacture of equipment for television broadcasting, and is once again a name recognized around the country.

Nevada City is very touristy but lots of fun with its wooden sidewalks and the usual hokeyness of restored mining camps. There are pleasant bars as well as restaurants, museums, antique stores and what's claimed as the oldest theater in the state (built 1865). The **National Hotel** still puts up overnight visitors in rooms tastefully furnished with antiques. There are regular readings/performances at **The Poets' Playhouse**.

Ten miles (16 km) to the north is a large state park at the old **Malakoff Diggings**, a place that generated one of the very earliest environmental laws. Visitors to the Malakoff mine can see the effects of hydraulic mining, a method of gold extraction in which high-powered streams of water are directed from cannons at the side of the mountain. This method was effective, but it devastated the mountain, and waterways were clogged with mud as far as San Francisco Bay. The technique was banned in 1884 but the scars are still awesome.

It's an hour's drive from Nevada City to **Downieville**, a fitting end to a tour of the Gold Country. The countryside here is higher, cooler and much less crowded than further south.

From **Camptonville**, midway along the route from Nevada City, the lovely **Henness Pass Road** veers off into the mountains. In good weather, it is a lovely side trip. There are a number of campgrounds a few miles toward the pass.

Downieville itself is almost as perfect as a picture, a tiny remote place hemmed in by steep hillsides, with a population of not more than 500 with a handful of places to eat or stay the night.

Right, wishful thinking.

253

YOSEMITE AND THE HIGH SIERRA

Standing in yet another line in the crowded Yosemite Valley, the idea of getting away from it all can seem like a cruel joke. Is this any way to celebrate the park's beauty, jostled and jammed together in a supposed wilderness setting?

Unfortunately, if you're one of the 3½ million annual visitors to the park – most of whom in the summer months end up in the 7-sq.-mile (11-sq.-km) Yosemite Valley – Yosemite can certainly feel like any other urban vacation, complete with overflowing parking lots, elbow-to-elbow shuttle buses and packed grocery stores.

Still, Yosemite, in writer Edward Abbey's words, is "a place where a man should count himself lucky to make one pilgrimage in a lifetime. A holy place." That place includes some 760,917 acres (308,000 hectares) of parkland – nearly the size of the state of Rhode Island – and is the third most visited national park in the United States. Ninety-four percent of its area is designated wilderness. In this, perhaps, there is hope for preservation.

All the congestion and overcrowding can't take away the magnificence that defines Yosemite, from the sheer granite walls to the multitude of spraying waterfalls. And the inescapable fact is that to truly experience or know Yosemite – as well as the rest of the High Sierra's wonders – you need to get out on a trail, preferably one that isn't paved from beginning to end.

Variety of torrents: Nowhere else in the world are there so many big falls in such a small area, including 2,425-ft (739-meter) **Yosemite Falls**, the highest in North America. When Ice Age glaciers scoured out the 8-mile (13-km) long and 1-mile (1.5-km) wide Yosemite Valley, they left behind several smaller hanging valleys on either side, conduits for free-leaping torrents whose very names suggest their variety: Ribbon, Bridalveil, Silver Strand, Staircase, Sentinel, Lehamite, Vernal, Nevada.

In early June, one of the rarest of Yosemite sights – the "moonbow" at the foot of lower Yosemite Falls – will sometimes appear. It shows up only in the spring, when the falls are running full, and only in the days around the full moon, when the moonlight shines on the spray from the falls, producing a ghostly rainbow – silver and white with a touch of blue.

"Great is granite," wrote New England clergyman Thomas Starr King in 1878, "and Yosemite is its prophet." As the prehistoric ice flows melted and retreated they exposed the colossal building blocks of the Sierra Nevada, shaped and polished into scenery on a grand scale – **El Capitan, Cathedral Rock, Three Brothers, Royal Arches, Half Dome, Clouds Rest**. In the daredevil world of technical rock climbing, from Austria to Australia, there is only one true triumph, Yosemite Valley.

The history: A holy place, as Abbey wrote, is exactly what Yosemite (*"yo-SEH-mih-tee"*) Valley was to its original inhabitants, the Ahwahneechee tribe.

Preceding pages: sunset over Half Dome. *Left* and *right*, Yosemite is nearly the size of the state of Rhode Island.

Because of Yosemite's isolation, the tribe managed to keep its mountain retreat a secret from whites until 1851, a full year after California attained statehood, when the US Cavalry arrived and herded the Ahwahneechees across the Sierras to a barren reservation situated near Mono Lake.

As with much of the Old West, subjugation of the Native Americans paved the way for settlement. During the decade following its "discovery," Yosemite Valley was fenced, farmed and logged by homesteaders. Visitors, drawn in increasing numbers by newspaper and magazine accounts of Yosemite's marvels, were appalled to find cow pastures instead of mountain meadows. In 1864, public pressure on the California legislature resulted in the Yosemite Grant, the first attempt in the nation's history to preserve a natural scenic area from commercial exploitation.

There are many who will argue today that the attempt has failed. With thousands of hotel rooms and nearly 2,000 campground sites, restaurants, super-markets, liquor stores, gift shops and even a jail, Yosemite Valley has become the textbook example of over-developed parkland. In a controversial, decade-long planning effort, the US National Park Service spent millions of dollars trying to determine what to do about degradation of the Yosemite environment; the principal recommendation, elimination of the private automobile from the valley, seems unlikely to be implemented before the year 2000, if ever, although every year there is new talk of restricting access to the park in some manner.

In the meantime, roads in the east end of the valley near **Mirror Lake** have been restricted to shuttlebuses, bicycles and pedestrians. A convoluted one-way traffic pattern almost everywhere else makes driving a truly masochistic experience, especially in summer.

If you can resist the valley's shuttlebuses, you might want to take a guided horseback trip. This can be arranged through the valley stables, near **Curry Village** (the first large developed area

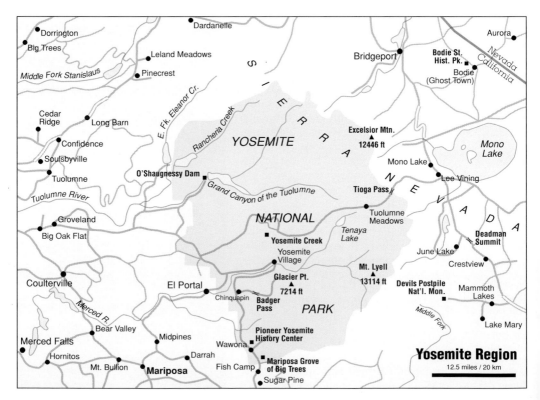

Yosemite Region
12.5 miles / 20 km

on the Yosemite loop road). Bicycles may be rented at both Curry Village and **Yosemite Lodge**, and several bikeways make two-wheeled travel the most efficient way for getting around.

In summer, Yosemite Valley plays host to more than 90 percent of all the park's overnight visitors. Lodging runs the gamut from inexpensive cabins at Curry Village to the palatial suite atop the beautiful **Ahwahnee Hotel**, with Yosemite Lodge occupying the middle ground. The surest way of seeing Half Dome without crowds and an enveloping wreath of smog is during the off-season, September–May.

Cool nights: Autumn brings a rich gold to the leaves of the valley's oak trees, and the sun's lowering angle etches the granite domes and spires into sharper relief. Nights are cool, mornings apple-crisp. It's a good time to focus binoculars on rock climbers, lured back to Yosemite's great walls by mild daytime temperatures.

Autumn also brings herds of wild deer, migrating through the valley en route to winter forage in the Sierra foot-hills. An early-morning stroller may not see another soul on his way through a meadow in October, but chances are excellent he'll see at least half a dozen deer, bounding fleet and silent through the golden grass like dancers.

Yosemite Valley is emptiest in winter, when most of the action shifts to the ski resort of **Badger Pass**, 21 miles (34 km) away and 3,000 ft (900 meters) higher. Badger's gentle pine-fringed slopes offer few challenges for accomplished skiers, but are ideal for family groups and novice-to-intermediate skiers who don't mind the 45-minute commute by car or bus from the valley. In the valley, the Yosemite Mountaineering School at Curry Village offers instruction in nordic (cross-country) skiing, as well as beginning and advanced rock climbing. An outdoor ice-skating rink boasts views of Glacier Point, Half Dome, and the frozen remnants of Yosemite Falls.

Spring is the favorite season of many Yosemite residents. Wildflowers carpet

Mammoth Lakes.

the meadows, and the roar of wild water resounds throughout the valley. The force of the runoff is such that most of the waterfalls are unapproachable; gale-force winds and drenching spray enliven the normally placid one-quarter mile walk from Yosemite Lodge to the base of Yosemite Falls.

Seeing Yosemite when the crowds have gone home is the best way to experience the tranquility that inspired the words of John Muir and the photographs of Ansel Adams. But even on the Fourth of July there are several routes of escape, if you're willing to venture off the well-worn paths.

To the south, State Highway 41 climbs 9 miles (15 km) to **Chinquapin** junction, where a 15-mile (25-km) paved road departs for **Glacier Point**. From this famed viewpoint, 3,200 ft (975 meters) above the floor of Yosemite Valley, the entire park comes into unforgettable stomach clutching focus. Directly below, the meadows, forest and waterfalls of the valley appear in dollhouse scale, dwarfed by the awesome verticality of the huge northside cliffs and domes. No less compelling is the 80-mile (129-km) vista to the east and south, a panorama of lakes, canyons, waterfalls and the rugged peaks of Yosemite's High Sierra. Close at hand are the granite steps of the **Giant's Staircase**, where Vernal and Nevada falls drop the raging waters of the **Merced River** 320 and 594 ft (98 and 181 meters) respectively.

From Glacier Point, **Half Dome** is the most prominent landmark, a great solitary stone thumb thrusting skyward. Park rangers are accustomed to one question more than any other: what became of Half Dome's other half? The answer is that the dome never had another half of solid rock, only slabs of granite on the sheer north face that were peeled away like onionskin by advancing glaciers during the Ice Age.

At the height of glaciation, 250,000 years ago, Glacier Point itself lay under 700 ft (213 meters) of ice, and interpretive markers explain how the 2,000-ft (610-meter) thick Merced and Tenaya glaciers ground down from the high country to merge near Half Dome and quarry out Yosemite Valley. The glacier filled the valley to its brim, and extended down the Merced canyon to **El Portal**, 15 miles (24 km) to the west.

Giant trees: Five miles (8 km) south of **Wawona**, just inside the park's southern boundary, a short side road leads to the **Mariposa Grove** of giant sequoias, a 250-acre (100-hectare) preserve containing more than 500 mammoth redwood trees. It was here that John Muir slept under the stars alongside President Theodore Roosevelt, and persuaded the chief executive that the ancient forest should be added to the infant Yosemite National Park.

The Mariposa Grove's largest tree, the **Grizzly Giant**, is at least 3,800 years old, with a height of 200 ft (61 meters) and a girth of 94.2 ft (28.7 meters). The best way to experience the big trees is to walk: leave the pavement and wander at random among trees that were already giants when Christ walked the Holy Land.

If Wawona and the Mariposa Grove

Yosemite Falls.

are Yosemite's Black Forest, **Tuolumne Meadows** is its Switzerland. Reached by an hour's drive north from the valley on the scenic **Tioga Road**, and situated at 8,600 ft (2,620 meters) above sea level, Tuolumne is the gateway to an alpine wilderness.

Perhaps not surprisingly, becoming totally familiar with such a wilderness is far from easy. The only way to see the more remote areas of the Tuolumne backcountry is to hike, with all creature comforts carried in a backpack that may tip the scales at 50 lbs (23 kg) or more. A less arduous alternative, at least on some of the smoother trails, is to arrange a horsepacking trip, details of which can be discovered locally or through Yosemite Park information services.

Tuolumne is also the site of **Tuolumne Meadows Lodge**, central star in the summer constellation of High Sierra Camps. Arranged in a rough circle, about 9 miles (14.5 km) apart, these six permanent tent camps provide lodging, meals and hot showers to hikers and horsepackers taking the High Sierra Loop trail.

Elevations of the camps vary from 7,150 ft (2,180 meters) to 10,300 ft (3,140 meters), and a night of acclimatization in Tuolumne is recommended before departure. In a typical year, camps are open from mid-June through September 1, with advance reservations essential. Wilderness permits, available free of charge at park ranger stations and visitor centers, are required for *all* overnight trips in the Yosemite backcountry.

Sequoia and Kings Canyon: It is tempting to dismiss **Sequoia** and **Kings Canyon** national parks as Yosemite without Yosemite Valley. Judging from park visitation figures, many California travelers do just that. In any given year, more than 3 million visitors converge on Yosemite; the comparable figure for Sequoia/Kings Canyon barely reaches 400,000. (Although Sequoia and Kings Canyon parks were established separately, their adjoining areas are administered as one unit.)

Lambert Dome and the Tuolumne River, Tioga Road.

262

Even though 7,000-ft (2,130-meter) deep Kings Canyon exceeds Yosemite Valley in sheer vertical relief, and the sequoia forests of the southern park are larger and more numerous than Yosemite's groves, the absence of waterfalls and striking rock formations make them pale alongside their more celebrated northern cousin. The result is a national park bereft of the most common national park headaches and reason enough for solitude-seeking vacationers to beat a hasty path to the entry station.

Much more so than Yosemite, Sequoia/Kings Canyon is a wilderness park, with only two developed areas near its western boundaries. The backcountry extends east across the west slopes of the Sierras as far as the crest of the range, encompassing the headwaters of the Kern and San Joaquin rivers and the highest Sierra summits, including Mount Whitney. Ironically, a majority of the park's mountain trails are most easily reached from trailheads out of Lone Pine, Big Pine and Bishop on

the Sierra's east side, a 250-mile (400-km) drive from park headquarters near **Three Rivers**. As in Yosemite, wilderness permits are required for overnight backcountry camping.

The most scenic approach to the Kings Canyon section of the park, State Highway 180, begins in the sprawling agricultural city of Fresno. A 52-mile (84-km) drive through the Sierra foothills leads to the **General Grant Grove**, a stand of massive 3,000-year-old sequoias notable for the wide-open parkland that surrounds their bases.

Thirty-eight miles (61 km) past the Grant Grove (where campground sites are available by advance reservation), the road drops into Kings Canyon at **Cedar Grove**. In contrast to Yosemite Valley, this gaping chasm is V-shaped rather than U-shaped; the smaller flow of the **Kings River** has yet to deposit enough alluvium to level out the canyon's floor. Cedar Grove offers idyllic camping and fishing alongside the placid waters of the Kings, and rustic lodging is also available. Two trailheads lead

Sequoia National Park.

north and east toward the High Sierra, but the 6,500-ft (1,980-meter) climbs on south-facing (and sun-broiled) slopes are only for the fit and experienced.

After backtracking to Grant Grove, you can proceed into the park's Sequoia section by following State Highway 198 south for 28 miles (45 km) to **Giant Forest**. A short nature trail here leads to the **General Sherman Tree**, believed to be the earth's largest living thing. California's coastal redwood (*sequoia sempervirens*) are taller than the Sierra subspecies (*sequoia gigantea*), but in terms of girth and overall volume the mountain redwoods come out on top.

Hotel rooms, restaurants, a grocery store and a visitor center make Giant Forest the closest approximation of an urban center Sequoia/Kings Canyon has to offer. Three campgrounds lie a few miles farther south on Highway 198. The road continues southward past good camping and boating at **Lake Kaweah**, and drops back into the San Joaquin Valley at **Visalia**, 50 miles (80 km) from the park boundary

The Eastern Sierra: Approached from the west, through the foothills of the Gold Country and on into Yosemite or Sequoia/Kings Canyon, the Sierra Nevada begins gently. Low, rolling hills studded with oak trees give way to higher hills blanketed with pines, which in turn give way to an accelerating crescendo of granite domes, spires and ridges, culminating in the 13,000- and 14,000-ft (4,000-meter) peaks of the crest.

But there is nothing gradual about the Sierra when approached from the east, up US Highway 395 from Southern California. On the east side, the mountains of the crest drop precipitously, nearly 10,000 vertical ft (3,000 meters) in the space of a few miles, a single great front nearly 200 miles (320 km) long. From **Walker Pass** at the southern end of the range to **Tioga Pass** on the eastern Yosemite boundary, not a single highway cleaves the scarp, the longest contiguous roadless area in the United States outside Alaska.

Owens Valley: Driving north from Los Angeles, the dramatic scenery begins

Mono Lake is the oldest body of water in North America.

on the shores of **Owens Dry Lake**, near the hamlet of **Olancha.** To the left, the tawny, unforested peaks of the southern Sierrras rise abruptly, cresting in granite pinnacles 12,000 ft (3,600 meters) high. To the right, across the wide, shimmering lake bed, the softer, more rounded contours of the somewhat lower **Inyo Range** dissolve into black and purple foothills. These are the portals of **Owens Valley,** deepest in America, "The Land of Little Rain." The vegetation here is hardy desert flora – scrub oak, mesquite, sagebrush. Owens Valley and the Inyos receive less than 10 inches (25 cm) of rain yearly.

Just past the northern end of the lake bed, 21 miles (34 km) north of Olancha, State Highway 136 departs east for Death Valley. Located at the junction is the **Interagency Visitor Center** which dispenses maps, information and wilderness permits for the extensive public lands under federal jurisdiction. In winter, the center is a mandatory stop for the latest word on campground closures and road conditions. In the busy summer season, rangers will steer travelers to campgrounds with spaces still available. Unlike the national park camping areas on the west side of the Sierras, many east-side campgrounds do not accept advance reservations, and the arrangement tends to be first come, first served.

Mount Whitney: On a patio outside the Visitor Center building, telescopes are trained on the summit of Mount Whitney, at 14,495 ft (4,418 meters) the highest mountain in the United States outside Alaska. A trail leads to the very top of Whitney where portable latrines have been set up to cope with the tide of visitors. It's a strenuous three-day hike (two up, one down) from where the trail begins at 8,360 ft (2,548 meters), but no technical skills are required, and therefore thousands of adventurers make the trip every summer.

The most difficult part of the 22-mile (35-km) journey in fact, can prove to be getting a reservation: many Whitney trail permits are snapped up a year in advance. For reservations, which are

free of charge, write to Inyo National Forest, Mount Whitney Ranger District, Lone Pine, CA 93545.

North of Crowley Lake, a 2-mile (3-km) road leads to **Mammoth Lakes**, the largest downhill ski resort in America. In winter, Mammoth is where residents of Los Angeles go skiing, and it is not uncommon to find yourself sharing lift lines with 20,000 other powder hounds. On the plus side, Mammoth offers gourmet dining, good wine and several cheese shops.

A summer (not winter) attraction is **Devils Postpile National Monument**, a 30-minute drive west of Mammoth Lakes into the Sierras. About 630,000 years ago, dark molten lava poured through Mammoth Pass and flowed into the deep canyon of the middle fork of the San Joaquin River, where it cooled, solidified and cracked into astonishingly uniform vertical columns. Successive glaciation scraped and polished the tops of the columns into a smooth, tile-like surface. Today, the abrupt geometric pickets of Devils Postpile (80 ft/

24 meter high, 0.2-mile/0.4 km long) offer mute testimony to the power of the twin forces that shaped the entire Sierras – fire and ice. Limited camping is available in summer at **Agnew Meadows** (just before the monument boundary on State Highway 203) and **Red's Meadows** (just after the boundary).

At **Deadman Summit**, north of June Mountain, US Highway 395 begins a long descent into Mono Basin, once the site of an inland sea and today the focal point of an ongoing controversy over Los Angeles' appropriation of eastern Sierra water.

Mono Lake, the last remnant of that sea, is the oldest continuously existing body of water in North America, and islands near the lake's northern shore are breeding grounds for 90 percent of the world's California seagulls. Eerie calcified rock formations on the shoreline are called *tufa*, examples of which are strikingly preserved at **Moon Lake State Tufa Reserve**.

From May until November, or until the first winter snow falls, the town of **Lee Vining** on Mono Lake's western shore is the east entry to Yosemite National Park, via 9,991-ft (3,045-meter) **Tioga Pass**. From Lee Vining, Tuolumne Meadows is a 45-minute drive away; it takes at least two hours to reach Yosemite Valley.

Campgrounds are spaced every 15 miles (24 km) or so, but, unlike the rest of the park's sites, they do *not* take reservations in advance.

North of Mono Lake, the Sierra crest begins to lower, although "lower" in this case still means snowy summits 11,000 ft (3,350 meters) high. Eleven and a half miles (18 km) north of Lee Vining, a graded side road leads 13 miles (21 km) to **Bodie State Historic Park**, which offers both an excellent view of the northern Sierras and a fascinating glimpse into the life of a '49ers boomtown.

Once the wildest camp in the West, Bodie was home to a ragtag collection of miners and confidence men who made silver fortunes by day and squandered them by night in opium dens, saloons and bawdyhouses.

Left, Mount Whitney climber. Right, towards the summit of Sentinal Rock.

LAKE TAHOE

Of Lake Tahoe, Sierra explorer and America's most famed naturalist, John Muir once wrote, "a fine place this to forget weariness and wrongs and bad business." Mark Twain was no less impressed. "The lake burst upon us," he wrote in *Roughing It* as he reached the summit overlooking the lake. He went on to describe the "noble sheet of blue water lifted 6,300 ft (1,920 meters) above the level of the sea, and walled in by a rim of snow-clad mountain peaks... I thought it must surely be the fairest picture the whole earth affords."

Twain might eat his words today. Several communities – and countless casinos, fast-foot joints, strip malls, and water and snow-sports outfitters – now dot the 71-mile (114-km) shoreline of this crystal-blue lake, which straddles Nevada and California, and stands at 6,229 ft (1,898 meters) in the Sierra Nevada. But in many ways, especially during winter, the words of Muir and Twain ring true. Tahoe still has a unique allure that can convert postcard admirers into would-be residents at the drop of a snowflake.

When Twain and Muir discovered Tahoe, the lake was as pure and sparkling as the silver being dug out of the nearby Comstock Lode. These days, Lake Tahoe's blue waters are sometimes green with algae, its blue skies dimmed somewhat by smog. The indoor attractions (roulette wheels and crap tables) rival the outdoor ones (sun, water, and winter snow) for the attention of the travelers, while an array of fast-food outlets, motels, condominiums, video arcades and miniature golf courses cater to their every need.

But only a few miles from the furious bustle of the Nevada casinos are wilderness, hiking trails, hidden lakeshore caves, snow-covered backroads ideal for cross-country skiing and quiet beaches that look much the same as when Twain dug a toe into them.

Despite the popularity of *Bonanza*, America's most popular television show

of the 1960s, Lake Tahoe was never adjacent to "The Ponderosa," the fictional 19th-century Cartwright ranch. This has not, however, prevented a goodly number of Tahoe establishments from calling themselves "Ponderosa." These include a flower shop, a glazier and a delicatessen.

The area's real story, however, would probably get equally high ratings. It involves explorers, cannibalism, silver and gold fever, the construction of a trans-Sierra rail line (the biggest engineering feat of its day), forestry and mining, the Winter Olympic Games and, these days, lots of bickering between developers and conservationists, with the developers seeming to win most of the big ones.

It was in 1844 that explorer John C. Fremont scrambled to the top of 10,100-ft (3,080-meter) **Steven's Peak**, gazed down on the lake, and proclaimed himself the lake's discoverer. That must have come as a surprise to the Piute, Lohantan and Washoe Indians who had been living there for hundreds of years.

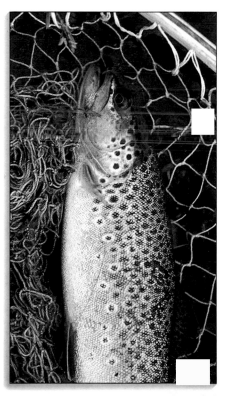

Preceding pages: Lake Tahoe's lucrative resource, snow. **Left**, afloat on McKinney Bay. **Right**, a fisherman's finest.

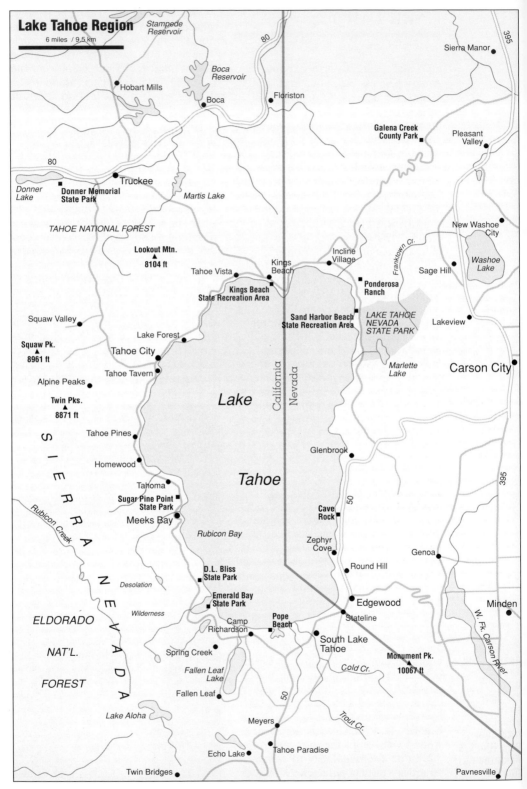

Lake Tahoe Region

6 miles / 9.5 km

Stampede Reservoir

Boca Reservoir

Sierra Manor

80

395

Hobart Mills

Boca

Floriston

Galena Creek County Park

Pleasant Valley

80

Truckee

Donner Lake

Donner Memorial State Park

Martis Lake

New Washoe City

TAHOE NATIONAL FOREST

Lookout Mtn. 8104 ft

Tahoe Vista

Kings Beach

Incline Village

Franktown Cr.

Sage Hill

Washoe Lake

Squaw Valley

Kings Beach State Recreation Area

Ponderosa Ranch

Squaw Pk. 8961 ft

Lake Forest

Sand Harbor Beach State Recreation Area

LAKE TAHOE NEVADA STATE PARK

Lakeview

Tahoe City

Alpine Peaks

Tahoe Tavern

California

Nevada

Lake

Marlette Lake

Carson City

Twin Pks. 8871 ft

Tahoe Pines

S
I
E
R
R
A

Glenbrook

Tahoe

Homewood

Tahoma

N
E
V
A
D
A

Sugar Pine Point State Park

Rubicon Creek

50

Cave Rock

Meeks Bay

Rubicon Bay

Zephyr Cove

Genoa

395

Desolation

D.L. Bliss State Park

Round Hill

ELDORADO

Wilderness

Emerald Bay State Park

Edgewood

Minden

Camp Richardson

Pope Beach

Stateline

NAT'L.

Spring Creek

South Lake Tahoe

Monument Pk. 10067 ft

W. Fk. Carson River

FOREST

Fallen Leaf Lake

Cold Cr.

50

Fallen Leaf

Lake Aloha

Meyers

Trout Cr.

Echo Lake

Tahoe Paradise

Twin Bridges

Pavnesville

272

The Indians hunted deer, fished for trout and, in general, did a lot of other things for survival that today's visitors do for recreation.

Two years after Fremont stumbled across the lake, a party of 82 settlers from Illinois, led by George Donner, became snowbound while trying to pass through the Sierra Nevada about 20 miles (32 km) north of the lake. The Donner Party ate twigs, mice, shoes and finally its own dead in order to survive. **Donner Pass**, now the route of Interstate 80 over the crest of the Sierras, is named in its honor.

Just east along this highway, past the Tahoe turnoff, is **Truckee,** a historic railroad town whose museum chronicles the horrific journey across the mountains of the Donner Party in the winter of 1846-47. In a macabre story known to every American schoolboy, the Donner family and others left the main party of a cross-country caravan in a futile search for a shorter route, ending up stranded in the early winter snows and finally resorting to cannibalism.

Along the south shore of the lake runs US Highway 50, the old overland route connecting Salt Lake City with Sacramento that brought so many settlers to California. In 1859, more than 3,000 covered wagons and stagecoaches passed by the lake, bound for the valley and farmlands below. The next year, for the first time, a young man on horseback sped along the lakeshore carrying a sack of tissue-paper letters. It was the inaugural run of the Pony Express, which cut in half the time required to send a letter from coast to coast. It was, however, no match for the railroad which was to follow by the end of the decade.

In the mid 1860s, the sound of 16-pound (7.2-kg) hammers rang through Donner Pass as tens of thousands of laborers, many of them low-paid Chinese immigrants, struggled to pound rail spikes and lay the first transcontinental railroad track. In 1869, the Central Pacific line, of which the trans-Sierra stretch was a portion, met the Union Pacific line in Utah and travelers could finally forsake the rigors of covered wagons and stagecoaches.

Uses and abuses: In the years that followed, the beauty of the lake became the area's drawing card for tourists. Campers, hikers, fishermen and skiers came for the spectacular alpine setting, clear water and pristine skies. In the 1940s, at Sugar Bowl west of Truckee, developers erected a cable lift to enable skiers to end the drudgery of climbing back up hills, and the area's ski industry was born. In 1960, the Winter Olympic games were held at Squaw Valley, 10 miles (16 km) north of **Tahoe City**, despite a meager snowfall that threatened the entire event. The Lake Tahoe area now has a dozen major ski areas, although weekend skiers, waiting in 30-minute lines for a ride to the top, probably think there are still too few.

Legalized gambling, among the lake's biggest attractions, is also among its biggest problems. One-third of the lake lies in the state of Nevada, one of the few places in the United States where casino gambling is legal. High-rise casinos – looking more at home in San Francisco's financial district than amidst

Gambling is legal on the Nevada side of the lake.

the jewel of the Sierras – are a main cause of the growing traffic jams, smog, lake pollution and sewage problems.

Since 1972, development at the lake has been governed by the Tahoe Regional Planning Agency. For years, critics claimed it was a rubber-stamp for every hotel, casino and taco stand looking for a home. In 1980, reacting to increasing pressure and deterioration of the lake, Congress expanded the agency, changed its charter to make the approval of new developments more difficult, banned the construction of new casinos and hotels, and restricted the expansion of existing ones. In 1982, California voters approved an $85 million bond act to buy environmentally sensitive lands and spare them from development. Some said the changes came just in time; others said it was far too late.

The fight over the lake's future continues. The water is no longer clear enough for a fisherman to drop a silver dollar into, and see it sparkle 100 ft (30 meters) down. Charles Goldman, professor of limnology (the study of lakes) at the University of California at Davis, warned that the lake will lose all its clarity and be deprived of oxygen within 40 years unless stricter controls are undertaken now.

Snowbound: Recreation is the lifeblood of the Lake Tahoe area, and in winter that means downhill and cross-country skiing, and snowboarding. On Friday nights, the weekend exodus from the Bay Area begins. Tens of thousands of cars with skis strapped on their roofs like sections of picket fences stream up Interstate 80 or US Highway 50 toward the lake.

The largest ski areas are **Squaw Valley**, at the northwest side of the lake, and **Heavenly Valley**, on the south side. Each has more than two dozen ski lifts and terrain to satisfy skiers of every ability, including novices. (Heavenly also has a "Sky Express" high-speed detachable quad, and a few triple chairs, plus expanded snow-making facilities). Another local favorite, the family-run Sierra Ski Ranch, 12 miles (19 km) west

Boating on Emerald Bay.

of South Lake Tahoe on Highway 50, also has high-speed detachable quads, and snowboarding.

Heavenly Valley is the favorite ski area for those who like to duck into the casinos at night, as it is located at **South Lake Tahoe**, the busiest part of the lake and just a stone's throw from Nevada. For all their commotion, the casinos can actually come in handy for skiers in the evening – most offer inexpensive all-you-can-eat buffet dinners, to lure customers to the gambling tables. There's no law, however, that says a person can't just visit the dining room, eat a filling meal after a tough day of skiing, and depart with the family fortune still jingling in his pocket.

In general, though, gambling and skiing don't mix, which is why the majority of skiers prefer the northern half of the lakeshore on the California side, particularly the area around Tahoe City. It's quieter, cleaner and the selection of ski areas is better. In addition to Squaw Valley, skiers can choose **Alpine Meadows, Sugar Bowl, Boreal Ridge** and **Northstar**. The latter caters particularly to families – its gentler slopes keep most of the show-offs away. Boreal, perched on the edge of four-lane I-80, is perhaps the easiest to reach. Sugar Bowl is the matriarch, having been around longest. Alpine Meadows is preferred by experienced skiers, as 40 percent of the runs are rated "expert."

Skiing is easy to learn and difficult to master. It should not be undertaken by anyone reluctant to fall down. A candy bar or wineskin containing stronger refreshments is invaluable. The novice skier should have the foresight to include at least one of these among the gloves, hat, lip balm, sunscreen, goggles and sweaters he must somehow find room for in the pockets of his parka.

After the lifts close, skiers usually retire to a bar with a fireplace. In any given bar are apt to be 100 skiers and only one fireplace, so it is usually impossible to get a ringside seat.

Cross-country skiing, which is more like a hike in the woods than a flight down a mountainside, is attracting more and more people each year. The skis are longer and narrower, the uphill stretches can make the legs ache, but the silence and solitude are blessed. It can be done on any snow-covered back road or meadow, or at Nordic ski-touring areas.

Even in winter, the outdoors is the central focus of travelers' Tahoe experience. To get off the beaten track, **Lake Tahoe Winter Sports Center**, 3071 Highway 50 in Meyers, leads snowmobile tours through meadows, lakes and mountain forest. Wilderness dinners, weddings and accommodation in igloos can be arranged.

At **Northstar Stables**, off Highway 267 between Kings Beach and Truckee, visitors can explore the terrain by horse and sleigh. To take the chill off, try a hot soak at **Walley's Hot Springs Resort**, 12 miles (19 km) east of South Lake Tahoe on Foothill Road in Genoa.

Summertime exploits: In the summer, camping, swimming, fishing, hiking and boating take over, and none of them requires a parka. Marinas at South Lake Tahoe and Zephyr Cove, Nevada, offer daily cruises aboard large vessels, in-

Peace and pipe.

cluding an authentic paddlewheel steamer. A daytime cruise on the *MS Dixie*, departing from Zephyr Cove, takes 2½ hours; evening cruises include dinner or cocktails and cost more. The 140-ft (43-meter) *Tahoe Queen*, another steam paddlewheeler, can carry 500 passengers. Both boats cruise through spectacular **Emerald Bay State Park**, an isolated, tree-lined wilderness tucked into the southwest corner.

Independent-minded visitors can rent motorboats and rowboats for their own exploring, or even waterski boats. If the latter is the choice, would-be skiers are advised to stick an exploratory toe into the lake before signing any papers – Lake Tahoe can be very cold.

Trout fishermen have good luck in the **Truckee River** and the river basin at the north end of the lake. Truckee itself abounds with sporting-goods stores that offer more shiny devices to catch the unsuspecting than DeBeers Limited. On any summer weekend, joggers and bicyclists take to the roads ringing the lake. The 75-mile (120-km) circle makes

a strenuous one-day bike ride, or a more leisurely two-day trip.

Hikers and backpackers usually head for **Desolation Wilderness**, a lake-studded area west of Emerald Bay. Nearby is the **El Dorado National Forest** Visitor Center, offering orientation programs and guided walks. A wilderness permit must be obtained for backpacking in Desolation Wilderness – it's a popular place that frequently fills to capacity in summer. The **Granite Peak** area is also good for backpacking, and Emerald Bay and **D.L. Bliss** and state parks are excellent for short walks and picnics. In **Sugar Pine Point park** is the spectacular **Ehrman Mansion**, a 12,000 sq. ft (1,100 sq. meter) summer house with pine-shaded lawns built by a wealthy banker almost a century ago.

In the midst of Tahoe's isolated splendor, it's easy to believe in myths and magic. The Washoe Indians called the area "big water," based on a legend involving the Evil Spirit and the Great Spirit. Coming to the aid of an innocent, the Great Spirit gave the Indian a branch of leaves; each leaf would create a pool of water which the Evil Spirit could not navigate. But the young brave dropped the entire branch at once, hence the huge body of water known as Lake Tahoe.

Getting there is simple, and, thanks to the many casinos seeking to lure fresh blood from the Bay Area, inexpensive. The drive from San Francisco takes four to five hours in good weather and light traffic. Chains should always be carried in winter, and drivers should be prepared to either lie on their backs in roadside slush to put them on, or to pay one of the "chain monkeys," young people who cluster on the side of the road hoping to earn money.

Probably the most spectacular way to get to the lake is on Amtrak's daily cross-country train, the *California Zephyr*, which leaves Emeryville in the morning and arrives in Truckee well in time for dinner. The train follows the same trans-Sierra route that was carved so laboriously in the 1860s, and the view is spectacular. Passengers may also disembark in Reno just in time for the dinner show.

Left and right, recreation is the lifeblood of Lake Tahoe.

THE NORTH COAST

There are few places in America as wild as California's North Coast. Developers may have recreated Southern California's coastline in their own image, but in the upper reaches of the north, the elements still rule and the eye can track miles of majestic coastline and inland hills without spotting a living soul – except perhaps the legendary Sasquatch, who supposedly roams throughout the redwood forests.

Although most of the delightful coastal towns tend to be small, visitors are welcome and accommodations are plentiful. Coastal State Highway 1, while offering glorious scenery, is a narrow, twisting, two-lane road for much of the way and all-too-often one tends to be behind an oversized motor home or logging truck. But courtesy still rules here and usually slower vehicles will move aside allowing you to pass at the occasional turn-outs. North and southbound traffic that is in more of a hurry will choose US Highway 101 through Santa Rosa, Ukiah and Willits, the lumber town from which California Western Railways' Skunk Train ("you can smell 'em before you can see 'em") runs to the coast at Fort Bragg.

Trucks loaded with fir and redwood logs hurtle along Highway 1 toward Fort Bragg at the rate of one every two or three minutes. The shoulders of the highway north of the city are strewn with red fuzz from redwood bark blown off the trucks.

The absence of development along the North Coast is partly due to the California Coastal Commission, formed in the 1970s when the state seemed fated to become a 400-mile (640-km) ribbon of private marinas and ocean-view condominiums.

The only sign of unchecked development on the North Coast is the Sea Ranch, a chic subdivision north of Marin County designed to blend into the environment and where vacation homes are for rent. There are tricky codes forbidding residents to paint their homes or to do anything but minimal landscaping.

Comfortable coast: North of **Bodega Bay**, most of the Sonoma County coast is a state beach, with comfortable access, plenty of parking, thrilling views, no camping, and appropriate beach names like Mussel Point, Salmon Creek, Hog Back, Shell Beach and Goat Rock.

The prevailing scenery is fog, cypress trees, pines, old barns and grazing sheep and cows. As real estate, this grazing land is so valuable that local ranchers are termed "boutique farmers," because they don't really have to farm. They could sell the land immediately for more money than they'd make in a lifetime of working in agriculture.

"I'd rather look at my cows than count money in a bank," said one North Coast dairyman not long ago. "If my cows are happy, I'm happy." This same man once owned a chunk of Marin County pasture land that he sold for millions to filmmaker George Lucas for his renowned Skywalker Ranch.

Tourism is the growth industry on the North Coast, overtaking logging and

fishing which are both suffering from depression. Demand for trees and fish is on the increase but the supply is diminishing.

The boats in the Bodega Bay salmon fishery, declared an "economic disaster" in the early 1980s, remain berthed during the salmon season because it is too expensive to cruise for a product that may not be there. Bodega salmon fishermen sell freshly caught albacore directly from their boats to recoup losses. The winner in this market may be the camping traveler. Fresh barbecued albacore is far better than the deep-fried frozen fish served with professional indifference in tourist cafes along Highway 1.

North of **Jenner**, Highway 1 weaves through daily fog, rolling pastures and sudden canyons that drop 1,000 ft (over 300 meters) into the blue and foamy Pacific. The road passes historic **Fort Ross**, a careful reconstruction of the original fort built by Russian traders in the early 19th century. The best way to see the fort is to stroll through on your own, being sure to inspect the small Russian Orthodox chapel.

One of the more compelling ways to pass an afternoon in north Sonoma County is to visit the coastal tidepools. At **Stewart's Point State Park**, a popular place for abalone divers, the pools are accessible at most tides, and there is little risk (present at some North Coast beaches) that the explorer will be swept to a majestic death at sea by what the California state's warning signs call "sleeper" waves.

Bayside beaches: Travelers enter Mendocino County just north of Sea Ranch at **Gualala**. Gualala is a former lumber port, many of whose fine Victorian homes have become elegant inns or B&Bs, and which are especially popular during the August arts festival.

The St Orres inn, famous for its redwood cottages, goose down comforters, and excellent California cuisine, was built from century-old timber. It has Russian-inspired onion shaped copper domes, stained glass and lovely weathered turrets.

Mendocino Victorian House.

Fifteen miles (24 km) north, a coastal access path leads to **Point Arena Harbor**, a tiny bayside beach that comprises several dozens of weathered mobile homes, a fishing pier popular with springtime whale-watchers and with a good wharfside place to eat, the Galley restaurant. An "underwater preserve" attracts scuba divers. The harbor was a major shipping point for tambark, the bark from oak trees from which tannic acid (for leather tanning) was obtained and which was also used on circus floors to control dust and cut down the considerable animal odors.

The clifftop **Point Arena Lighthouse**, 115 ft (35 meters) high, is a couple of miles down a dead-end road off Highway 1 at the nearest point of the US mainland to Hawaii. Rebuilt after the 1906 earthquake, the lighthouse is open most days for a couple of hours around noon, and offers spectacular views of the coast. Inland, between Boonville and Navarro, is the fertile Anderson Valley best known for apples, sheep and lush vineyards.

In a sense, **Mendocino** is a victim of its own beauty: it's just too lovely to be ignored. A century-old former logging village just small enough to walk around (once you've found a place to park), it's set on a long bluff above a small bay and is full of picturesque Victorian structures. Water is still in short supply and at one time everybody had to dig their own well.

A handful of the town's original 83 water towers or windmills survive, one of them adjoining the pre-Civil War home of William Kelley on Albion Street, which is now the historical museum. The **Ford House** on Main Street was the second house to be built here – in 1854 – two years after Jerome Bursley Ford discovered the redwoods which became responsible for the logging business in these parts. Mendocino's sawmill, erected in 1852, closed in 1931.

Dominating the main street is the century-old **Mendocino Hotel** ("we're just a stone's throw getting here – but a long way off when you arrive"). There are a dozen or so B&Bs, many in old

Mendocino barber shop.

houses built in lumber-town days. Because of the many Danish, Norwegian and Swedish sailors manning the lumber boats, the fleet became known as the Scandinavian Navy.

Mendocino has stood in for Maine in various TV episodes of *Murder She Wrote* and several movies have been made here: *East of Eden, Johnny Belinda, Frenchman's Creek* and also *Same Time Next Year*, a 1975 weepie in which Alan Alda and Ellen Burstyn have an annual illicit liaison in the town's **Heritage House,** a romantic, antique-filled haven.

A small gallery opened by Bill and Jennie Zacha in 1958 grew into the flourishing **Mendocino Arts Center** which offers dozens of creative classes and stages theatrical performances. Worth checking out, on the highway just north of town, are the **Mendocino Coast Botanical Gardens**, which were begun by Ernest Schoefer and his wife, who spent 30 years clearing out the underbrush from their 49-acre (20 hectare) backyard. While still well into his seventies, Schoefer was working 12 hours a day filling the grounds with year-around flowers. Two nearby state parks, **Van Damme** and **Russian Gulch**, offer camping, hiking, beach-combing and other quiet pleasures.

To the north, the city of **Fort Bragg** is an unpretentious, working-class, beer-bellied, hick town that greets the wayfarer with roadside cafés bearing such names as Jerko's Koffee Kup. Its impact comes as a bit of a shock after genteel Mendocino but it does have a batch of interesting 19th-century buildings (and, along Main Street several reconstructed ones).

These include the 1885 depot of the California Western "Skunk" Railroad, originally built to transport lumber from Willits to the harbor here, but now a popular tourist ride. Operating over 41 miles (66 km) of track, 34 bridges and trestles, two tunnels and 381 curves, it covers what would be only 23 miles (37 km) as the crow flies.

Adjoining the station, the Fort Bragg Depot reproduces a tiny village with 21 **Repairing the nets.**

284

interior stores and food stands bearing colorful period facades.

Noyo Harbor, just south of town, is lined by docks, charter boats and seafood restaurants. The cloud of steam over Fort Bragg, the largest coastal settlement between San Francisco and Eureka, is produced by the Georgia-Pacific Corporation's lumber mill.

Some of the earliest mills appeared in 1850 on Humboldt Bay, incongruously named after the celebrated 18th-century Prussian explorer Alexander von Humboldt who never visited here. The mills were powered from steamships run ashore, their bunks housing the millhands.

Redwood country: Much of the North Coast's mystique lies in the tall redwood trees, which for environmentalists are disappearing much too fast but, loggers claim, are protected by too many restrictions. Some groves of the remaining old-growth redwoods are now protected in parks, where tourists are invited to look up at the trees, to drive through holes burnt or cut through them, and to buy objects made of their wood.

Notices tacked to buildings and utility poles all along the North Coast offer "Sinsemilla Tips," a reference to the high-grade seedless marijuana, the area's lucrative black market commodity. Until 1981, it was listed in the annual Mendocino County agricultural report as the county's largest cash crop. Since then, state and federal authorities have mounted a disproportionally costly assault with helicopters, jets and jeeps on those who nurture it on secluded mountain farms. Sometimes the planters win; sometimes the law. Raids on dope fields and questionably-legal confiscation of properties have driven away many of these enterprising entrepreneurs.

Garberville, a small town with lots of ex-hippies, feisty dope lawyers, two weekly newspapers and an active library, is the bustling center of all kinds of activity. EPIC, the environmental group is here, and an Alternate Energy company ships out its solar and wind-power equipment over the world. The second-largest abalone shell in the world

Brown pellican, a common coastal sight.

sits in Brown's Sporting Goods store, which Darrell Brown has been stocking with every conceivable type of outdoor merchandise – as well as dispensing fishing advice – for 50 years.

Two miles (3 km) south of town, overlooking a lovely lake, is the famous Tudor-style **Benbow Inn**. This was once a presidential retreat (Herbert Hoover, Eleanor Roosevelt) as well as being a movie-star hideaway (Spencer Tracy, John Barrymore and Gertrude Lawrence all stayed here) in Hollywood's heyday.

North of Garberville, a diversion into **Humboldt Redwoods State Park** will take you through the **Avenue of the Giants**, which follows the South Fork of the Eel River for 32 miles (52 km) passing through tiny hamlets. At **Phillipsville**, the **One Log House** is on everybody's itinerary. Floods in 1955 and 1964 wiped out several small communities and left hilltop **Redcrest** with the only working sawmill out of the hundreds that were operating in these woods half a century ago.

The giant redwoods, otherwise known as *Sequoia sempervirens*, are around 300 ft (90 meters) tall and sometimes as much as 12 ft (3.7 meters) wide. In the midst of the redwoods is **Leggett** (population 400), a former logging town 175 miles (282 km) north of San Francisco at the junction of Highways 1 and 101. One of the northernmost towns in Mendocino County, it is popular in summertime with campers and hikers and in late fall with fishermen in pursuit of the salmon's rush to spawn up the south fork of the Eel River.

One mile north of town is a 200-acre (80-hectare) redwood forest with black-tailed deer, raccoon, grey fox and the **Drive-Thru Tree Park**. The **Chandelier Tree**, its fabulous centerpiece, is said to be 2,400 years old and is 315 ft (96 meters) high. In its 21-ft (6-meter) base is a corridor barely bigger than a car, carved 75 years ago by Charles Underwood whose family still runs the attraction.

Millions of trees have been cut down and harvested for paper since 1870 but attention is now turning to some older

Left, Avenue of the Giants. Below, the Benbow Inn.

alternatives: a few companies already use a combination of hemp and cereal straw to produce a paper that is reputed to last 20 times longer than that made from wood pulp. (*see page 291*). Not far from Leggett, the **Standish-Hickey State Recreation Park,** in redwoods beside the **Eel River**, offers around 160 campsites in three different campgrounds. About 20 miles (32 km) to the north a difficult road heads over the King Mountains to **Shelter Cove** in an area unvisited enough to be tagged the Lost Coast. King's Peak (4,086 ft/1,245 meters) is the highest point on the continental US coastline. North of this isolated outpost is **Petrolia**, site of the first oil well in California.

Company town: Logging fans are the inhabitants of **Scotia**, a tidy little company town where the largest redwood mill in the world is operated by the Pacific Lumber Company. Targeted constantly by environmentalists, the company tries hard to be visitor-friendly, issuing passes for self guided tours through the vast mill where one ob-

serves the transformation of immense hairy logs into the smoothest of planks and boards. There are no trees growing in Scotia's gardens, nor is there any distinctly modern architecture, but the town's market stocks everything from liquor to video tapes.

Just before Fortuna, Highway 36 winds eastwards through **Grizzly Creek Park** (there are no grizzly bears here now) along the Van Duzen river. **Fortuna** is the site of an annual rodeo every July. It has half a dozen motels and lovely Rohner Park in which eagles, deer and raccoon can sometimes be seen beside the fern-lined creek.

Don't miss seeing **Ferndale**, 10 miles (16 km) southwest of Eureka, a village of visually-stunning Victorian houses (mostly painted in bizarre pastel colors) which has deservedly been named a Historical Landmark. Several films have been shot here, including *Outbreak*, starring Dustin Hoffman. Beg, borrow or rent a camera before your visit, and especially on Memorial Day weekend (late May) when the town is the termi-

Lumber is the area's main industry.

nus for the annual three-day World Championship Great Arcata to Ferndale Cross Country Kinetic Sculpture Race.

This amusing event, recently the subject of a documentary film, features dozens of pedal-powered cars in the shape of lobsters, ducks, shoes and dinosaurs, all of which compete more than 38 miles (61 km) of rough, muddy terrain including a bay crossing at low tide.

The **Loleta** Cheese Factory, just west of the highway, invites visitors to the little dairy town to tour its plant and sample its cheeses.

Often shrouded in fog, **Eureka** (population 27,000) is the largest Pacific Coast enclave in North America north of San Francisco. It is a sprawling semi-industrial place on Humboldt Bay whose major interest to visitors is the historic old town section between 6th Street and the waterfront. The Chamber of Commerce (2112 Broadway, as you enter town) hands out a free map to some of the hundreds of Victorian homes around town.

Boats line the marina across Samoa Bridge on **Woodley Island** where the **Samoa Cookhouse** has been filling its long tables since 1885. The *Madaket*, the coast's oldest passenger ship, cruises around Humboldt Bay from the waterfront at C Street

Grotto with a motto: For half a century, until 1987, **Lazlo's** shipped out briny barrels of salmon from lst Street along the bay. Now the restaurant is in a sturdy, old building around the corner on 2nd Street. Over on Broadway (US 101 entering town), the **Seafood Grotto** serves stacks of clams piled up like pancakes. "We Ketch 'em, Cook 'em, Serve 'em" its motto acclaims. Whimsical murals are spreading around town due to a grant-financed program to train young artists.

The star of Eureka's ubiquitous and impressive Victorian architecture is the 1885 **Carson House**, now a private club. Lumber tycoon William Carson is said to have commissioned this extravagant whimsy to keep his workers busy in the slow seasons. There are many attractive little shops and restaurants

The Carson House, Eureka.

along 2nd Street, near D Street; the **Maritime Museum** (1854) is situated in the town's oldest bulding at 1410 2nd Street. The bigger stores are in the **Bayshore Mall** out on Broadway.

Across the bay, the university town of **Arcata**'s spacious plaza sports palm strees and, incrongruously, a statue of Ohio-born President William McKinley (assassinated in Buffalo, NY in 1901). The city won a $100,000 Ford Foundation grant for the ingenious way it filtered its sewage by creating a 154-acre (62 hectare) Marsh and Wildlife Sanctuary. The sanctuary has abundant and vibrant birdlife, and guided walks on Saturday mornings.

On the coast 50 miles (80 km) to the north, **Orick** is the entrance to **Redwood National Park**, established in 1968 to consolidate 40 miles (64 km) of majestic forested coastline under federal jurisdiction. A visitors' center in Orick gives out directions and shuttle-bus information for southeastern excursions up **Redwood Creek** where three of the six tallest trees ever identified are

clustered in the unimaginatively named **Tall Trees Grove**. The record holder is 368 ft (112 meters) in height, the equivalent of a 35-story building.

McKinleyville, with its bulb and tree farms, dairies and truck gardens is the country's fastest-growing community – but horses still have the right of way. It's the actual site of the so-called Eureka-Arcata airport.

It is difficult to recommend much of the scenery north of the **Klamath River** bridge, because you probably won't see much of it. The stands of redwood in **Del Norte Coast Redwoods State Park** and **Jedediah Smith Redwoods State Park**, both extensions of Redwood National Park, are noteworthy, but the foremost fact of life in this area is fog. About 3,000 members of the Yurok tribe live along the banks of the Klamath, and their salmon festival should not be missed by lovers of good fish.

At tiny **Trinidad** (population 450) on US 101 the phone rings constantly at the local real estate office where an employee talks of the intense demand for

property from people outside the area. "They are coming from Los Angeles, San Diego and San Francisco," she says. "And they all want ocean views. People just can't stand the cities anymore." This entire area has for some time been popular with counter-culture devotees, but interest has now spread far beyond that group, to the wider world of lawyers and yuppies and media people.

In 1964, the town of **Klamath** was washed away in a flood, the result of a storm that dumped 40 inches (over 100 cm) of rain in just 24 hours. The newer town boasts a very commercial souvenir marketing outlet, known to the people who visit the North Coast as the **Trees of Mystery**. Each motorist who leaves a vehicle in the parking lot runs the risk of a sign wired to his bumper while his back is turned. A statue of the mythic lumberjack **Paul Bunyan** and his blue ox, Babe, overlooks the Trees of Mystery souvenir shop, which includes "the largest display of sculptured redwood in the world." It might well include, in addition, the world's largest display of small. stuffed blue ox toys.

In **Crescent City**, one of the principal civic ironies is that someone had the chutzpah to name a seaside restaurant "Harbor View." To be charitable, though, Crescent City – a grim, gray gathering of plain houses and vacant lots around a semi-circular harbor – has never fully recovered from a 1962 typhoon which devastated the town.

For the traveler looking for a place to have a pleasant time, the best bet is to head inland to higher and hotter ground. Fifteen minutes east of Crescent City, on US Highway 199 toward Grants Pass, Oregon, the last un-dammed river in California flows gin-clear through the 90°F (32°C) summer twilight.

The **Smith River region** combines majestic redwoods with some excellent fishing. There are clean campgrounds, public and private, under the peeling red madronas. At the Ship Ashore Resort with its restaurant, motel rooms and RV camping is a 16-ft (5-meter) former luxury yacht which has been turned into a gift shop and museum.

Yurok Indian at the salmon festival in Klamath.

HEMP INITIATIVE

Hemp, one of America's most valuable crops, became too popular for its own good in the 1960s, when it hit the headlines as *cannabis sativa*, or marijuana, but there are signs that it might still regain a place in the country's agricultural economy.

The first American farmer of the new era is likely to be John Stahl in Leggett. A paper-maker by trade, Stahl claims he has met all the stringent governmental requirements for growing a 3,000-ft (279-meter) square area of hemp on his farm for research, paper making and seed production. He was required by law to construct a cyclone fence topped with barbed wire, as well as security lights, alarm systems and a 24-hour guard. "Professionally I am indifferent to the THC content; I'm a paper maker," says Stahl. (It is the THC that produces the plant's renowned euphoria.)

Not all of his neighbors feel the same way. The cultivation of high-grade marijuana is a multi-million-dollar black market commodity in Humboldt County, one to which many of its residents are dedicated. Feisty lawyers in Garberville and Eureka devise strategies to counter CAMP, the federal Campaign Against Marijuana Planting. Helicopters fly over the area constantly, a tactic the growers have countered by setting up "mobes," plants in pots that can be taken indoors during flyover searches.

Thoughout much of America's history, however, hemp was a major crop. Widely used for fabric, oil, paper, paints, sailcloth, clothing, fuel, rope and twine as well as food for livestock, the plant had became so essential that, by the 17th century, there were mandatory laws in some countries requiring its cultivation.

The world hemp industry, once controlled by Russia and its neighbors, prompted a war when Napoleon invaded Russia over hemp trade rights. At the dawn of the New World, Benjamin Franklin, Thomas Jefferson and George Washington all cultivated it, and Benjamin Franklin started America's first hemp paper mill. By 1850, the US Census was able to count 8,327 large plantations.

Stahl is printing a 400-copy edition of the Declaration of Independence on hemp paper. The first and second drafts were originally written on hemp, the second draft being signed on July 4, 1776 a few months before it was copied onto vellum. In the production of making paper, hemp stalks are dried and cleaned, shredded and cooked with a 20 percent solution of sodium hydroxide, a strong alkali.

In the early part of the 20th century, scare stories began to appear about the plant's hallucinogenic propensities. In 1937, the Federal Bureau of Narcotics and Dangerous Drugs pushed through Congress the Marijuana Tax Act which required growers to register and pay a 100 percent tax on its selling price of $1 an ounce. Although the seed and oil lubricating industries protested (as did doctors, aware of the drug's therapeutic qualities), the politicians wouldn't budge.

By 1942, when it was realized how much hemp would be needed to make ropes and rigging for the fast-growing wartime fleet, certain farmers were subsidized to cultivate 42,000 tons annually. Since then, North American hemp fields have lain fallow. A proven cash crop, it could be a lifesaver for small family farms, say backers of the Hemp Initiative, who make repeated attempts to get onto the voting ballot. ∎

CAMP officials raid a Humboldt County marijuana plantation.

THE HIGH NORTH

The key to unlocking the secrets of California's High North – at least from a limited traveler's perspective – is State Highway 299. Native American tribes, some of which still inhabit these parts and fish its rivers, know more than we'll ever know about the sparsely populated end of the state – including, probably, whether the legendary Sasquatch is just that – legendary. But there's plenty you can cover on your own. Running 321 miles (517 km) from the Humboldt County redwoods to the Nevada border, one could easily drive the highway in two days. But that's not the idea.

This mountainous journey should be savored like a fine wine, but the restaurant guides can be left behind; no one undertakes this trip for the cuisine. Highway 299 is the only paved highway that crosses the state's isolated north. On its winding, two-lane blacktop trek, it cuts across some of California's least populated wilderness – a remote domain of mountains, valleys, volcanoes, rivers, canyons, basins and, at the end, desert.

Other paved roads penetrate the High North, including the north–south Interstate 5, running roughly along the boundary between the Klamath and Cascade mountain ranges. Every journey through this region should include side trips on secondary roads. But when it comes to offering visitors the most topographically varied exposure to the region, Highway 299 is the road to ride.

The time to visit is between mid-April and mid-November. The northern third of California gets two-thirds of the state's precipitation. Winter snows and spring floods make Highway 299 dangerous; they often close the route altogether. Even under the best conditions, rock slides and heart-stopping curves make driving in this district no experience for the timid, the drunk or the impatient.

Anyone hell-bent on winter travel should bring their own tire chains, but local police can recommend reputable garages if mechanical assistance is needed. The California Highway Patrol will give current road conditions over the telephone.

Sasquatch Territory: Coming from the Pacific Coast, Highway 299 branches off US Highway 101 at Arcata, north of Eureka, and crosses the low Coast Range to the **Klamath** and **Trinity rivers**. These main two rivers drain the Coast Range and the Klamath Mountains.

The **Klamath Mountains** comprise a series of smaller ranges – the Siskiyou, the Trinity, the Trinity Alps, the Marble, the Scott Bar, the South Fork and the Salmon mountains, which together cover 12,000 sq. miles (about 31,000 sq. km) of Northern California and southern Oregon. **Mount Hilton**, 8,964 ft (2,732 meters), is the region's highest peak; most vary between 5,000–7,000 ft (about 1,500–2,100 meters).

The Klamaths are famous as the home of Bigfoot, also known as Sasquatch, the giant humanoid who – according to legend – stalks these mountains. Whether or not Bigfoot really exists, it is an appropriate and popular myth.

There *is* something wild about the Klamaths: with some areas receiving more than 70 inches (180 cm) of annual rainfall, they sustain a lush forest of ferns, hemlocks, pines and spruce. Some native tribes still inhabit the area. Except for the highest of the Trinity Alps, glaciers are rare, so most peaks have a raw, jagged quality.

Three national forests cover most of California's Klamaths – Klamath, Shasta and Trinity. Within these forests are more strictly protected wilderness areas. The best-known and most popular is the **Salmon-Trinity Alps Primitive Area**, laced with hundreds of miles of trails for hiking and camping. Ranger stations along Highway 299 at **Burnt Ranch, Big Bar** and **Weaverville**, and on Highway 3 at **Trinity Center**, will issue free permits, answer flora and fauna questions, and provide information on weather and trail conditions.

Ten miles (16 km) east of the Trinity River bridge marking the Humboldt-Trinity county line, near the community of Burnt Ranch, Highway 299 passes just south of **Ironside Mountain** (5,255 ft/1,602 meters). Ironside's sheer, scenic face is the eroded, exposed tip of a much larger piece of granite, the Ironside Mountain Batholith. **Blue Lake** was formed in the 1860s by receding floodwaters of the Mad River. It dried up 70 years ago but the residents never got around to changing the name.

People power: The Klamath–Trinity drainage system includes hundreds of smaller creeks, lakes and rivers. In high mountain streams, the spring melting of snowpacks creates a fearsome torrent of a volume and velocity that can move large boulders more than a mile downstream. Taking advantage of the federal law mandating local power companies to purchase any electricity generated by small entrepreneurs, some residents have developed small hydroelectric plants – like the one run by Mom & Pop Power Company in Trinity's tiny **Minersville**. Only a few such plants now operate, but others are planned.

For residents of this region, a "night on the town" usually means a trip to **Weaverville,** a former supply post for gold prospectors. in a valley below the Trinity Alps. Its drugstore, dating back to 1853, is the oldest in the state and its Trinity County Courthouse was built in 1857 as a hotel and saloon. California's oldest Chinese temple still in use is the **Joss House**, a tribute to the Chinese miners of Gold Rush days. There are tours most days. Nearby is the eclectic **J.J. "Jake" Jackson Museum** featuring everything from Indian relics to Chinese weapons.

Weaverville is also the gateway to Clair Engle and Lewiston Lakes, part of the expansive **Whiskeytown-Shasta– Trinity National Recreation Area** north of town. Created by damming the upper Trinity River, the lakes are good for fishing, boating and camping.

At **Willow Creek**, where a statue of Bigfoot adorns the plaza, there's a celebration of "Bigfoot Daze" every September. A side road from here leads into the 93,000-acre (37,600-hectare) **Hoopa Valley Reservation,** the largest in California, with a tribal museum, fish hatchery and traces of Indian dwellings thousands of years old.

Inside the Weaverville Joss House.

Federal land: As is typical in rural California, 72 percent of Trinity County is owned by the federal government, and another 10 percent by Southern Pacific Railroad, although no railroads actually cross the county. Southern Pacific received huge 19th century land grants here as elsewhere in the West.

Although lumber ranks first, marijuana ranks second in the local cash crops. This juxtaposition of enterprises – one traditional, one contraband – is typical of Trinity, whose population is split between true locals, and those who have come here since the end of the 1960s. Generally, locals tend to be conservative; the newcomers less so.

Despite their differences, Trinitarians share an individualism and a jealous regard for the natural environment. While Trinity often votes conservative in general elections, it also displays an abiding sensitivity to ecological issues – a sort of environmental populism. This is not so much a matter of ideology as one of simple self-interest.

Some residents hunt their own food and draw water directly from springs, rivers and creeks. So when the county recently tried to stop the federal government from spraying Trinity's woodlands with a herbicide that many feared would end up in water supplies, no politician – either Democrat or Republican – openly opposed the grass-roots effort. This closeness to each other and to the land seems to breed a native suspicion of most outsiders.

Frontier heritage: Visiting motorists should know that **Trinity County**, like most of California's north, has "open range." Cattle has never been a major part of the economy here, and the term is mainly a symbolic vestige of the region's frontier heritage. Open range means that cattle wander beyond their owner's unfenced lands. It also means that any driver whose vehicle strikes a cow has probably just purchased damaged livestock.

Hikers must be careful to stay away from creek bottoms on which gold prospectors have staked claims. Likewise, those who come across a patch of mari-

Lumber and marijuana are Trinity's two major cash crops.

juana should leave quickly before (a) they are shot at by its grower or (b) they are arrested on suspicion of being its grower.

East of Weaverville, Highway 299 crosses **Buckhorn Summit** (elevation 3,125 ft/980 meters) then quickly loses altitude. Douglas firs, ponderosa pines and the occasional redwood give way to manzanitas (whose gray-green leaves look ghostly under headlights) and digger pines.

Coming out of the Klamaths, a few miles past the Shasta County line, the highway skirts **Whiskeytown Lake**, a reservoir for which locals have mixed feelings. Both this lake and nearby Shasta Lake hold waters from the **Sacramento River**. Like Clair Engle and Lewiston lakes, they are part of a huge federal project, completed in the 1960s, that diverted Klamath Mountain water from the range's east slope. They have now become part of the region's national recreation area.

An extensive system of tunnels, penstocks, dams and aqueducts directs Klamath water into California's Central Valley where it irrigates cash crops for huge agribusinesses. Residents here say they like the lakes but liked even more the wilder, more plentiful waters that once flowed from the mountains. A native businessman put it this way: "We've had our water taken and exported south, our timber cut and our farmlands flooded. We feel like we've been colonized up here."

There is an information sign by the Whiskeytown dam. Beside it is a button one can push to hear the speech given by President John F. Kennedy when he dedicated the dam. It echoes across the still lake, with the sure cadences of manifest destiny.

Not far from the dam access road, Highway 299 leads into the town of **Shasta** (population 750), until 1888 the county seat. Now it's mostly a tourist stop: the whole community has been declared a state historic park.

Free of franchisers: Conspicuous by their absence along most of Highway 299 are traffic lights, franchise motels

Butch Marks, Yurok Indian and salmon fisherman.

and restaurants. According to the marketing strategists, none of the highway's towns has developed enough to warrant franchise food. None, that is, except the sprawling valley town of **Redding** – population 43,500.

As Highway 299 metamorphoses into a four-lane highway and straggles into Redding, the usual fast-food jungle begins: McDonald's, Long John Silver's, Shakey's Pizza and the rest. On Market Street, Highway 299 passes Redding's old **City Hall**, built in 1907, then hitches a ride north on Interstate 5. Redding sits at the northern end of the 450-mile (724-km) long Central Valley. These 2 miles (3 km) are Highway 299's only exposure to the valley. Northeast of Redding, the highway resumes its eastward passage and returns to being two lanes.

Less than 15 miles (24 km) up Interstate 5 from Redding is one of California's largest lakes, many-coved **Shasta Lake**. A popular resort for fishing, hiking, camping, and boating, it comprises the largest section of Whiskeytown-Shasta-Trinity National Recreation Area. As with its counterparts, this reservoir was created by the damming of rivers – in this case, the **Sacramento**, the **McCloud** and the **Pitt**. Lake Shasta's shoreline stretches for 370 miles (595 km). Visitors can rent houseboats or explore the **Lake Shasta Caverns**, an array of underground wonders accessible only by boat or (with difficulty) by foot. Full information is available at the Shasta Dam Area Chamber of Commerce, just west of the Shasta Dam exit on Interstate 5.

North of Lake Shasta is **Dunsmuir** and the granite outcroppings of **Castle Crags State Park**, favored by rock climbers. Above that – some 50 miles (80 km) north of Redding – is magnificent **Mount Shasta**, the highest mountain in the California Cascades at 14,162 ft (4,316 meters). Unlike the Sierras' Mount Whitney, which, although higher, is lost among myriad other summits, Shasta stands alone, a majestic monarch dominating the countryside for miles around.

This mountain has five glaciers, fine

skiing, and covers a very large area. For a sense of its awesome proportions, take the scenic highway that winds 7,880 ft (2,400 meters) up its slopes – barely halfway to the top. There's a ranger station on the mountain's western flank in the tiny town of Mount Shasta.

The only town of significant size on Interstate 5 between Mount Shasta and the state of Oregon border, another 55 miles (89 km) to the north, is **Yreka** (population 6,000). The government seat of Siskiyou County, it features a museum with restored buildings from its 19th-century mining past.

Just north of Yreka, State Highway 96 heads west, giving access to otherwise isolated stretches of the beautiful Klamath River country. It eventually joins Highway 299 at Willow Creek in Humboldt County.

The Volcanic Cascades: The Cascades run almost due north from California to Canada's British Columbia. In California, the range runs 40–50 miles (70–80 km) across, in Washington state more than 80 miles (130 km). Farther north,

glaciers dominate the range but the dominant snow-capped Cascade peaks are young, inactive volcanoes. There are few better places to study volcanology than **Lassen Volcanic National Park**.

The park is reached via Highway 36 east from Red Bluff, Highway 44 east from Redding, or from Highway 89 south from Highway 299 beyond **Burney Lassen Peak** (elevation 10,457 ft/3,187 meters).

Much of 108,000-acre (43,700-hectare) Lassen Park lies within a caldera, the giant crater left by the collapse of an ancient volcano. Out of this caldera, Lassen Peak later rose to dominate this expanse of wilderness, but there are small volcanoes in the park as well. There is also **Bumpass Hell**, a steaming valley of active geothermal pools and vents. And there are lakes, rivers, meadows, pine forests and fine trails for hiking and camping.

Between Redding and Burney, a distance of 53 miles (85 km), Highway 299 climbs into a gently undulating country of ranches and volcanic debris. The red

Hill Road winds through Lava Beds National Park.

rocks that litter the landscape and pastures to the south of the road were deposited by hot mud flows from the eruption of Mount Maidu, seven million years ago. This posthumously named volcano collapsed to form the caldera within Lassen Park.

East of Bella Vista, on the south banks of **Cow Creek**, are the ruins of **Afterthought Mine**, a resource of zinc and copper from the late 19th century until the end of World War II.

Just beyond the lumber and livestock marketing center of **Burney** (population 3,200) is the State Highway 89 intersection. South is Lassen Park; north is Mount Shasta.

About 6 miles (10 km) north is lovely 129-ft (39-meter) **Burney Falls**. Volcanic terrain is inhospitable to rivers, and this state park gives a clear indication why. Before it gets to the falls, Burney Creek disappears into a porous lava flow, but reappears just in time to drop over the spectacular moss-covered precipice.

East of Burney is **Fall River Mills**,

and from here to the Nevada border, Highway 299 runs across the basins and fault-block mountains of the Modoc Plateau covering 13,000 sq. miles (33,670 sq. km). For a large part of its route, the highway follows the deep canyon of the Pitt River, the plateau's main drainage.

The Modoc doesn't look like a plateau but more like a scrubby basin on which someone left block-like piney mountains that don't seem to belong. Vestiges of volcanism make up much of the **Modoc National Forest**, which covers 1.97 million acres (797,000 hectares). A pristine example of this volcanic past is **Glass Mountain,** a huge flow of obsidian lava on the forest's western edge.

The focus of any geologic tour of the Modoc Plateau is **Lava Beds National Monument**, a moonlike landscape of lava flows, columns and caves. In one of the **caves**, a Modoc chief known as "Captain Jack" and the warriors of his tribe held out against the US Army during the final days of the 1872–73

Shadowlands in ranch country.

Modoc Indian War – one of the last such conflicts in American history.

Pahoehoe (smooth) lava flows created the national monument's 300 lava "tubes" – cylindrical caves often only a few feet underground. Some are too small for humans to walk through; others are multi-leveled and exceed 75 ft (23 meters) in diameter. Some of these caves contain prehistoric Indian petroglyphs. There is a visitors' center at **Indian Wells**, but no lodging, supplies or gasoline are available. The closest community of any size is **Tulelake** (population 800), about 10 miles (16 km) north on the Oregon state border.

The 46,500-acre (18,800-hectare) national monument lies in Siskiyou County on the western edge of the Modoc Plateau. From Highway 299 east, travelers should turn north near the **Canby** ranger station and proceed on State 139 about 40 miles (72 km) via **Tionesta**.

Eagles and geese: In the region surrounding Lava Beds National Monument are three national wildlife refuges – **Tule Lake** (north), **Lower Klamath** (northwest) and **Clear Lake** (east). More than one million water-fowl populate these lakes in the fall; there are also significant numbers of bald eagles in January and February.

Another refuge, the 6,000-acre (2,400-hectare) **Modoc National Wildlife Refuge**, lies a few miles south of the county seat of **Alturas**, at the confluence of the North and South forks of the Pitt River. Located on the Pacific Flyway, it provides nesting for Canada geese, ruddy ducks, green-winged teal and other native and migratory fowl.

Elsewhere in Modoc National Forest, however, there is extensive hunting of these same waterfowl, as well as other game birds, deer and antelope. Trout fishing is popular in the occasional streams. More universal recreations are hiking and camping.

Between Canby and Alturas, a distance of 18 miles (29 km), Highway 299 crosses part of a higher, rocky central plateau known as the **Devil's Garden**, covered with pines, sage and juniper.

Alturas (population 3,000) is a farming center with a history dating to the mid-19th century. Its **Modoc County Museum** has a 500-year collection of firearms plus exhibits of regional Indian artifacts. Of greater interest, however, may be its marvelous Basque restaurant – the Brass Rail.

Here, at 4,400 ft (1,340 meters) altitude, away from the Cascade rainshadow, the terrain is dry and vegetation sparse. Annual precipitation is less than 12 inches (30 cm). Summer temperatures often exceed 100°F (38°C); in the winter, they frequently drop below 0°F (–18°C) and snow covers the ground. Cattle graze on a brown-and-purple landscape; alfalfa is the cash crop.

East of Alturas, Highway 299 rises into the **Warner Mountains**, which form the boundary between the Modoc Plateau and the even more arid high-desert country of the **Great Basin**. Pine forests, rivers and streams cover the Warner range. And while some of its peaks reach as high as 9,900 ft (3,000 meters), most of it is half that altitude. It is a gently rolling upland that's especially suited to hiking and camping. But outdoorsmen should remember that it's wise to bring water purification tablets: extensive cattle ranging makes these pills essential.

There is a small ski resort at **Cedar Pass**, elevation 6,305 ft (1,922 meters). Then the highway drops down into **Surprise Valley** and the hamlet of **Cedarville** (population 800). Cedarville has ailanthus trees, poplars and one pay telephone. No building is over two stories high. If it weren't for the automobiles, the Visa stickers on shop windows and a Bank of America branch, this town could still be slumbering in the 19th century.

Residents are loathe to leave, and the reasons are obvious. "In the winter," says one, "I can get in my snowmobile and go east of here for hundreds of miles and not see another person. We were in San Francisco not long ago, and a friend of mine said, 'You know, you're living a life that most people just dream about.' He's right: I don't have to go to Alaska to find unspoiled wilderness. I've got everything I want right here."

Right, Hot Springs Creek, near Drakesbad.

INSIGHT GUIDES
Travel Tips

FOR THOSE
WITH MORE THAN
A PASSING INTEREST
IN TIME...

Before you put your name down for a Patek Philippe watch *fig. 1*, there are a few basic things you might like to know, without knowing exactly whom to ask. In addressing such issues as accuracy, reliability and value for money, we would like to demonstrate why the watch we will make for you will be quite unlike any other watch currently produced.

"Punctuality", Louis XVIII was fond of saying, "is the politeness of kings."

We believe that in the matter of punctuality, we can rise to the occasion by making you a mechanical timepiece that will keep its rendezvous with the Gregorian calendar at the end of every century, omitting the leap-years in 2100, 2200 and 2300 and recording them in 2000 and 2400 *fig. 2*. Nevertheless, such a watch does need the occasional adjustment. Every 3333 years and 122 days you should remember to set it forward one day to the true time of the celestial clock. We suspect, however, that you are simply content to observe the politeness of kings. Be assured, therefore, that when you order your watch, we will be exploring for you the physical—if not the metaphysical—limits of precision.

Does everything have to depend on how much?

Consider, if you will, the motives of collectors who set record prices at auction to acquire a Patek Philippe. They may be paying for rarity, for looks or for micromechanical ingenuity. But we believe that behind each $500,000-plus

bid is the conviction that a Patek Philippe, even if 50 years old or older, can be expected to work perfectly for future generations.

In case your ambitions to own a Patek Philippe are somewhat discouraged by the scale of the sacrifice involved, may we hasten to point out that the watch we will make for you today will certainly be a technical improvement on the Pateks bought at auction? In keeping with our tradition of inventing new mechanical solutions for greater reliability and better time-keeping, we will bring to your watch innovations *fig. 3* inconceivable to our watchmakers who created the supreme wristwatches of 50 years ago *fig. 4*. At the same time, we will of course do our utmost to avoid placing undue strain on your financial resources.

Can it really be mine?

May we turn your thoughts to the day you take delivery of your watch? Sealed within its case is your watchmaker's tribute to the mysterious process of time. He has decorated each wheel with a chamfer carved into its hub and polished into a shining circle. Delicate ribbing flows over the plates and bridges of gold and rare alloys. Millimetric surfaces are bevelled and burnished to exactitudes measured in microns. Rubies are transformed into jewels that triumph over friction. And after many months—or even years—of work, your watchmaker stamps a small badge into the mainbridge of your watch. The Geneva Seal—the highest possible attestation of fine watchmaking *fig. 5*.

Looks that speak of inner grace *fig. 6.*

When you order your watch, you will no doubt like its outward appearance to reflect the harmony and elegance of the movement within. You may therefore find it helpful to know that we are uniquely able to cater for any special decorative needs you might like to express. For example, our engravers will delight in conjuring a subtle play of light and shadow on the gold case-back of one of our rare pocket-watches *fig. 7*. If you bring us your favourite picture, our enamellers will reproduce it in a brilliant miniature of hair-breadth detail *fig. 8*. The perfect execution of a double hob-nail pattern on the bezel of a wristwatch is the pride of our casemakers and the satisfaction of our designers, while our chainsmiths will weave for you a rich brocade in gold *figs. 9 & 10*. May we also recommend the artistry of our goldsmiths and the experience of our lapidaries in the selection and setting of the finest gemstones? *figs. 11 & 12.*

How to enjoy your watch before you own it.

As you will appreciate, the very nature of our watches imposes a limit on the number we can make available. (The four Calibre 89 time-pieces we are now making will take up to nine years to complete). We cannot therefore promise instant gratification, but while you look forward to the day on which you take delivery of your Patek Philippe *fig. 13*, you will have the pleasure of reflecting that time is a universal and everlasting commodity, freely available to be enjoyed by all.

Should you require information on any particular Patek Philippe watch, or even on watchmaking in general, we would be delighted to reply to your letter of enquiry. And if you send us

fig. 1: *The classic face of Patek Philippe.*

fig. 4: *Complicated wristwatches circa 1930 (left) and 1990. The golden age of watchmaking will always be with us.*

fig. 6: *Your pleasure in owning a Patek Philippe is the purpose of those who made it for you.*

fig. 9: *Harmony of design is executed in a work of simplicity and perfection in a lady's Calatrava wristwatch.*

fig. 2: *One of the 33 complications of the Calibre 89 astronomical clock-watch is a satellite wheel that completes one revolution every 400 years.*

fig. 5: *The Geneva Seal is awarded only to watches which achieve the standards of horological purity laid down in the laws of Geneva. These rules define the supreme quality of watchmaking.*

fig. 7: *Arabesques come to life on a gold case-back.*

fig. 10: *The chainsmith's hands impart strength and delicacy to a tracery of gold.*

fig. 11: *Circles in gold: symbols of perfection in the making.*

fig. 3: *Recognized as the most advanced mechanical regulating device to date, Patek Philippe's Gyromax balance wheel demonstrates the equivalence of simplicity and precision.*

fig. 8: *An artist working six hours a day takes about four months to complete a miniature in enamel on the case of a pocket-watch.*

fig. 12: *The test of a master lapidary is his ability to express the splendour of precious gemstones.*

PATEK PHILIPPE
GENEVE

fig. 13: *The discreet sign of those who value their time.*

INSIGHT GUIDES

COLORSET NUMBERS

Getting Acquainted

Unless otherwise stated, all telephone numbers are prefixed by 415. Numbers beginning with 800 are toll-free if dialed in the United States.

The Place

California, on the west coast of the United States, is bordered by Mexico to the south, Oregon to the north and Nevada and Arizona to the east. Covering an area of 163,707 sq. miles (423,999 sq. km) – 7,734 sq. miles (20,031 sq. km) of which is water – it ranks third in size and first in population of all the states. It is in the Western Time Zone.

It comprises the highest mountain range in the continental US, the Sierra Nevadas, with deserts to the south and northeast; temperate rain forest in the northwest and a vast Central Valley (once the bed of an inland sea) which is one of the country's biggest agricultural regions. Mount Whitney (14,494 ft/4,418 meters) is its highest point and Death Valley (282 ft/86 meters below sea level) its lowest. Muir Woods is among Northern California's best known national monuments and Yosemite among its best-known national parks. State parks are visited by 77 million people each year.

Climate

San Francisco's climate is typical of the Northern California coast. Daytime temperatures average in the mid-50s (10°–15°C) and drop as much as 10 degrees at night. Average temperatures are significantly higher in the South Bay and inland valleys. In fact, in the Sacramento and San Joaquin valleys summer temperatures often reach above 90°F (32°C). Summers tend to be warm and dry. Winters are generally rainy; temperatures rarely go below freezing along the coast.

The average daily highs in San Francisco are:

Month	°C	°F
January	12.8	55
February	14.4	58
March	16.7	62
April	17.8	64
May	19.4	67
June	21.1	70
July	22.2	72
August	22.2	72
September	23.3	74
October	21.7	71
November	17.8	64
December	13.9	57

The People

At the 1990 census, California's population was a shade under 30 million, of which about two-thirds was white, one quarter Hispanic, roughly 10 percent Asian, 8 percent black and 6 percent Native American. Of the state's 58 counties, Los Angeles with 8.3 million is the biggest, followed by Orange and San Diego counties, each with about 2.2 million. More than 92 percent of the state's population is urban.

The Economy

California's economy is the world's sixth largest, its agricultural crops and livestock bringing in around $17.5 billion each year. (Unofficially, marijuana with revenues of $2 billion annually, is said to be the largest crop). It is a leading state in fishery production and its mineral wealth includes oil, natural gas, iron ore, tungsten and boron. Aerospace, construction and electronics are its major manufacturing industries with Silicon Valley (south of San Francisco) regarded as the nation's center for eletronic, computer and software development.

Government

The state legislature comprises the Senate (40 members serving four-year terms) and the Assembly (80 members serving two-year terms) with powers, if necessary, to pass laws over the veto of the governor and the authority to conduct impeachment proceedings. The governor, in whom the California Constitution invests supreme authority, serves a four-year term from the capital, Sacramento.

Planning the Trip

What to Bring

Northern California shares with the rest of the state a generally moderate climate although coastal areas invariably suffer from morning fogs and both the coast and desert areas can get quite cold once the sun goes down. Although casual clothing is the general rule, San Francisco offers opportunities for dressing up and many of the better restaurants expect formal wear. Rain is always a possibility, even in summertime, so bring a raincoat.

Film of all kinds is widely available and often cheaper than elsewhere in the world, so allow your stocks to run low and buy it in California.

Maps

Maps are widely available at any bookstore and free city maps for San Francisco are available at the city's **Visitor Information Center** in Hallidie Plaza on Market Street. For long-term visitors, membership in the American Automobile Association is well worth while, bringing with it access to free maps for just about any US, Canadian or Mexican destination and also comprehensive tour books packed with information about accommodations and restaurants.

Entry Regulations

Most foreign travelers to the US must have a passport, visa and, depending on where you are coming from, a health record. In addition, you must make prior arrangements to leave the country. Those exempt from these rules are:
● Canadian citizens.
● British subjects from Bermuda or Canada entering from the western hemisphere.
● Certain government officials.

Any person who enters the US can visit Mexico or Canada for a period of less than 30 days and still be re-admitted to the US without a new visa. Visas can be obtained from any US embassy. If a visitor loses his or her visa while in this country, a new one may be obtained from the embassy of the visitor's home country. Extensions are granted by the **US Immigration and Naturalization Service**, 425 I Street, Washington, DC 20536, tel: (202) 514-2000.

Quarantine Regulations

At the Mexican, Nevada and Oregon borders, the State Department of Food and Agriculture inspects all produce, plant materials and wild animals to see if they are admissable under current quarantine regulations. If you want to avoid a lengthy inspection, don't bring any agricultural products into California.

Customs

Whether or not you have anything to declare, all people entering the country must go through US Customs. This can be a time-consuming process, but to speed things up, be prepared to open your luggage for inspection and keep the following restrictions in mind:

- There is no limit to the amount of money you can bring in with you. If the amount exceeds $10,000, however, you must fill out a Customs report.
- Anything you have for your own personal use may be brought in duty- and tax-free.
- Adults are allowed to bring in 1 quart (1 liter) of alcohol for personal use.
- You can bring in gifts valued at less than $400 duty- and tax-free. Anything over $400 is subject to duty charges and taxes.
- Dogs, cats and other animals may be brought into the country with certain restrictions. For details, contact the US consulate nearest you or alternatively write to the Department of Agriculture.

Should you have any queries about Customs, contact:
US Customs, 1301 Constitution Avenue NW, Washington, DC, tel: (202) 566-8195.

Health

In the event you need medical assistance, consult the local Yellow Pages for the physician or pharmacist nearest you. In large cities, there is usually a physician referral service number listed. If you need immediate attention, go directly to a hospital emergency room. Most emergency rooms are open 24 hours a day.

There is nothing cheap about being sick in the United States. It is essential to be armed with adequate medical insurance and to carry an identification card or policy number at all times. If expense is a concern, turn first to county hospitals, which offer good service and do not charge indigent patients a fee.

Currency

Current exchange rates are listed on the inside back page of the *Los Angeles Times'* Sunday Travel section each week and usually in the *San Francisco Examiner's* Sunday travel section.

Travelers checks are accepted in many places (when accompanied by identification) but, as with foreign currency, can be exchanged only at certain banks. Credit cards are widely accepted (again with ample identification). It is wise to acquire at least some dollars from one of the airport currency exchange booths on arrival.

Public Holidays

New Year's Day	January 1
Martin Luther King Jr's Birthday (Observed)	January 15
Presidents' Day	Third Monday in February
Easter Sunday	
Memorial Day	Last Monday in May
Independence Day	July 4
Labor Day	First Monday in September
Veteran's Day	November 11
Thanksgiving Day	Fourth Thursday in November
Christmas	December 25

Getting There

By Air

In addition to the international airports listed below, there are smaller, regional airports in several locations throughout the northern part of the state, including Fresno and San Jose. Shuttle flights are available at all of the larger air terminals.

San Francisco International: SFO is 14 miles (23 km) south of downtown San Francisco near the town of San Mateo. Transportation to and from the airport is provided by Airport Coaches 24 hours a day. SamTrans, San Mateo's bus system, makes several stops between downtown San Francisco and the airport and also has services to nearby towns. A free information service, giving details of the best way to travel to and from the airport, is available by calling (800) SFO-2008.

Oakland International: Oakland Airport is located on the east side of the Bay. It is often less crowded than SFO and parking is more convenient. Local bus service to and from Oakland is offered by AC Transit (number 57 line) between 5am and midnight daily. A shuttle van links the airport with the Bay Area Rapid Transit system (BART) as well as with SFO.

Sacramento Airport: Twelve miles (19 km) west of downtown on Interstate 5. Taxi costs around $25; van service about $10.

San Jose Municipal Airport: An international facility with 30 gates in operation and five terminals. Fourteen airlines operate out of San Jose: Alaska, American, Pacific Coast, Pacific East, Republic, TWA, United, West-Air, Western and Wings West. The San Jose Chamber of Commerce has an information booth at the airport, tel: (408) 287-9849.

Transportation linking the San Jose, the San Francisco and the Oakland airports is provided by Airport Connection, contacted at (415) 885-2666.

Airlines

Alaska Airlines	(800) 426-0333
America West	(800) 247-5692
American Airlines	(800) 433-7300
Continental Air	(800) 525-0280
Delta Airlines	(800) 221-1212
Northwest	(800) 225-2525
Sky West Airlines	(800) 453-9417

Southwest	(800) 453-9729
TWA	(800) 221-2000
United Airlines	(800) 241-6522
USAir	(800) 428-4322

By Rail

Amtrak's *California Zephyr* is the main rail line into Northern California, stopping at Sacramento, Colfax, Davis, Martinez and Richmond before reaching Oakland's 16th Street Station, where a free bus service to San Francisco is provided.

Southern Pacific Railroad also runs passenger trains between San Francisco and San Jose with several stops along the peninsula. Commonly called Cal-train, this rail service operates from the terminal which is located at Fourth and Townsend streets in San Francisco.

By Bus

The national bus line, Greyhound (find their toll-free number in your local phone book), as well as a number of smaller charter companies provide an impressive network of ground travel throughout California, offering daily service to major towns and cities. Routes and schedules are subject to change; it is a good idea to check all arrangements with local stations, in advance. San Francisco, Oakland, Los Angeles, San Diego and other large towns also have municipal bus systems. Be warned that bus stations are often located in undesirable parts of town, so it pays to remain alert.

By Car

Highways 1, 5, 15, 99, 101 and 395 are the principal north–south arteries in California. State Highway 1, also known as the Pacific Coast Highway, runs the full length of the state and is famous for its hairpin curves and spectacular views of the California coast. The principal east–west highways are Interstates 8, 10 and 40, all of which head directly out of the state.

People with Disabilities

The US Welcomes Handicapped Visitors is a 48-page booklet available from the Advancement of Travel for the Handicapped, 1012 14th Street, Number 803, Washington DC 20005. Or you can write to Consumer Information Center, Pueblo, CO 81109.

San Francisco has a **Recreation Center for the Handicapped** at 207 Skyline Boulevard, tel: (415) 665-4100. The facility includes an adapted gymnasium, sports/physical fitness area, therapeutic warm water swimming pool, dining facility, arts and local crafts.

Senior Citizens

If you are a senior citizen (over 65 for men, over 62 for women) you are entitled to many benefits, including reduced rates on public transportation and museums. Some restaurants also give a discount. Seniors who want to be students should write to Elderhostels, 80 Boylston Street, Suite 400, Boston, MA 02116, Massachusetts for information on places that provide both accommodation and classes. The Bay Area has a number of Elderhostel locations where rooms are reasonably priced.

Practical Tips

Security & Crime

Like big cities all over the world, Californian cities have dangerous neighborhoods. Common sense is your most effective weapon. Don't walk alone at night. Keep an eye on your belongings. Never leave your car unlocked. Never leave small children by themselves.

If you are driving, never pick up anyone you don't know, especially if you are alone. Always be wary of who is around you. If you have trouble on the road, stay in the car and lock the doors, turn on your hazard lights and

leave the hood up in order to increase your visibility and alert any passing police cars.

Hotels usually warn that they do not guarantee the safety of belongings left in the rooms. If you have any valuables, you may want to lock them in the hotel safe.

In the case of an emergency dial 911 from any telephone for the police, fire department or ambulance service.

Medical Services

Most hospitals in the Bay Area have 24-hour emergency rooms. No matter what your problem is, you usually end up waiting longer at these "emergency rooms" than you feel you should but the eventual care and treatment is thorough and professional. The biggest and busiest of the emergency rooms in San Francisco are at:
Children's, 3700 California, tel: 750-6031.
Mount Zion, 1600 Divisadero, tel: 885-7520.
Saint Francis, 900 Hyde, tel: 775-4321.
San Francisco General, 1001 Potrero, tel: 821-1111
University of California's Moffitt, 500 Parnassus, tel: 476-1037.

Outside San Francisco, the biggest and busiest emergency rooms can be found at:
Alta Bates, 1 Colby Plaza, Berkeley, tel: (5100 540-4444.
Highland General, 1411 East 31st, Oakland, tel: (510) 534-8055.
Marin General, 250 Bon Air Road, Greenbrae, tel: (415) 461-0100.
Mount Diablo, Bacon and East streets, Concord, tel: (510) 682-8200.
Stanford University Medical Center, Palo Alto, tel: (415) 497-2300.
Valley Medical, 751 South Bascom, San Jose, tel: (408) 279-5100.

If you need non-emergency medical care, look under "Physicians" in the Yellow Pages. In San Francisco, call the San Francisco **Medical Society Referral Service**, tel: 567-6234, or the **Dental Society Referral Service**, tel: 421-1435.

Pharmacies

Certain drugs can only be prescribed by a doctor. Most modern drugstores stock a variety of low-level drugs and have a pharmacist on duty. The stores listed below are open for long hours and have pharmacists on duty.

San Francisco
Mission Geneva Pharmacy, 5125 Mission Street, tel: 333-5266. Opens daily 11am–9pm.
Rexall Reliable Drug, 801 Irving, tel: 664-8800. Opens Monday–Saturday 8am–9pm.
Walgreen Drugs, 1524 Polk, tel: 673-4701. Opens Monday–Friday 9am–10pm, and Saturday and Sunday 9am–5pm.

Bay Area
Day and Night Pharmacy, 1776 Broadway, Oakland, tel: (510) 451-3965. Opens Monday–Friday 7am–7pm, Saturday 8am–7pm.
Long's Drug Store, San Bruno Bayhill Shopping Center, tel: (415) 873-9522. Opens Monday–Friday 9.30am–9pm, Saturday and Sunday 10am–7pm.
Marin Town & Country Pharmacy, Tiburon Boulevard and Blackfield, Tiburon, tel: (415) 388-6300. Opens Monday–Saturday 9am–9pm, and Sunday 10am–6pm.
Thrifty, 345 South B Street, San Mateo, tel: (415) 342-6264. Opens Monday–Friday 9am–9pm, and Saturday 10am–6pm.

Weights & Measures

The US uses the Imperial system of weights and measures. Metric is rarely used. Below is a conversion chart.

1 inch	=	2.54 centimeters
1 foot	=	30.48 centimeters
1 mile	=	1.609 kilometers
1 quart	=	1.136 liters
1 ounce	=	28.40 grams
1 pound	=	0.453 kilograms
1 yard	=	0.9144 meters

Business Hours

Standard business hours are from 9am to 5pm weekdays; some businesses operate weekend hours. Most department stores open at 10am and many stores, especially those in shopping malls, stay open until 9pm. San Francisco and some of the bigger towns have a number of 24-hour restaurants or an all-night convenience store. A few supermarkets and convenience stores are also open around the clock. Bank hours usually run from 9am–3pm, although some stay open later, especially on Friday. Although some branch offices keep Saturday morning hours, most banks are closed on weekends. However, most banks are equipped with 24-hour automated teller machines on the outside of their building, and if you have an account card you can use these machines for simple transactions at your convenience. Be careful at night.

Keep in mind that during the holidays, post offices, banks, government offices and many private businesses are closed.

Tipping

Like other parts of the country, service personnel in California rely on tips for a large part of their income. In most cases, 15–20 percent is the going rate for tipping waiters, taxi drivers, bartenders and barbers. In the larger cities, taxi drivers tend to expect around 20 percent.

The accepted rate for baggage handlers at airports and hotels is around 50¢ per bag. For overnight stays, it is not necessary to tip the chambermaid. For longer stays, the rule of thumb is to leave a minimum tip of one or two dollars per day. A doorman expects to be tipped for helping unload your car or for other services; 50¢ to $1 should cover it, depending on the nature of the service.

The final and the only tasteful rule in tipping is that the tip should be fair and commensurate with the service provided.

Media

Newspapers & Magazines
San Francisco has two major daily newspapers, the *San Francisco Chronicle* in the morning and the *San Francisco Examiner* in the afternoon. The two papers combine into one large edition on Sunday. Across the Bay is the *Oakland Tribune*. Other papers in Northern California include the *Sacramento Bee*, the *San Jose Mercury-News*, *Eureka Times-Standard*, *Ukiah Daily Journal* and the *Monterey Herald*. The *Bay Guardian*, an alternative weekly, carries comprehensive listings of local activities.

Television

Television and radio are invaluable sources of up-to-the-minute information about weather, road conditions and current events. It is now almost standard for decent hotels and motels to include televisions in the price of a room, although you sometimes have to pay extra for cable service. Television and radio listings are published in local newspapers. Sunday papers usually have a detailed weekly guide. Besides the national networks and cable TV options, most towns in California have their own local TV station. In the Bay Area, the major stations are:

Channel

2:	KTVU, Oakland (Independent)
3:	KCRA, Sacramento (NBC)
4:	KRON, San Francisco (NBC)
5:	KPIX, San Francisco (CBS)
6:	KVIE, Sacramento (PBS)
7:	KGO, San Francisco (ABC)
8:	KSBW, Salinas (NBC)
9:	KQED, San Francisco (PBS)
10:	KXTV, Sacramento (CBS)
11:	KNTV, San Jose (ABC)
13:	KOVR, Sacramento (ABC)

Radio

Most American radios (in cars, hotel rooms, and hand-held instruments) pick up two frequencies; AM and FM. FM has fewer commercials and a greater range of programs. The most popular stations in the Bay Area include:

AM

560:	KSFO, popular music, talk shows
610:	KFRC, big band
680:	KNBR, pop, sports (NBC)
740:	KCBS, news, talk (CBS)
810:	KGO, news, talk (ABC)
910:	KNEW, country-western
960:	KABL, easy listening
1220:	KDFC, classical
1260:	KOIT, light rock
1310:	KDIA, soul
1510:	KTIM, big band
1550:	KKHI, classical

FM

88.5: KQED, classical, talk, community affairs including excellent news programs from National Public Broadcasting

93.3: KLHT, light rock

94.1: KPFA, talk, classical, community affairs

94.9: KSAN, country-western

102.9: KBLX, modern jazz

104.5: KFOG, rock, from oldies to New Wave

106.1: KNEI, rock

Cities with all-Spanish-speaking AM stations include: Fremont (KDOS), Fresno (KGST, KSJV-FM, KXEX), Gilroy (KAZA), Hayward (KIQI), Hollister (KMPG), King City (KLFA-FM), Lodi (KCVR), Roseville (KPIP-FM), Salinas (KRAY-FM, KCTY), San Francisco (KBRG-FM), San Mateo (KPFY), Santa Clara (KNTA), Santa Rosa (KBBF-FM), Stockton (KSTN-FN) and Watsonville (KOMY).

Some radio stations run occasional programs in foreign languages lasting from 2–20 hours a week. Sunday nights have an international flair at KQED, San Francisco's public radio station (88.5 FM). At 9pm, it's the Chinese Community Hour; at 10pm, it's Israel Calling; at 11pm, it's the Filipino Community Hour; and at midnight it's the Arab Radio Hour.

Postal Service

Post offices open between 7 and 9am and usually close at 5pm, Monday–Friday. Many of them are also open for a few hours on Saturday morning. All post offices are closed on Sunday. If you don't know where you will be staying in any particular town, you can receive mail by having it addressed to General Delivery at the main post office in that town. You have to pick up General Delivery mail in person and show proper identification.

Telecoms
Telephone

Coin-operated telephones are ubiquitous – in hotels, restaurants, shopping centers, gas stations and booths on street corners. To operate, deposit 20 cents (note that you may use a quarter, but the phone will not give change) and dial a local number. To place a long distance call, dial 1–area code–local number. Be sure to have plenty of change with you to deposit on the operator's prompting.

The quickest way to get assistance for a telephone-communications problem is to dial "0" for the operator from any phone. If the operator cannot be of assistance, he or she will most likely be able to connect you with the proper party. Another indispensable number is for information assistance, which can provide telephone listings if you do not have a phone book handy. For local information dial 411; for long distance dial 1–area code–555-1212. For a toll-free number directory dial 1-800-555-1212. Make use of toll-free numbers when possible. For personal calls, take advantage of lower long-distance rates after 5pm on weekdays and during weekends.

Telegram & Telex

Western Union tel: 800-325-6000 and International Telephone and Telegraph (ITT) will take telegram and telex messages as well as orders to wire money over the phone. Check the local phone directory, or call Information for local offices. The area code for San Francisco is (**415**); for Sacramento it's (**916**); for the Napa Valley (**707**); and for Lake Tahoe (**916**).

Tourist Offices

Visitors' Bureaus: When in doubt, use the telephone. Local Visitor Bureaux are happy to give information over the phone and will also mail maps, lists of upcoming events or other literature in advance of your trip.

Berkeley Convention & Visitors Bureau, 1834 University Avenue, CA 94703, tel: (510) 5449-7040 or (800) 846-4823.

Calaveras County Lodging & Visitor Center, 1301 S. Main Street, PO Box 637, Angels Camp, CA 95222, tel: (209) 736-0049 or (800) 225-3764.

Carmel Valley Chamber of Commerce, 71 W. Carmel Valley Road, PO Box 288, CA 93924, tel: (408) 659-4000.

Eureka/Humboldt County Convention & Visitors Bureau, 1034 Second Street, Eureka, CA 95501, tel: (707) 443-5097 or (800) 346-3482 from outside California.

Kern County Board of Trade, 2101 Oak Street, PO Box 1312, Bakersfield, CA 93302, tel: (805) 861-2367.

Lake Tahoe Visitors Authority, PO Box 16299, South Lake Tahoe, CA 96151, tel: (916) 544-5050 or (800) AT-TAHOE.

Lone Pine Chamber of Commerce, 126 Main Street, PO Box 749, tel: (619) 876-4444.

Monterey Peninsula Convention & Visitors Bureau, 380 Alvarado Street, PO Box 1770, Monterey, CA 93942, tel: (408) 649-1770.

Sacramento Convention & Visitors Bureau, 1421 K Street, CA 95814, tel: (916) 264-7777.

San Francisco Convention & Visitors Bureau, 201 Third Street, CA 94103, tel: (415) 974-6900.

San Francisco Visitor Information Center, 900 Market Street, San Francisco, CA 94101, tel: (415) 391-2000.

San Luis Obispo Convention & Visitors Bureau, 1041 Chorro Street, CA 93401, tel: (805) 541-8000 or (800) 634-1414.

San Jose Convention & Visitors Bureau, 333 W. San Carlos Street, CA 95110, tel: (408) 296-9600 or (800) SAN-JOSE.

Chambers of Commerce

Berkeley Chamber of Commerce, 1835 University Avenue, Berkeley, CA 94703-1500, tel: (510) 549-7000.

Big Bear Lake Valley Chamber of Commerce, 630 Bartlett Road, Big Bear Lake, CA 92315. Mail: PO Box 2860, Big Bear Lake, CA 92315, tel: (714) 866-4608.

Fort Bragg-Mendocino Coast Chamber of Commerce, PO Box 1141, Fort Bragg, CA 95437, tel: (707) 961-6300.

Monterey Chamber of Commerce, 380 Alvarado Street, Monterey, CA 92940. Mail: PO Box 1770, Monterey, CA 93942, tel: (408) 649-1770.

Oakland Chamber of Commerce, 100 Broadway, Suite 200, Oakland, CA 94607, tel: (510) 839-9000.

Sacramento Chamber of Commerce, 917 7th Street, Sacramento, CA 95814, tel: (916) 552-6800.

San Francisco Chamber of Commerce, 465 California Street, San Francisco, CA 94104, tel: (415) 392-4511.

San Jose Chamber of Commerce, 180 South Market Street, San Jose, CA 95113, tel: (408) 998-7000.

San Simeon Chamber of Commerce, 9511 Hearst Drive, CA 93452, tel: (805) 927-3500 or (800) 342-5613.

Santa Cruz Area Chamber of Commerce, 1543 Pacific Avenue, Santa Cruz, CA 95060. Mail: PO Box 921, Santa Cruz, CA 95061, tel: (408) 423-1111.

Shasta Cascade Wonderland Association, 1250 Parkview Avenue, Redding, CA 96001, tel: (916) 243-2643 or (800) 326-6944.

Solvang Visitors Bureau, 1511A Mission Drive, PO Box 70, CA 93463, tel: (805) 688-6144 or (800) 468-6765.

Sonoma County Convention & Visitors Bureau, 5000 Roberts Lake Road, Rohnert Park, CA 95928, tel (707) 686 8100.

Walnut Creek Chamber of Commerce, 1501 N. Broadway, CA 94596, tel: (510) 934-2007.

Yosemite Park & Curry Co, 5410 E. Home, Fresno, tel: (209) 252-4848.

Consulates in San Francisco

Foreign visitors looking for local representatives can find consulates in San Francisco (listed below) and Los Angeles. Check in the Yellow Pages of local telephone books, available in libraries and post offices, or call Information (411 if calling within town; 1–area code of city–555-1212 if calling from out of town).

Argentina: Suite 1083, 870 Market Street, tel: 982-3050.
Australia: 1 Bush Street, tel: 362-6160.
Bolivia: 870 Market Street, tel: 495-5173.
Brazil: 300 Montgomery Street, tel: 981-8170.
Canada: 50 Fremont Street, tel: 495-7030.
Chile: 870 Market Street, tel: 982-7662.
Colombia: 595 Market Street, tel: 495-7195.
Costa Rica: 870 Market Street, tel: 392-8488.
Dominican Republic: 870 Market Street, tel: 982-5144.
Ecuador: 455 Market Street, tel: 957-5921.
El Salvador: 870 Market Street, tel: 781-7924.
France: 540 Bush Street, tel: 397-4330.

Germany: 1960 Jackson Street, tel: 775-1851.
Great Britain: 1 Sansome Street, tel: 981-3030.
Greece: 2441 Gough Street, tel: 775-2102.
Honduras: 870 Market Street, tel: 392-0076.
India: 540 Arguello Boulevard, tel: 668-0683.
Ireland: 655 Montgomery Street, tel: 392-4214.
Israel: 220 Bush Street, tel: 398-8885.
Italy: 2590 Webster Street, tel: 931-4924.
Japan: 50 Fremont Street, tel: 777-3533.
Luxembourg: 1 Sansome Street, tel: 788-0816.
Mexico: 870 Market Street, tel: 392-5554.
Netherlands: 1 Maritime Plaza, tel: 981-6454.
Norway: 20 Californis Street, tel: 986-0766.
People's Republic of China: 1450 Laguna Street, tel: 563-4885.
Peru: 870 Market Street, tel: 362-5185.
Philippines: 447 Sutter Street, tel: 433-6666.
Portugal: 3298 Washington, tel: 346-3400.
Spain: 2080 Jefferson Street, tel: 922-2995.
Sweden: 120 Montgomery Street, tel: 788-2631.
Switzerland: 456 Montgomery Street, tel: 788-2272.
Venezuela: 455 Market Street, tel: 512-8340.

Getting Around

Public Transportation

By Train

Bay Area Rapid Transit (**BART**) is one of the most efficient and modern rail lines in the US. Often compared to the super-subways of Europe and Russia, BART serves 34 stations in three counties, from San Francisco to Daly City and throughout the East Bay. Hours are Monday–Friday, 4am–midnight; Saturday, 6am–midnight; and Sunday 8am–midnight. Tel: (415) 788-BART.

Amtrak offers several major rail lines in California although most of them are in the south. The *Sunset Limited* from New Orleans stops at Indio, Ontario and Pomona before reaching Los Angeles. The *Desert Wind*, from Chicago to Los Angeles stops at Barstow, Victorville, San Bernardino and Fullerton. The *San Diegan* runs between Los Angeles and San Diego, with stops at Santa Ana, San Juan Capistrano, Oceanside and Delmar.

The state is tied together by the *Coast Starlight*, which travels north from Los Angeles all the way to Seattle, stopping at Glendale, Simi Valley, Oxnard, Santa Barbara, San Luis Obispo, San Jose, Oakland (from here there's a bus transfer to San Francisco before the route continues), Martinez, Davis, Sacramento, Marysville, Richmond, Chico, Reading and on across the Oregon border. Amtrak offers some local service also. Amtrak, tel: (800) 872-7245.

By Bus

The national bus line, Greyhound, runs throughout the state and every region has its local bus company. Check the Yellow Pages of the telephone book for details or call the local tourist office. San Francisco, Oakland, San Jose and other large towns have municipal bus systems. For information about traversing San Francisco, call MUNI at (415) 673-6864. In the East Bay call AC Transit at (510) 839-2882.

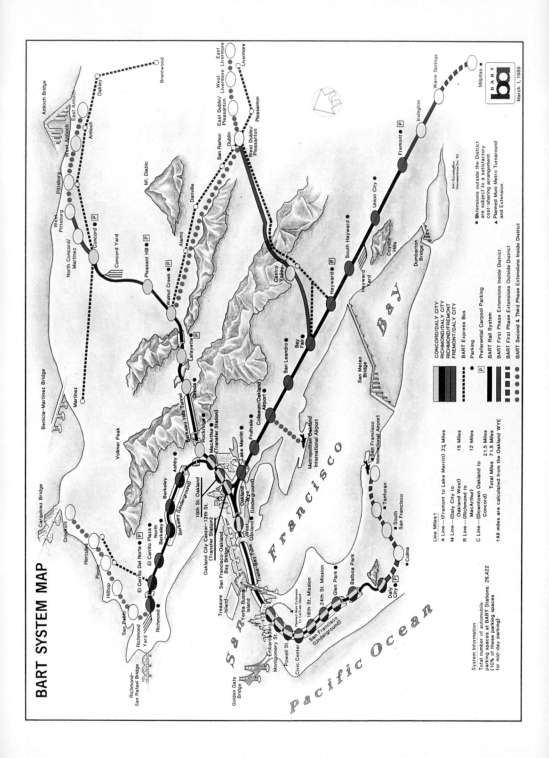

BART SYSTEM MAP

March 1, 1989

Line Miles †

A Line—(Fremont to Lake Merritt) 2¾ Miles
M Line—(Daly City to
   Oakland West) 15 Miles
R Line—(Richmond to
   MacArthur) 12 Miles
C Line—(Downtown Oakland to
   Concord) 21.5 Miles
            Total Miles 71.5 Miles
†All miles are calculated from the Oakland WYE

System Information
Total number of automobile
parking spaces at BART Stations: 26,422
(10% of these parking spaces
for mid-day parking)

CONCORD/DALY CITY
RICHMOND/DALY CITY
RICHMOND/FREMONT
FREMONT/DALY CITY

BART Express Bus

Parking

Preferential Carpool Parking

BART Rail System

BART First Phase Extensions Inside District

BART First Phase Extensions Outside District

BART Second & Third Phase Extensions Inside District

■ Extensions outside the District
are subject to a satisfactory
cost-sharing arrangement.

▲ Planned Muni Metro Turnaround
and Extension.

By Car

Driving is by far the most flexible and convenient means of travel in California, although newcomers are often confused by the many freeways. Roads are well-maintained throughout the state, and gasoline is relatively inexpensive. Before you set out, however, there are some important things to keep in mind.

In most cases you must be at least 21 years old to rent a car (often 25), and you must have a valid driver's license and at least one major credit card. Foreign travelers may need to produce an international driver's license or a license from their home country. Always take out collision and liability insurance, which may not always be included in the base price of the rental. Insurance usually costs somewhere between $40 and $150 per week, depending on the type of coverage. It is also a good idea to inquire about an unlimited mileage package, especially on a long trip. If not, you may be charged 5–25¢ per mile in addition to your rental fee, and considering the vast area of California, your vacation miles add up quickly.

National car rental companies are located at all airports and large towns. These major rental agencies provide the widest selection of cars and the most extensive services. They are also usually the most expensive. Smaller, regional rental agencies tend to cost less, but their selection and services are limited. Still, they may be perfectly suitable for local driving.

Alamo	(800) 327-9633
Avis	(800) 331-1212
Budget	(800) 527-0700
Dollar	(800) 800-4000
Enterprise	(800) 325-8007
Hertz	(800) 654-3131
National	(800) 227-7368
Thrifty	(800) 331-4200

ADVICE FOR MOTORISTS

Your greatest asset as a driver is a good road map. It is absolutely essential to make sense of the tangle of highways surrounding most large cities. Maps can be obtained directly from the state tourism office, or they can be purchased at most book stores, convenience stores, drug-stores and service stations. It is also advisable to listen to local radio stations for updates on traffic and road conditions, and to check with highway officials for the latest information on weather and road conditions if you are planning a lengthy drive.

Keep in mind that the national speed limit on all interstate highways is 65 miles per hour, and 55 miles per hour on most other local highways. California law requires that every passenger wears a seat belt, that small children and babies be secured in youth or infant seats and that drivers carry a valid license. There is also a state law that requires all motorcycle riders to wear helmets.

If you plan on driving any distance, it's a good idea to join the American Automobile Association (based at 811 Gatehouse Road, Falls Church, VA 22047, tel: (703) 222-6334) or a similar organization. In addition to emergency road service, AAA offers maps, guidebooks, insurance, bail bond protection and a $200 arrest certificate to its members.

Travelers should check local listings for the AAA office closest to them. There are reciprocal arrangements with many international AAA organizations throughout the world.

DESERT AND MOUNTAIN TRAVEL

A word of caution for desert travelers: the single most important precaution you can take is to tell someone your destination, route and expected time of arrival. Check tires carefully before long stretches of desert driving. Heat builds pressure, so have them at slightly below normal air pressure. The desert's arid climate makes carrying extra water – both for passengers and vehicles – essentials. Carry at least one gallon (4 liters) per person. Keep an eye on the gas gauge. It's a good idea to have more than need. Remember, if you should have car trouble or become lost, do not strike out on foot. A car, visible from the air and presumably on a road, is easier to spot than a person, and it affords shelter from the weather. Wait to be found rather than pursue your rescuers.

Mountain drivers are advised to be equally vigilant about weather conditions. Winter storms in the Sierras occasionally close major roads, and at times chains are required on tires.

Phone ahead for road conditions before you depart.

Hitchhiking

Hitchhiking is a hazardous and unpredictable way to travel. Because traffic is sparse in some regions, it can also be quite difficult. Hitchhiking is illegal on all main highways and interstates and on many secondary roads as well. However, if you do decide to hitch, it is best to do it from an exit ramp (if legal) or a highway rest stop rather than on the road itself. For long distances, it is advisable to make a sign clearly stating your destination. To find the safest situations, check ride services and college campus bulletin boards for posted ride shares.

Where to Stay

Hotels

California offers the complete spectrum of accommodations – from elegant European-style hotels to inexpensive motels rented by the week. In San Francisco, the most expensive hotels are situated in the Nob Hill area and the Financial District. These grand hotels are particularly well-suited to the international traveller, and many are attractive landmarks in their own right. The concierge at most finer hotels will arrange theater tickets, tours, telexes, limousines with bilingual drivers and airline reservations. Rates average anywhere from $125–$250 per night, double occupancy.

There are also a number of smaller hotels and hotel chains to chose from. These establishments usually offer all of the essential comforts without the high prices of the grand hotels.

The price guide listed below indicates approximate rates for a standard double room

$	=	under $100
$$	=	$100–150
$$$	=	over $150

Arena Cove

Coast Guard Inn, 695 Arena Cove, Point Arena, tel: (707) 882-2442 or (800) 524-9320. Turn-of-the-century inn and grounds overlook whale migration route. Big breakfasts. $$

Wharfmaster's Inn, 785 Port Road, tel: (707) 882-3171 or (800) 932-4031. This 120-year-old inn, once the wharfmaster's house, has private spas, fireplaces and restaurant. $$

Big Sur/Monterey

Post Ranch Inn, Big Sur, tel: (408) 667-2200 or (800) 527-2200. Spectacular setting between redwoods and the ocean. Pool and gourmet restaurant. $$$

Ventana Inn, Big Sur, tel: (408) 667-2331 or (800) 428-6500. Hot tub, tennis, all-around luxury. $$$

Bodega Bay

Inn at the Tides, 800 Coast Highway 1, tel: 707) 875-2751 or (800) 541-7788. Overlooking the harbor, near the site of Alfred Hitchcock's *The Birds*. $$$

Sonoma Coast Villa, 16702 Coast Highway 1, tel: (707) 876-9818. Mediterranean-style residence in terraced grounds with fireplaces, Jacuzzis, pool. $$

Calistoga

Calistoga Inn, 1250 Lincoln Avenue, tel: (707) 942-4101. Almost a century old. Two restaurants, garden patio and its own micro-brewery. $$

Calistoga Village Inn & Spa, 1880 Lincoln Avenue, tel: (707) 942-0991. Mud baths, mineral and steam baths, massage, indoor swimming pool. $

Indian Springs, 1712 Lincoln Avenue, tel: (707) 942-4913. Founded 1860. Mud baths, steam baths, massage, pool, tennis. $$

Roman Spa, 1300 Washington Street, tel: (707) 942-4441. In tropical gardens. Mud baths, mineral pool, massage. $

Carmel

Carmel River Inn, Highway 1 at Carmel River Bridge, tel: (408) 624-1575. Rooms and some cottages in peaceful grounds. One mile (1½ km) from town near shopping mall. Kitchens, fireplaces, pool. $

Coachman's Inn, San Carlos Street, tel: (408) 624-6421 or (800) 336-6421. Free breakfast in the morning and sherry in the evening. Near golf course and shops. $

Cypress Inn, 7th Avenue and Lincoln Street, tel: (408) 624-3871. Center of town. Rooms around a pleasant patio. $$

Crescent City

Best Western Northwoods Inn, 655 US 101, tel: (707) 464-9771 or (800) 528-1234. Opposite harbor. Restaurant, picnic area, spa. $

Curly Redwood Lodge, 701 Redwood Highway South, tel: (707) 464-2137. Built entirely from one tree in the heart of the park. Restaurants nearby. $

Pacific Motor Hotel, PO Box 595, on Highway 1, tel: (707) 464-4141. Sauna, whirlpool. Adjoins restaurant. $

Eureka

An Elegant Victorian Mansion, 1406 C Street, tel: (707) 444-3144 or (800) 386-1888. Splendidly opulent, friendly service and gourmet breakfasts. $$

Downtowner Motel, 424 8th Street, tel: (707) 443-5061. Central but quiet. Bar, free breakfast, pool. $

Eureka Inn, 518 7th Street, tel: (707) 442-6441 or (800) 862-4906. Impressive and luxurious mock Tudor behemoth, built 1922 but looks older. Pool, sauna, retaurant. $$$

Matador Motel, 129 4th Street, tel: (707) 443-9751. Pleasant, inexpensive two-story motel centrally located in old town. $

Red Lion Inn, 1929 4th Street, tel: (707) 445-0844 or (800) 547-8010. Large hotel at eastern edge of town. Pool, steakhouse restaurant. $$$

Ferndale

The Gingerbread Mansion, 400 Berding Street, tel: (707) 786-4000. Large elegant rooms with enormous bathtubs. Afternoon tea. Bicycles available for exploring town. $$$

Victorian Inn, 400 Ocean Avenue, Ferndale, tel: (707) 786-4949 or (800) 576-5949. Deluxe rooms. Restaurant with vast wine and beer selection. $$$

Fort Bragg

Anchor Lodge, Noyo Harbor, tel: (707) 964-4283. Private decks overlook water. Restaurant. $

Beachcomber Motel, 1111 N. Main Street, CA 95437, tel: (707) 964-2402 or (800) 4400-SURF. Ocean views, hot tub suites. Near Skunk train. $$

The Grey Whale Inn, 615 N. Main Street, tel: (707) 964-0640 or (800) 382-7244. Attractive B&B. $$$

Pudding Creek Inn, 700 N. Main Street, tel: (707) 964-9529 or (800) 227-9529. Victorian manor with fireplaces, enclosed garden, lavish breakfast. $$

Garberville

Benbow Inn, 445 Lake Benbow Drive, on US 101 south of town, tel: (707) 923-2124. Historic old place amidst the redwoods. Boating lake on the grounds. $$$

Humboldt House Inn, 701 Redwood Drive, CA 95542, tel: (707) 923-2771 or (800) 525-1234. Best Western Inn, garden pool, attractive views. $$

Shelter Cove Bed & Breakfast, 148 Dolphin, CA 95589, tel: (707) 986-7161. Ocean views, suites with Jacuzzis, beach and airport nearby. $$

Gualala

Seacliff, 39140 S. Highway 1, CA 95445, tel: (700) 884-1213 or (800) 400-5053. Luxurious clifftop suites, fireplaces, bubble baths. $$$

Surf Motel, tel: (700) 884-3571. Central; restaurant and, if you're lucky, whale watching from your window. $$

Whale Watch Inn by the Sea, 350100 Highway 1, tel: (700) 884-3667. Gardens with wildlife, unique rooms with different decor. $$$

Hopland

Thatcher Inn, Highway 1, Hopland, CA 95449, tel: (707) 744-1890. Restored 1894 hotel near wineries. Restaurant, bar. $$$

Wine Country Cottage, 14594 S. Highway 101, tel: (707) 744-1396. Operated by Milano Winery which offers discount on wines, tour of its 64 acres. $$

Inverness

Golden Hinde Inn & Marina, 12938 Sir Francis Drake Boulevard, tel: (415) 669-1389 or (800) 339-9398. Fireplaces, pool, fishing pier. $$

Patterson House, 12847 Sir Francis Drake Boulevard, tel: (415) 669-1383. A country inn overlooking Tomales Bay. $$$

Jenner

Salt Point Lodge, 23255 Highway 1, tel: (707) 847-3234. Sundeck overlooks garden and ocean cove. Hot tub, sauna. $$

Stillwater Cove Ranch, 22555 Coast Highway 1, tel: (707) 847-3227. Intimate retreat on 50 acres next to redwoods and sea cove. $$

Lake Tahoe

Holiday Inn Express, 3691 Highway 50, tel: (916) 544-5288. Pool, sauna, adjoins restaurant. $$

Mayfield House, Tahoe City, tel: (916) 583-1001. Wood panelling, hand-hewn beams, comfortable. $$

Rockwood Lodge, Homewood, tel: (916) 525-5273 or (800) LE TAHOE. Converted from a private home half a century ago and beautifully restored. $$$

South Tahoe Motor Lodge, 954 Park Avenue, South Lake Tahoe, tel: (916) 544-5266. Near the casino and the ski area. $

Little River

The Inn at Schoolhouse Creek, 7051 N. Highway 1, tel: (707) 937-5525. Ocean view rooms and cottages on 10 acres (4 hectare) of forest, meadow and gardens. $$

SS Seafoam Lodge, PO Box 68, Mendocino, tel: (707) 937-1827. Ocean view staterooms. $$

Los Alamos

Victorian Mansion & Union Hotel, 362 Bell Street, Box 616, CA 93440, tel: (805) 344-2474. Unique theme rooms in two elegant Victorian structures. $$

Mendocino

Blair House Inn, 45110 Little Lake Road, PO Box 1608, tel: (707) 937-1800. Victorian house familiar as Angel Lansbury's television "home." Near art center. $$$

Little River Inn, Little River, CA 95456, tel: (707) 937-5942. Two miles (3 km) south of Mendocino. Charming 225-acre (91-hectare) coastal estate built by a lumberman in 1853 and operated by his great granddaughter. $$$

McElroy's Inn, Main and Evergreen, tel: (707) 937-1734. Some rooms with ocean views. Trail to beach. $$

Mendocino Coast Accommodations, tel: (707) 937-1913.

Mendocino Hotel, 45080 Main Street, PO Box 587, CA 95460, tel: (707) 957-0511 or (800) 548-0513. Victorian furnishings, fireplace lounge, garden suites, restaurant. $$

Mendocino Village Cottages, 406 Little Lake Street, tel: (707) 937-0866. $$

Monterey

Californian Motel, 2042 N. Fremont Street, tel: (408) 372-5851. Kitchenettes, pool, whirlpool, free movies. $

Cannery Row Inn, 200 Foam Street, tel: (408) 649-8580 or (800) 876-8580. Central. Garden courtyard, whirlpool. $$

Holiday Inn Resort, 100 Aguajito Road, tel: (408) 373-6141 or (800) 234-5697. Restaurant, pool, sauna, tennis, putting green. $$

Quail Lodge Resort, 8205 Valley Greens Drive, tel: (408) 624-1581 or (800) 538-9516. Out of town in gardens with golf course, hot tubs, nature trails, tennis. $$$

Scottish Fairway Hotel, 2075 Freemont Street, tel: (408) 373-5551. Near fairgrounds. Pool, free breakfast and movies. $$

Steinbeck Lodge, 1300 Munbras Avenue, tel: (408) 373-3203 or (800) 528-1234, Opposite shopping center. Pool, free breakfast and movies. $$

Mount Shasta

Pine Needles Motel, 1340 S. Mount Shasta Boulevard, tel: (916) 926-4811. Heated pool, whirlpool. $

The Tree House Best Western, PO Box 236, CA 96067, tel: (916) 926-3101 or (800) 528-1234. Pool, hot tub, picnic area. $

Napa Valley/Wine Country

Auberge du Soleil, 186 Rutherford Hill Road, Rutherford, CA 94573, tel: (707) 963-1211 or (800) 348-5406. Cottages discreetly placed in 33-acre (13 hectare) terraced olive grove. $$$

Beazley House, 19010 First Street, Napa, CA 94559, tel: (707) 257-1649 or (800) 559-1649 A cosy, almost 100-year-old mansion in a lovely garden. $$

The Inn at Napa Valley, 1075 California Boulevard, Napa, tel: (707) 253-9540 or (800) 433-4600.

Rancho Caymus, 1140 Rutherford Cross Road, Rutherford, tel: (707) 963-1777 or (800) 845-1777. Haci-

enda-style inn with attractive furnishings, stained glass. $$

Silverado Country Club & Resort, 100 Atlas Peak Road, Napa, tel: (707) 257-0200 or (800) 532-0500. About 300 fully-equipped suites on 1,200 acres (486 hectares). Three restaurants, golf, tennis. $$$

White Sulphur Springs Spa, 3100 White Sulphur Springs Road, St Helena, tel: (707) 963-4361. Established in 1852 in the redwood forest. Herbal or mud wraps, sulphur pools, near a waterfall. $$

Wine Country Reservations. For information about upscale inns, tel: (707) 257-7757.

Nevada City

Best Western Gold Country Inn, 11972 Sutton Way, Grass Valley, tel: (916) 273-1393. Kitchenettes and swimming pool. $

Holiday Lodge, 1221 E. Main Street, Grass Valley, tel: (916) 273-4406. Some rooms in "gold rush" style. Pool, sauna. $

Nipomo

Kaleidoscope Inn, 130 East Dana Street, CA 93444, tel: (805) 929-5444. Century-old Victorian mansion with gazebo, popular with wedding couples. $$

Paso Robles

The Paso Robles Inn, 1003 Spring Street, tel: (805) 238-2660. Downtown with bungalows and lovely garden. $$

Petaluma

Best Western Petaluma Inn, 201 S. McDosell Boulevard, tel: (707) 763-0994 or (800) 297-3864. Pool, restaurant, near shops. $$

Cavanagh Inn, 10 Keller Street, tel: (707) 765-4657. Victorian B&B near river and historic downtown section. $$

Quality Inn, 5100 Montero Way, tel: (707) 664-1155 or (800) 221-2222. Restaurant, free continental breakfast. $$

Pismo Beach

Sandcastle Inn, 100 Stimson Avenue, tel: (805) 773-2422. On beach. Whirlpool. $$

Seaview Motel, 230 Five Cities Drive, tel: (805) 773-1841. Just a few yards off US 101. $

Point Arena

Wharf Master's Inn, 785 Port Road, CA 95468, tel: (707) 882-3171. "An aromatic peaceful hideaway." Hot tubs, fireplaces, 4-poster beds. $$$

Point Reyes

Holly Tree Inn, PO Box 642, CA 94956, tel: (415) 663-1554. Quiet place in the woods. $$$

Inns of Point Reyes. An agency that handles reservations for half a dozen small inns in the area, tel: (415) 485-2649.

Marsh Cottage, PO Box 1121, CA 94956, tel: (415) 669-7168. Fireplaces, kitchens, tranquility. $$

Point Reyes Hostel, tel: (415) 663-8811. Inexpensive overnight dormitory accommodations for all ages. $

Sacramento

Canterbury Inn, 1900 Canterbury Road, tel: (916) 927-3492 or (800) 932-3492. Pool, whirlpool, restaurant, free movies. $

Clarion Hotel, 700 16th Street, tel: (916) 444-8000 or (800) 443-0880. Downtown. pool, restaurant. $

Central Motel, 818 16th Street, tel: (916) 446-6006. Next to the Governor's Mansion. $

Delta King Hotel, 1000 Front Street, tel: (916) 444-5464 or (800) 825-5464. Sleep aboard a historic riverboat. $$

Harbor Inn & Suites, 1250 Halyard Drive, tel: (916) 371-2100 or (800) 371-2101. Close to Old Town, pool and spa, adjoining restaurant. $

Red Lion Hotel, 2001 Point West Way, tel: (916) 929-8855 or (800) 547-8010. Restaurant, coffee shop, two pools. $$$

Sacramento Hilton, 220 Harvard Street, tel: (916) 922-4700 or (800) 344-4321. Pool, hot tub, sauna, restaurant, free movies. $$

San Simeon

San Simeon Lodge, 9520 Castillo Drive, CA 93452, tel: (805) 927-4601. $

Silver Surf Motel, 9390 Castillo Drive, CA 93452, tel: (805) 927-4661. $

Whitewater Inn, San Simeon, CA 93452, tel: (805) 927-1066. Very small and pretty, hot tub. $$

San Luis Obispo

Budget Motel, 345 Marsh Street, CA 93401, tel: (805) 543-6443. Near downtown, pool, laundromat. $

Madonna Inn, 100 Madonna Road, CA 93405, tel: (805) 543-3000. Outrageous rooms in Western, Hawaian, Austrian styles etc. $$

San Francisco

Reservations may be made through San Francisco Reservations, 22 Second Street, San Francisco, 94102, tel: (415) 227-1500. All telephone numbers are prefixed by (415).

Fairmont Hotel, 950 Mason Street, tel: 772-5000 or (800) 527-4727. One of San Francisco's landmarks. Located atop elegant Nob Hill. $$$

Four Seasons-Clift, 495 Geary, tel: 775-4700. Just west of Union Square downtown. Old, conservative and elegant. $$$

Hilton San Francisco, 333 O'Farrell, tel: 771-1400. At Union Square downtown. Pool, excercise room, five restaurants. $$

Holiday Inn, tel: 626-6103 or (800) 465-4329. At five locations (all but Union Square). All hotels have swimming pools. $$

Hotel Bedford, 761 Post Street, tel: 673-6040 or (800) 652-1889. Reasonable and popular Café Bedford. $

Hotel Britton, 112 7th Street, tel: 621-7001 or (800) 444-5819. Cable cars nearby. Coffee shop, laundromat, cable TV. $

Huntington Hotel, 1075 California Street, tel: 474-5400 or (800) 277-4683. A favorite celebrity haunt, especially with opera stars. Great views and gourmet restaurants. $$$

Hyatt Regency, 5 Embarcadero Center, tel: 788-1234. Spectacular architecture: the triangular lobby atrium rises 170 ft (52 meters), lined with interior balconies, cascading plants, and glassed-in elevators. $$$

Mark Hopkins Intercontinental, Nob Hill, tel: 392-3434 or (800) 327-0200. Famous Top of the Mark restaurant and many rooms with panoramic views. $$$

Miyako, 1625 Post Street, tel: 922-3200. Attractive Japanese decor. $$

Monticello Inn, 127 Ellis Street, tel: 392-8800. Central. Restaurant, bar, cable TV. $$

Petit Auberge, 863 Bush Street, tel: 928-6000. Near Union Square. Gourmet breakfast buffet. $$

Queen Anne Hotel, 1590 Sutter Street, tel: 441-2828 or (800) 227-3970. A Victorian girls' school which became an exclusive men's club before its incarnation as a B&B. $$

Royal Pacific Motor Inn, 661 Broadway near Chinatown, tel: 781-6661. Sauna, excercise room. $

St Francis, 335 Powell, tel: 397-7000. A 1907 landmark on Union Square. Part of the Westin hotel chain. $$$

Shannon Court Hotel, 550 Geary Street, tel: 775-5000. Central. Restaurant, free movies, refrigerators. $

Sheraton Palace, 2 New Montgomery Street, tel: 392-8600. A historical landmark featuring the famous Garden Court Restaurant. $$$

Sir Francis Drake Hotel, 450 Powell Street, tel: 392-7755. Stylish old place near Union Square. Restaurant. $$

Stanyan Park Hotel, 750 Stanyan Street, tel: 751-1000. Listed on the National Register of Historic Places, near Golden Gate Park and the Haight-Ashbury district. $$

The Wharf Inn, 2501 Mason Street, tel: 673-7411 or (800) 548-9918. Right at Fisherman's Wharf. Free parking. $$

Vagabond Inn, 2550 Van Ness Avenue, tel: 776-7500 or (800) 522-1555. Cocktail lounge, pool, cable TV. $

Victorian Inn on the Park, 310 Lyon Street, tel: 931-1830. Classic century-old house with style. That's now a B&B. $$

Sonoma

Madrona Manor, 1001 Westside Road, Healdsburg, tel: (707) 433-4231 or (800) 258 4003. Victorian mansion lised in The National Register of Historic Places. Three suites and 18 rooms with lovely landscaped grounds. $$–$$$

Sonoma Mission Inn & Spa, PO Box 1447, CA 95476, tel: (707) 938-9000 or (800) 862-4945. An on-the-site replica of a century old hot springs resort whose fitness program includes hikes and picnics. Attractive grounds. Pools, restaurants, tennis. $$

Ukiah

Discovery Inn Motel, 1340 N. State Street, tel: (707) 462-8873. Pool, sauna, tennis. $

Lantern Inn Motel, 650 S. State Street, tel: (707) 462-6601. Non-smokers' rooms. Restaurant nearby. $

Vichy Springs, 2605 Vichy Springs Road, CA 95482, tel: (707) 462-9515. Hot springs bed and breakfast ranch with mineral baths, pool. $$$

Weaverville

Trinity Motel, 1112 Main Street, tel: (916) 623-2129. Pool, whirlpool, nice views. $

Victorian Inn, 1709 Main Street, tel: (916) 622-4432. $

Yosemite

Ahwahnee House, tel: (209) 372-1406. Stone and wood landmark that's hosted European royalty and Fresno farmers. Reservations essential. $$$

Curry Village, on the Valley floor, tel: (209) 372-1233. Several hundred units from "tent cabins" to large rooms. $

Yosemite Lodge, across from the trail to the falls, tel: (209) 372-1274. Pool, restaurants, bike rentals. $$

Motels

Motel quality varies considerably, but you can usually expect clean and simple accommodations. This is especially true for most of the national chains. A restaurant or coffee shop, swimming pool and sauna are often found on the premises. Room facilities generally include a telephone, television and radio, but don't hesitate to ask the manager if you may inspect a room before agreeing to take it.

Other than their accessibility by auto, the attraction of motels is their price. Motels in California range from $50 to $100 per night, double occupancy. They are less expensive in the outlying areas, usually from $35–$75.

NATIONAL HOTEL/MOTEL CHAINS

Best Western	(800) 528-1234
Embassy Suites	(800) 326-2779
Hilton	(800) 445-8667
Holiday Inn	(800) 465-4329
Hyatt	(800) 233-1234
Marriott	(800) 228-9290
Motel 6	(800) 437 7486
Quality Inn	(800) 228-5151
Ramada	(800) 272-6232
Sheraton	(800) 325-3535

Bed & Breakfast Inns

Country inns have become extremely popular in the last decade throughout the United States, especially in New England and Northern California. Most cluster in such scenic areas as the Wine Country, Gold Country, North Coast and Monterey Peninsula. Situated in such beautiful rural settings, they do a thriving business with city dwellers in search of a romantic weekend retreat.

Converted from mansions and farmhouses with five to 15 rooms, these inns offer the traveler a highly individual experience; no two inns are alike, and in most inns, no two rooms are alike. For those accustomed to the strict uniformity of large hotels and motel chains, the inns provide a warm, hospitable and quaint alternative.

Many inns have shared bathrooms and only a few have televisions or telephones in the rooms. Most include breakfasts with the room rental, hence the name bed-and-breakfast inns.

Prices vary greatly from inn to inn, but they tend to be pricey. Call or write in advance – the inns are particularly popular on weekends and in the summer. In fact, they are so popular that small intimate inns are even popping up in large urban cities to compete with the large hotels. Here is an incomplete but wide-ranging (north to south) sampling of the B&Bs in Northern California.

Big Bear Lake

The Knickerbocker Mansion, 869 S. Knickerbocker, PO Box 3661, CA 92315, tel: (714) 866-8221.

Calistoga

Scott Courtyard, 1443 2nd Street, CA 94515, tel: (707) 942-0948.

Cambria

The Blue Whale Inn, 6736 Moonstone Beach Drive, CA 93428, tel: (805) 927-4647.

Carmel

The Pine Inn, Ocean Avenue and Lincoln, CA 93921, tel: (408) 624-3851.

Inverness

The Ark, Inverness Way, CA 94956, tel: (415) 455-8424.

Mendocino

Sea Gull Inn, 44594 Albion Street, tel: (707) 937-5204.

Monterey

Old Monterey Inn, 500 Martin Street, CA 93940, tel: (408) 375-8284.

Napa/Wine Country

Bed & Breakfast Inns, 1400 South Coast Highway, Suite 104, Laguna Beach, CA 92651, tel: (714) 376-0305 or (800) 424-0053.

Bed & Breakfast International, 1181 Solano, Albany, CA 94706, tel: (510) 525-4569.

La Residence Country Inn, 4066 St Helena Highway North, CA 94558, tel: (707) 253-0337.

Oak Knoll Inn, East Oak Knoll Avenue, CA 94558, tel: (707) 255-2200.

Sacramento

Amber House, 1315 22nd Street, CA 95816, tel: (916) 444-8085 or (800) 755-6526.

San Luis Obispo

The Garden Street Inn, 1212 Garden Street, CA 93401, tel: (805) 545-9802.

San Francisco

Bed & Breakfast Inn, 4 Charlton Court, San Francisco, CA 94123, tel: (415) 921-9784.

The Inn at the Opera, 333 Fulton Street, CA 94102, tel: (415) 863-8400.

The Mansions Hotel, 2220 Sacramento Street, CA 94115, tel: (415) 929-9444.

Petite Auberge, 863 Bush Street, CA 94108, tel: (415) 928-6000.

Queen Anne Hotel, 1590 Sutter Street, CA 94109, tel: (415) 441-2828 or (800) 227-3970.

Victorian Inn on the Park, 310 Lyon Street, tel: (415) 931-1830.

Washington Square Inn, 1660 Stockton Street, CA 94133, tel: (415) 981-4220.

Specialty reservation services include:

American Family Inn, 2185A Union Street, San Francisco, CA 94123, tel: (415) 479-1913.

Visitors' Advisory Service, 1530 Fountain, Alameda, CA 94501, tel: (510) 521-9366.

Hostels

Some travelers may also want to take advantage of California's chain of hostels. Hostels are clean, comfortable and, on the opposite end of the spectrum from B&Bs, very inexpensive (as low as $10 per night). Although suitable for people of all ages, they are definitely for the young at heart. Beds are provided in dormitory-like rooms. Hostelers carry their own gear (silverware, sleeping bag, towel, etc.) and are expected, following breakfast each day, to take 15 minutes to help clean up and perform other communal tasks. Hostels are closed from 9.30am–4.30pm, so most guests fill their days with nearby outdoor activities. Reservations are highly recommended.

Northern California has a chain of more than 20 hostels up and down the Pacific coast, from Jedediah Smith Redwood State Park at the Oregon border down to John Little State Beach. All the hostels are along the shoreline; many are located inside old lighthouses. For lists of hostels in both Northern and Southern California, try these numbers:

Central California Council, PO Box 3645, Merced, CA 95344, tel: (209) 383-0686.

Golden Gate Council, 425 Divisadero Street, #307, San Francisco, CA 94117, tel: (415) 863-1444.

Los Angeles Council, 3601 South Gaffey Street, San Pedro, CA 90731-6969, tel: (310) 831-8109.

Campgrounds

Public and private campgrounds are located in or near most of the parks in California. Most public campgrounds offer primitive facilities – a place to park, rest rooms within walking distance and outdoor cooking. Private campgrounds are a little more expensive and offer additional facilities such as RV hook-ups, coin laundries, swimming pools and restaurants. Most campgrounds are busy from mid-June to early September and are allotted on a first-come-first-served basis. If possible, make reservations.

For more information on camping grounds call or write:

California State Parks System, PO Box 942896, Sacramento, CA 94296 tel: (916) 653-8380. Addresses of more than 200 state parks.

Reservations in campgrounds can be made by calling (800) 444-7275.

US Forest Service, Pacific Southwest Regional Office, 630 Sansome Street, San Francisco, CA 94111, tel: (415) 705-2874.

National Park Service, Western Regional Office. 600 Harrison Street, Suite 600, San Francisco, CA 94107-1372, tel: (415) 744-3876.

National Park Service, Department of the Interior, Washington, DC 20013-7127, tel: (202) 208-4747.

California Dept of Fish and Game (License & Revenue Branch) 3211 S. Street, Sacramento, CA 95815. For license information: tel: (916) 739-3380.

Eating Out

What to Eat

California is a food-lover's paradise and has the statistics to prove it. There are more restaurants in San Francisco, per capita, than any other US city, and many Californians dine out two or three times a week. The Golden State has also been the birthplace of several culinary trends over the years, including Szechuan, sushi, nouvelle, and of course, California cuisine.

Although the most prevalent ethnic food you'll encounter here is Mexican, there is an endless variety of other ethnic foods, as well as classic American cuisine. The following list is a mere sampling of some notable restaurants across Northern California.

Prices listed include meal for two without wine:

$	=	under $16
$$	=	$16-28
$$$	=	$28 and above.

Where to Eat

Boonville

Boonville Hotel, State Highway 128, tel: (707) 895-2210. California cooking, fresh, simple and sensitively prepared. All the food has been grown or raised right at the hotel. Dinner only. $$

Calistoga

Cafe Pacifico, 1237 Lincoln Avenue, tel: (707) 942-4400. Mexican cuisine, good seafood. $

Checkers, 1414 Lincoln Avenue, tel: (707) 942-9300. Pasta, pizza, sandwiches, frozen yogurt. $

Lord Derby Arms, 1923 Lake Street, tel: (707) 942-9155. Lively pub/restaurant. $

Carmel

Hog's Breath Inn, San Carlos Street, tel: (408) 625-6765. Clint Eastwood's pub with an outdoor patio. Dishes named after some of the star's movies. $$

Clam Box, Mission Street at 6th Avenue, tel: (408) 624-8597. Family place with accent on chicken and seafood. $$

Gualala

St Orres, 36611 State Highway 1, tel: (707) 884-3303. A beautiful restaurant emphasizing French cooking in a Russian-style hotel. Also serves Sunday brunch. $$

Eureka

Bon Boniere, 215 F Street, tel: (707) 444-8075. Attractive ice cream parlor. Soup, sandwiches, salads and sundaes. $

Cafe Marina, Woodley Island at the Eureka Marina, tel: (707) 443-2233. Serves very fresh scampi, scallops and sole. Also scrumptious sandwiches and Italian dishes. $

Lazlo's, 327 2nd Street, tel: (707) 443-9717. A century of excellent seafood. Try the sand dabs. The Windjammer Lounge is favored by the locals. $

Lost Coast Brewery & Cafe, 617 4th Street, tel: (707) 445-4480. Always lively, brew pub in century-old landmark. $

Samoa Cookhouse, off Highway 101 across the Samoa Bridge, tel: (707) 442-1659. Waitresses place huge loaves, large bowls of hot soup and cool salad onto long oil cloth-covered tables. Entrees, platters of potatoes and vegetables are all shared by a crowd as hungry as any since the first lumbermen ate here a century ago. $$

Fort Bragg

David's Deli & Restaurant, 450 S. Franklin, tel: (707) 964-1946. Big breakfasts, gourmet sandwiches, "fresh fruit creations." $

Rosie's, 223 N. Franklin, tel: (707) 051-1514. Mexican cuisine and celebrated margaritas. $

Home Style Cafe, 790 S. Main Street on Highway 1, tel: (707) 964-6106. Its name tells it all. Breakfast, lunch only. $

Egghead's Restaurant, 326 N. Main Street, tel: (707) 064-5005. Extensive breakfast menu, vegetarian dishes, espresso. $

Laurel Deli & Desserts, 136 E. Laurel Street, tel: (707) 964-7812. Sandwiches, soup, pies, coffee. Take-out only. Closes 4pm. $

High Sierra/Yosemite

Ahwahnee, Yosemite National Park, tel: (209) 372-1488. The *Grande Dame* of hotels nestled in breathtaking Yosemite Valley serves grand meals in its cathedral-like dining room. $$$

Erna's Elderberry House, 48688 Victoria Lane (Highway 41), Oakhurst, tel: (209) 683-6800. Elegant French country inn hidden in the forest. Stunning interior design mingles with superb classic European cuisine. Far from cheap but worth the trip. $$$

Inverness

The Gray Whale, tel: (415) 669-1244. Dining on outdoor deck. Pizzas, pastas, espresso. $$

Vladimir's Czech Restaurant, tel: (415) 669-1021. Weiner schnitzel, roast pork, roast duck are specialties. $$

Lake Tahoe

Le Petit Pier, 2572 North Lake Boulevard, Tahoe Vista, tel: (916) 546-4464. Classic French cuisine with many exotic touches. $$$.

Old Post Office Coffee Shop, 5245 North Lake Boulevard. Carnelian Bay, tel: (916) 546-3205. Crowded, friendly and inexpensive. $

Sunnyside Restaurant & Lodge, tel: (916) 583-7200. Popular with boaters who stop at this lakeside spot. $

Wolfdale's, Tahoe City, tel: (916) 583-5700. Great view over the lake as you savor California cuisine with a Japanese twist. $$$

Little River

Albion River Inn, 7051 State Highway 1, Little River, tel: (707) 937-0282. Hearty fare for moderate prices. $

Ledord House, 7051 State Highway 1, Little River, tel: (707) 937-0282. A rustic little house overlooking the sea. Locally-grown food is always cooked to order. Dinner only; closed Monday and Tuesday. $$

Mendocino

Bay View Cafe, 45040 Main Street, tel: (707) 937-4197. Second floor view of the bay. Wide menu. Music. $

Cafe Beaujolais, 961 Ukiah Street, Mendocino, tel: (707) 937-5614. A really cozy atmosphere. Beautifully-prepared dishes; fresh ingredients every night. $$

DeHaven Valley Farm Country Inn & Restaurant, 39247 N. Highway 1, Westport, tel: (707) 961-1660. Twenty-five minutes' drive north but worth it to see this charming Victorian place. Reservations essential. $$

MacCallum House, Albion Street, tel: (707) 937-5763. Elegant surroundings of an inn over 100 years old; late night cafe. $$

955 Ukiah Street, tel: (707) 937-1955. Wednesday–Sunday dinners only. Seafood a specialty. $$

Monterey/Big Sur

Casanova, Fifth Street near San Carlos, Carmel, tel: (408) 625-0501. Emphasis on seafood served with light sauces, but there are also veal, lamb and beef selections. Breakfast, lunch, dinner and Sunday brunch in a French cottage setting. $$ 5

Glen Oaks, State Highway 1, Big Sur, tel: (408) 667-2623. Rustic exterior belies elegant dining room filled with fresh flowers and fine music. Large, eclectic menu. $$$

Grenot's Victorian House, 649 Lighthouse Avenue, Pacific Grove, tel. (408) 646-1477. This Victorian home with just 12 tables requires reservations well in advance. Austrian food and more, including divine desserts. $$$

Nepenthe, State Highway 1, Big Sur, tel: (408) 667-2345. Spectacular view of waves crashing 800 ft (244 meters) below, homemade soups and enormous chef's salads. Tourists and locals mingle comfortably. $$

Ventana, State Highway 1, Big Sur, tel: (408) 667-2331. A luxurious and charming resort set back in the woods. Save room for the accomplished desserts. $$$

The Whaling Station Inn, 763 Wave Street, Monterey, tel: (408) 373-3778. Seafood predominates – grilled or sauteed. Dinners only. $$

Napa

Downtown Joe's, 902 Main Street, tel: (707) 258-2337. Century old restaurant and brewery beside the river; garden patio. $$

Kelley's, 1339 Pearl Street, tel: (707) 224-2418. A cafe complete with entertaining gadgets. $$

Pasta Prego, 2206 Jefferson Street, tel: (707) 224-9011. Fresh seafood, pasta, outdoor dining. $$

Sushi Bar Mari-Ya, 1015 Coombe Street, Napa, tel: (707) 257-6604. The expected and the unfamiliar. $$

Traditions, 1202 Main Street, Napa, tel: (707) 226-2044. Napa's first coffee house: 41 coffees, 25 teas and outdoor seating. $

Olema

Olema Farm House, Highway 1, tel: (415) 663-1264. Outdoor dining. Seafood, oysters, steak, pasta. $$

Point Reyes

Barnaby's by the Bay, one mile (1½ km) north of Inverness, tel: (415) 669-1114. Great view from deck. Barbecued oysters, local seafood, vegetarian dishes. $$

Roadhouse Oyster Bar, Highway 1, tel: (415) 663-1277. Pasta, pizza, seafood. $$

Station House Cafe, 11285 State Highway 1, tel: (415) 663-1515. Try the spinach salad with duck, blueberries and walnuts. $$

Taqueria La Quinta, Third Street and Highway 1, tel: (415) 663-8868. Mexican food. Espresso bar. $

San Francisco

Balboa Cafe, 3199 Fillmore, tel: 922-4595. This city's finest California cooking: warm salads, perfect pasta, handsome hamburgers and fresh fish. $$$

Caffe Sport, 574 Green Street, tel: 981-1251. Chaotic and crowded at all hours. Campy decor and superb shellfish. $$

Castagnola's, 286 Jefferson Street, tel: 776-5015. Italian cuisine near Fisherman's Wharf. $$

Chic's Place, Pier 39 at Fisherman's Wharf, tel: 421-2442. Interesting view over the water. $$

Donatello, Post and Mason, tel: 441-7182. Luxurious and expensive. Excellent pasta, fine carpaccio, good service; the perfect place for a business meeting. $$$

Gaylord, Ghirardelli Square, tel: 771-8822. Elegant Indian cuisine. Lovely view of the Bay, especially at lunchtime. $$$

Golden Turtle, 2211 Van Ness Avenue, tel: 441-4419. Lunch and dinner, Vietnamese cuisine, interesting decor. $$

Green's, Fort Mason, Building A, tel: 771-6222. Gourmet vegetarian restaurant managed by the Zen Center. Only takes reservations two weeks in advance, and they're hard to come by. $$$

La Rondalla, 901 Valencia Street, tel: 647-7474. Inexpensive Mexican food served until 3.30am. $

Little Joe's, 523 Broadway, tel: 433-4343. Large portions, hurly-burly atmosphere and mouth-watering pasta. $$

Mai's, 316 Clement, tel: 221-3046. Great Vietnamese, from the Saigon-style shrimp-and-pork-noodle soup to the Hanoi-style anise-and-lemon-flavor soup. $$

Mama's, 1701 Stockton Street, tel: 362-6421. Just plain good food. It's jammed on weekends, so try it during the week. Another branch on the north side of Washington Square. $

The Mandarin, 900 N. Point Street, tel: 673-8812. Atop renovated old building at far end of Ghiradelli Square. Delicious Chinese food. $$

Masa's, 684 Bush Street, tel: 989-7154. One of the finest French restaurants in town. Smoking is not permitted; coats and ties are required for men. It can be very expensive. $$$

Osome, 1923 Fillmore, tel: 346-2311. Excellent sushi bar plus usual range of cooked Japanese food. Closed Tuesday and for lunch on weekends. $$

Prego, 2000 Union, tel: 563-3305. The perfect place for pizza pie, baked in a wood-burning brick oven. $$

Yank Sing, 427 Battery, near Clay, tel: 781-1111. Classic *dim sum*, food unique to Hong Kong and San Francisco. A very San Francisco experience. $$

Zuni, 1658 Market Street, tel: 552-2522. Simply cooked California cuisine made from fresh local ingredients. $$

East Bay

Bay Wolf, 3853 Piedmont, Oakland, tel: (510) 655-6004. A lovely little restaurant that serves fine Mediterranean food. Sundeck. $$

Chez Panisse, 1517 Shattuck Avenue, Berkeley, tel: (510) 548-5525. One of the most famous restaurants in the country. $$$

Hunan, 396 Eleventh Street, Oakland, tel: (510) 444-1155. One of the few restaurants in Oakland's Chinatown serving excellent spicy food. Menus are impressive and amazingly inexpensive. Ask for the day's specials. $

Le Marguis, 3524-B Mount Diablo Road, Lafayette, tel: (510) 284-442. The finest French food in Contra Costa county. Dinner only; closed Sunday and Monday. $$$

Santa Fe Bar & Grill, 310 University Avenue, Berkeley, tel: (510) 841-4740. Restored train station and blues piano provide great atmosphere for California cuisine. $

Siam Cuisine, 1181 University Avenue, Berkeley, tel: (510) 548-3278. Exceptional Thai cuisine; spicy and irresistible. $

Peninsula/San Jose

Chantilly, 520 Ramona Street, Palo Alto, tel: (415) 321-4080. Wonderful small European restaurant; closed Sunday and for lunch on Saturday. $$

El Charro, 2169 Winchester Avenue, Campbell, tel: (408) 378-1277. Mexican fare – excellent margaritas and *chiles colorados* – plus some Argentinian steak specialties. $

Emile's, 545 S. Second Street, San Jose, tel: (408) 289-1960. French contemporary and Swiss cuisine. Open for dinner only; closed Monday. $$

Fung Lum, 1815 Bascom Avenue, Campbell, tel: (408) 377-6955. A sumptuous and elegant environment for sampling delectable Cantonese cuisine. $

Henry's Hi-Life, 301 W. Saint John Street, San Jose, tel: (408) 295-5414. Good barbecued food at reasonable prices. Dinner only. $$

La Foret, 21747 Bertram Road, San Jose, tel: (408) 997-3458. On the site of the first adobe hotel in California (built in 1848), this charming old house is graced with tuxedo-clad waiters, traditional continental entrees, fresh mussels and clams and tempting desserts. Dinner and Sunday brunch; closed Monday. $$$

La Hacienda Inn, 18440 Los Gatos Saratoga Road, Los Gatos, tel: (408) 354-6669. Get a full Italian dinner here at moderate prices. $

Original Joe's, 301 S. First Street, San Jose, tel: (408) 292-7030. Home of the famous "Joe's Special" – a tasty sandwich of spinach, ground beef, mushrooms, onions and scrambled eggs. $

St Michael's Alley, 800 Emerson Street, Palo Alto, tel: (415) 329-1727. The chalkboard menu at this pub/cafe changes daily. Excellent baked goods. Local folk musicians. $

Sacramento

Americo's, 2000 Capital, tel: (916) 442-8119. Perfect pasta and beautifully executed sauces. $$

Compadres Bar & Grill, Town & Country Village, 2713 El Paseo, tel: (916) 483-2336. First-rate Mexican food, excellent margaritas. $$

California Pizza Kitchen, Arden Market Square, 1735 Arden Way, tel: (916) 586-0932. A score or more of different wood-fired pizzas. $$

Il Fornaio, 400 Capitol Mall, tel: (916) 446-4100. First-rate Italian food, traditional breads. $$$

Fat City Bar & Cafe, 1001 Front Street, tel: (916) 446-6768. Century-old bar with art nouveau decor. $

Garbeau's Dinner Theatre, Highway 50 at Hazel Avenue, Rancho Cordova, tel: (916) 985-636. A short drive east for eating with entertainment. $$$

The Mandarin, 1827 Broadway, tel: (916) 443-5052. Good Szechuan and Hunan Chinese food. Spicy. $

Max's Opera Cafe, 1735 Arden Way,

tel: (916) 927-6297. Upscale New York style deli and restaurant. Singing waiters. $$

River City Brewing Company, 545 Downtown Plaza, tel: (916) 447-2739. Attractive setting for European, American cuisine with good ale. $

Wakano Ura, 2217 10th Street, tel: (916) 448 6231. An upstairs place in the Japanese district that can be a little noisy with Japanese revelers, although the fun becomes infectious. $

Stinson Beach

Parkside Cafe, tel: (415) 868-1272. Breakfast and lunch weekdays; Thursday–Monday nights feature "traditional Italian cooking." $$

Ukiah

The Pasta Shop, 108 N. School, tel: (707) 482-9541. Downtown, open late. $

El Sombrero, Mill and Main Street, tel: (707) 483-1818. Mexican cuisine, outside dining, music on Saturday. $

Wine Country

Auberge du Soleil, 180 Rutherford Hill Road, Rutherford, tel: (707) 963-1211. Creative French cuisine and a view of the vineyards. $$$

Calistoga Inn, 1250 Lincoln Avenue, Calistoga, tel: (707) 942-4101. Casual, friendly service, large portions and excellent food. $$

The Diner, 6476 Washington Street, Yountville, tel: (707) 944-2626. Good old American breakfasts, lunches and dinners. The malts are made with real ice cream. Inexpensive. Closed Monday. $

John Ash & Co, 4330 Barnes Road, Santa Rosa, tel: (707) 527-7687. California cuisine with both French and Chinese accents. $

Showley's, 1327 Railroad Avenue, Saint Helena, tel: (707) 963-3970. California cuisine with French and Italian influences. Everything is made from scratch and looks as good as it tastes. $$

Attractions

Museums

As anywhere else, Northern California has scores of museums exhibiting everything from Egyptian antiquities to surfboards. Here is a sampling of some of the more interesting ones:

Auburn

Gold Country Museum, 1273 High Street, CA 95603, tel: (916) 889 6500. Open Tuesday–Sunday 10am–4pm.

Bakersfield

California Living Museum, 14000 Old Alfred Harrell Highway, Bakersfield, tel: (805) 872-CALM. Native plants, indigenous animals, aviary, reptile house and childrens' park. Tuesday-Saturday 10am to sunset.

Calistoga

Sharpsteen Museum, 13211 Washington Street, CA 94515, tel: (707) 942-5911. What Napa Valley looked like in the old days.

Columbia

Miwok Heritage Museum, 11175 Damin Road, CA 95310, tel: (209) 533-8660. Cedar bark lodge, acorn bins etc. Open daily.

Crescent City

Battery Point Lighthouse Museum, Box 396, CA 95531, tel: (707) 464-3089. This 1856 lighthouse, lying 200 yards offshore, is open April–September.

Ferndale

Ferndale Museum, Shaw & 3rd streets, CA 95536, tel: (707) 786-4466. History of the preserved Victorian village. Wednesday–Sunday, year around.

Mendocino

Kelley House Museum, 45007 Albion Street, CA 95460, tel: (707) 937-

5791. Home (1861) of one of the town's founders. Open daily June–September, weekdays in winter.

Santa Cruz

Surfing Museum, Lighthouse Point, West Cliff Drive, CA 95062, tel: (408) 429-3429. Photos, boards, paraphernalia trace a century of surfing. Open Tuesday–Monday.

Santa Rosa

Robert Ripley Memorial Museum, 492 Sonoma Avenue, CA 95401, tel: (707) 524-5233. The man who originated *Believe It or Not!* Open April–October, Wednesday–Sunday.

San Andreas

Calaveras County Museum, 30 N. Main Street, CA 95249, tel: (209) 754-6579. Indians, Gold Rush and other 19th century memories.

San Jose

Rosicrucian Egyptian Museum, 1342 Naglee Avenue, CA 95191, tel: (408) 947-3636. Egyptian antiquities. Open daily.

Sonoma

Depot Park Museum, 270 First Street W, CA 95476, tel: (707) 938-1762. Depicts Bear Flag Revolt. Open Wednesday–Sunday.

St Helena

Silverado Museum, 1490 Library Lane, CA 94574, tel: (707) 963-3757. Thousands of items about the writer Robert Louis Stevenson. Open Tuesday–Sunday.

Sacramento

California State Railroad Museum, 125 I Street, CA 95814, tel: (916) BEE-LINE. Restored locomotives and other exhibits.

Crocker Art Museum, 216 O Street, tel: (916) 264-5423. The West's oldest art museum, built 1870. Open Wednesday–Sunday.

Folsom Prison Museum, near Folsom Lake Dam, CA 95821-0222, tel: (916) 372-6060 or (800) 821-6443. Visual record of this infamous jail's past.

San Francisco

Asian Art Museum, Golden Gate Park, tel: 668-8921. Nearly 10,000 bronzes, sculptures, paintings and porcelain from China, Japan, India, Korea, Tibet. Open Wednesday–Sunday.

Cable Car Museum, Mason and Washington streets, tel: 474-1887. Complete model collection of San Francisco cable cars. Daily all year.

Chinese Culture Center, on 3rd floor of the Holiday Inn at 750 Kearny Street, tel: 986-1822. Chinese arts and culture displays; frequent exhibit changes. Open Tuesday–Saturday 10am–4pm. Admission: free.

The Exploratorium and **Palace of Fine Arts**, near the Marina on Lyon Street, one wing houses one of the best science museums in the world. Visitors are encouraged to touch everything, including over 500 ever-changing exhibits. Open Tuesday–Sunday.

Fire Department Pioneer Memorial Museum, tel: 861-8000. Horse-drawn fire wagons, leather buckets, photos. Open Thursday–Monday.

M.H. de Young Memorial Museum, Golden Gate Park next to the Asian Art Museum, tel: 863-3600. This is the city's most diversified art museum with 21 galleries of everything. Closed Monday and Tuesday.

Mexican Museum, in Building D of the Fort Mason Center near the Marina (Buchanan and Marina streets), tel: 441-0404. Bilingual museum also organizes walking tours of Mission District murals. Wednesday–Sunday.

Museum of Russian Culture, 2450 Sutter Street, tel: 921-4082. Immigration to America is documented from various artifacts, books and 120 archival objects. Open Wednesday and Saturday.

National Maritime Museum, at the end of Polk Street at Beach Street, tel: 556-8177. The history of the port of San Francisco is represented with photos, art and displays. Daily in summer.

North Beach Museum, 1433 Stockton Street, tel: 391-6210. Historic photographs and artifacts of the Italian-American community.

San Francisco Museum of Modern Art, 151 Third Street, tel: 357-4000. The largest collection of modern art on the West Coast. Open Tuesday–Sunday 11am–6pm, Thursday 11am–9pm.

Submarine USS Pampanito. Tel: 929-0202. This 312-ft (95-meter) ship played a very important active role in World War II. Open daily in summer, Thursday–Sunday in winter.

Treasure Island Museum, tel: 395-5067. The 1939 Golden Gate International Exposition, the China Clipper flying boats and the history of Sea Services in the Pacific. On Treasure Island, halfway across the Bay Bridge. Daily to 3.30pm.

Stockton

Haggin Museum, 1201 N. Pershing, CA 95203, tel: (209) 462-4116. The history of the San Joaquin Valley. Tuesday–Sunday.

Tahoe City

Gatekeeper's Log Cabin Museum. Tel: (916) 583-1762. Tahoe's early days. Open May–October.

Taft

West Kern Oil Museum, Highway 33 at Wood Street, CA 93268. tel: (805) 765-6664. Early life in the oil fields. Open Tuesday–Sunday.

Yreka

Siskiyou County Museum, 910 Main Street, CA 96097, tel: (916) 842-3836. Exhibits from prehistoric fur trapping also mining, lumbering, railroad history. Open daily June–September, closed Sunday.

Tourist Attractions

Al Bussell Ranch, 26500 Stockdale Highway, Bakersfield, tel: (805) 589-2677. A working ranch where visitors can pick vegetables, pet farm animals and picnic. Open daily 7am–7pm, year around.

Alcatraz. In a two-hour excursion local ferries take you to The Rock and back, with the ferry leaving every 30 minutes between 9am and 2:45pm from Fisherman's Wharf, San Francisco's Pier 41. For a small fee, you can see where the Birdman of Alcatraz, Al Capone and Machine Gun Kelly lived out their sentences. Park rangers lead a walking tour covering much of the island and most of the prison. Wear comfortable shoes, and dress for winter because it gets quite cold in the middle of the Bay. Reservations are advised, tel: (415) 546-BOAT.

Balloon Rides. California Dreamin' launches three hot-air balloons daily for flights that overlook the Temecula wine country or the Del Mar coastal valley, tel: (800) 748-5959.

Skysurfer, tel: (800) 660-6809 also covers Del Mar; Dream Flights, tel: (619) 321-5154 overlooks Palm Desert; Gold Prospecting Expeditions is in Jarrestown near Fresno, tel: (209) 984-4653; and for a bird's-eye view of Napa Valley wineries call Napa Valley Balloons Inc., tel: (707) 944-0228 or (800) 253-2224 in California. Check local phone books for other listings.

Blue Diamond Growers, 4800 Sisk Road, Modesto, tel: (209) 545-3222. Free movie, almond tastings and a gift shop. Monday–Friday 9am–5pm, Saturday 10am–4pm.

Calico Ghost Town. East of Barlow and north of Interstate 15, tel: (619) 254-2122. This town produced $86 million worth of silver about a century ago, but its saloons and homes were deserted for years until the city of San Bernardino restored it as a regional park in 1966. It now survives on tourists who ride the (tiny) Calico and Odessa Railway, inspect a deserted mine and attend a performance at the town playhouse.
Information about the area is available from the **California Desert Information Center** at Barstow, tel: (619) 256-8617.

California Caverns, Box 78, Vallecito, tel: (209) 736-2708. Walking tours for all and spelunking trips for the adventurous. Daily May–December, weekends in winter.

California Hot Springs, tel: (805) 548-6582. Natural hot springs, swimming pool, massages; nature trail, adjoining RV park.

Delta Cruises. Rent a houseboat to explore the Delta country traversing leisurely some of the 1,000 miles (1,609 km) of waterways around Sacramento. Seven Crown Resorts, tel: (702) 293-7770 or (800) 752-9669, has 300 houseboats available which are pretty simple and safe to operate as they don't exceed 12 miles (19 km) per hour. Offseason (September–mid-June) rates for a houseboat sleeping 10 people begin at around $450 for three days, $750 per week.

Discovery Center, 1944 N. Winery, Fresno, tel: (209) 251-5531. Wildlife dioramas, hands-on science exhibits, picnic area. Tuesday–Sunday 11am–5pm.

Drive-Thru Tree Park, PO Box 10, Leggett, tel: (707) 925-6363. Among the 200 acres (81 hectares) of redwoods here off US 101 is the Chandelier Drive-Thru tree.

Duncan Water Gardens, 6901 E. Makenzy, Fresno, tel: (209) 252-1657. Acres of landscaped gardens with waterfall, babbling brooks, fish and locally created art. Weekends 9am–4pm.

Eureka Old Town, 123 F Street. Renovated Victorian buildings, waterfront restaurants, trolley cars, horse-drawn carriage rides.

Gold Prospecting Expeditions, 18170 Main Street, Jamestown, tel: (209) 984-4653. Trips arranged, panning equipment supplied.

Great Petaluma Mill, Petaluma, tel: (707) 762-1149. Riverfront landmark buildings around an 1864 warehouse. Shops, restaurants

Golden Gate Park. Formerly a parched expanse of sand dunes, this is a 1,000 acre (405 hectare) lush oasis in the city of San Francisco between Lincoln Way and Fulton. The park offers baseball and polo fields, hiking, horseback riding, rollerskating and blading, archery, a kids' playground, a lake for model boats, several man-made lakes for real rented canoes and rowboats, an arboretum and carefully tended gardens.

Don't miss the Japanese Tea Garden, the 1912 Herschel Spillman Carousel or the park's several museums.

Grass Valley. 10791 E. Empire Street, tel: (916) 273-8522. Site of the 784-acre (317-hectares) Empire Mine where hard-rock gold mining began in the US. Now a state park with a museum, exhibits, hiking trails and picnic areas.

Great American Melodrama, 1827 Pacific Coast Highway, Oceano, CA 93445, tel: (805) 489-2499. Turn of the century style productions. Open Wednesday–Sunday.

Hangtown's Gold Bug Park, 549 Main Street, Placerville, tel: (916) 642-5232. A 60-acre (24-hectares) site once dotted with more than 200 gold mines. Self-guided tours. Daily 10am–4pm in summer, weekends in winter.

Heavenly Tram, PO Box 2180 Stateline, NV, tel: (916) 544-6263. Ride 2,000 ft (610 meters) above Lake Tahoe (call in advance for dinner reservations). Open daily 10am–10pm spring and summer months, 9am–4pm in winter months.

Kern Valley Onyx Store, Highway 178,

east of Lake Isabella. A treasure trove of Western memorabilia, this 1851 shop is the oldest continuously operating store in the state.

Japanese-style Baths, Kabuki Hot Springs at the Japan Center in San Francisco, tel: (415) 922-6000. has sauna, steam room and massages. Massages also available at the Berkeley Massage & Self-Healing Center, 1962 University Avenue, tel: (415) 843-4422.

Living Memorial Sculpture Garden, 17211 Player Court, Weed, tel: (916) 938-2308. Thousands of trees planted over 136 acres (55 hectares) of forest in memory of victims of Korean and Vietnam wars.

Lake Shasta Caverns, PO Box 801, O'Brien, tel: (916) 238-2341. Stalagmite and stalactites 20 ft (6 meters) high with glittering crystals. Open daily except Thanksgiving and Christmas. Tours from 9am, 10am in winter.

Lake Tahoe Cruises, PO Box 14292, South Lake Tahoe, tel: (800) 23-TAHOE. Cruise year-around in glass-bottom sternwheeler *Tahoe Queen*.

Mammoth Lakes, tel: (800) 367-6572, A four-season recreational area with America's longest skiing season. Also fishing, sailing, swimming, horseback riding, tennis, mountain biking.

Mendocino Coast Botanical Gardens, 18220 N. Highway 1, Fort Bragg, tel: (707) 964-4352. Open March–October 9am–5pm, winter 9am–4pm.

Miller's California Ranch Horse & Buggy Display, 9425 Yosemite Boulevard, Modesto, tel: (209) 522-1781. An old store surrounded by hundreds of old vans, trucks, cars, hearses etc., some almost a century old. Call to book guided tour.

Moaning Cavern, PO Box 78, Vallecito, tel: (209) 736-2708. An enormous limestone cavern with 165-ft (50-meter) stairway to main chamber or an (optional) 180 ft (55 meter) descent by hanging rope.

Monterey Bay Aquarium, 886 Cannery Row, Monterey, tel: (408) 648-4888. Thousands of fish and some sharks roam kelp-strewn habitats recreating those of the adjoining bay. Open daily 10am–6pm.

Mount Tamalpais, six miles (10 km) west of Mill Valley, tel: (415) 388-2070. Spectacular views of the entire Bay Area can be enjoyed after driving up a winding road to the summits'

6,000-acre (2,428 hectares) state park. In spring and summer, plays and musical programs are presented in the amphitheater.

Mount Whitney, which towers an awesome 14,500 ft (4,420 meters) above sea level in the Sequoia National Park, is about 200 miles (322 km) north of LA via Palmdale on State Highway 14 and US 395. It can be seen from the highway, but the most beautiful, unobstructed views are from along Whitney Portal Road, which is westwards from Lone Pine.

Beginning at **Victorville**, US 395 offers numerous landmarks and diversions along its route: **Death Valley** to the east; **Edwards Air Force Base** (landing site for the space shuttle); the once-fertile **Owens Valley** from which LA's water supply was stolen in 1913; the desolate camp at **Manzanar** where Japanese-Americans were held in World War II; and the Indian museum at **Independence**. Further north the road leads to relaxing **Keough Hot Springs**, the resorts of the **Mammoth Lakes** skiing area and eventually **Lake Tahoe**.

Muir Woods, take State Highway 1 to Stinson Beach; from Muir Beach, follow the signs. The woods are 17 miles (27 km) northwest of San Francisco, tel: (415) 388-2595 for information. This 550-acre (223-hectare) redwood forest, a national monument, offers 6 miles (10 km) of trails. The main trail is an easy stroll and has trailside markers and exhibits. Seven unpaved trails offer greater challenges. The *Sequoia Sempervirens*, the tallest trees in the world, are in abundance here. Some coast redwoods are 200 ft (61 meters) tall with diameters in excess of 10 ft (3 meters). No picnicking, camping or pets in the park, but there are campsites nearby. Open daily 8am to sunset. Admission free.

Nuts & Candy packers, 1220 Madera Avenue (Highway 145), Kerman, CA 93630, tel: (800) 232-4SUN. Tour Scott Empire Food where candy, nuts and raisins are processed.

Old Faithful Geyser, 1299 Tubbs Lane, Calistoga, tel: (707) 942-6463. Erupts to 60 ft (18 meters) high about every 40 minutes, year in, year out. Open daily 9am–6pm, winter 9am–5pm.

Old Sacramento, downtown by the river, tel: (916) 443-8653 for events listings. More than 100 restored buildings from the Gold Rush era. Cobblestone streets, wooden sidewalks, horse drawn carriages, steam trains, paddlewheelers on the river.

Oroville Chinese Temple, 1500 Broderick Street, Oroville, tel: (916) 538-2496. An authentic Chinese temple built during the 1850s Gold Rush era. Open Tuesday, Wednesday, Thursday afternoons.

Pioneer Village, 1880 Art Gonzales Parkway, Selma, tel: (209) 896-3315. A village of historic buildings with farm implements and gadgets.

Pollardville Showboat & Ghost Town, 10480 N. Highway 99, Stockton, tel: (209) 931-0274. Theater performances with or without dinner; shops and train rides in adjacent ghost town. Open for performances Friday, Saturday evenings, some Sunday matinees.

Riata Ranch, PO Box 363, Exeter, tel: (209) 594-2288. Trick riding, roping techniques demonstrated by cowboys and cowgirls. Call to arrange visit.

Roaring Camp Mining Company, PO Box 278, Pine Grove, tel: (209) 296-4100. Four-hour guided tours of the Mokelumne Canyon with panning for gold, river swimming, rock collecting, etc. Wednesday evening tours include steak dinners beside the river. Open May–September. Call for reservations.

Rowdy Creek Fish Hatchery, 255 N. Fred Haight Drive, Crescent City, tel: (707) 487-3443. A public, non-profit fish hatchery. Open Monday–Friday, 9am–4.30pm. Admission free.

Santa Cruz Beach Boardwalk, 400 Beach Street, Santa Cruz, tel: (408) 426-7433. California's first and finest seashore amusement area (established in 1868) offers 24 rides, games, arcades, gift shops, entertainment and a mile-long beach. A magnificent casino, built here in 1907, has been renovated to house two restaurants. The carousel was built in 1911. The Giant Dipper is one of the world's best roller coaster rides. Winter hours 11am–6pm, weekends only; summer hours (beginning May 28) daily 11am–10pm. Admission free.

Seventeen-Mile Drive. This scenic drive from Pacific Grove to Carmel is a must for all coastal visitors. Points of interest along the way include Seal Rock, Cypress Point and four of the most beautiful golf courses in the country. It's also a great bicycle trip. Toll for cars is about $15.

Samoa Cookhouse, Humboldt Bay, Eureka, tel: (707) 442-1659. The last surviving lumber camp cookhouse in the west. Photos, paintings, historical artifacts. Open Monday–Friday 6am–3pm and evenings, Sunday all day.

Shasta Dam, Visitor Information, Redding, tel: (916) 275-1554. Spillway is three times higher than Niagara Falls. Vista House has photo displays and films.

Sonoma County Farm Trails, Write to PO Box 6032, Santa Rosa, CA 95406 for a free map showing trails to 100 farms in the region.

State Capitol, bounded by 10th, 12th, L and N streets, Sacramento, tel: (916) 324-0333. Built between 1861 and 1874 and recently restored, this seat of the state government is known for its fine proportions and lofty dome, which rises 237 ft (72 meters) above the street. The main building contains murals, historical exhibits and statues; the surrounding park boasts shrubs, trees and plants from all parts of the world. Free guided tours daily 9am–4pm; tickets are limited. East Annex is open daily 7am–9pm.

Undersea World, 304 Highway 101 South, Crescent City, tel: (707) 464-3522. Thousands of fish in their natural habitat. Feed the sealions. Open daily all year.

Vikingsholm, Emerald Bay, tel: (916) 541-3030. Daily tours in summer of this 38-room Scandinavian castle on an inlet of Lake Tahoe.

Wild Water Adventures, 11413, E. Shaw, Clovis, tel: (209) 297-6500. Family water amusement park with 17 rides, extensive picnic areas. Open daily in summer, some days in May and September.

Winchester Mystery House, Winchester Boulevard between Interstate 280 and Stevens Creek Boulevard, San Jose, tel: (408) 247-2101. This mansion belonged to eccentric rifle heiress Sarah Winchester, who had it designed to confuse evil spirits. With 160 rooms, 10,000 windows and more than 200 doors, as well as scores of fireplaces, stairways and secret passages. Tours about every 30 to 40 minutes daily between 9am and 4pm.

Farm Visits

If you want to avoid the "I Left My Heart In San Francisco" coffee mugs and other commercial souvenirs, and

return home with authentic made-in-California gifts, take a trip to the farm country. Apple wine, blackberry jam, dried fruits and herbs, fresh honey, jojoba oil – there are hundreds of products that you can buy direct from the producer, saving yourself money while visiting a real, working farm.

Sonoma County Farm Trails is an association of about 160 agricultural producers, from Buchan (famous for its oyster fresh from Tomales Bay) to the Petaluma Desert (potted cactus) with all kinds of imaginable fruits, vegetables, livestock and wines in between.

Free maps and brochures are available at all participating farms, and from the Santa Rosa Chamber of Commerce, tel: (707) 545-1414, or by writing to Farm Trails, PO Box 6674, Santa Rosa, CA 95406.

Santa Clara and Santa Cruz counties have teamed together in a similar program called **Country Crossroads**. Some 50 farms encourage visitors to pick their peaches, tour their egg ranches, and sample their apples. Maps and information are available at participating farms, from the Santa Cruz Visitors' Bureau, tel: (408) 423-6927, or by writing to Country Crossroads, 1368 North Fourth Street, San Jose, CA 95112.

Historical Monuments

Bodie State Historic Park, 13 miles (21 km) east of Highway 395, 7 miles (11 km) south of Bridgeport, tel: (619) 647-6445. A ghost mining town in a 500-acre (202-hectare) park. Museum open daily 10am–5.30pm during the summer. There is a vehicle entry fee. All roads are closed in winter.

Hearst Historical Monument, San Simeon, tel: (805) 927-2000 or (800) 444-7275. The phenomenal "castle" in which the publishing tycoon entertained the rich and famous from the 1920s onward. Art, antiques and memorable architecture abound. It's about midway between Los Angeles and San Francisco in the hills above San Simeon off coastal State Highway 1, and is well worth the four-hour drive. Because tycoon William Randolph Hearst (who died in 1951) pillaged all of Europe for his treasures, the castle has so much to see that it supports four different tours which overlap each day as well as an evening tour which features the highlights from the daily walks. Open winter 8am–3.20pm. Closed New Year's and Christmas days; summer 8am–5pm. Reservations are advised, tel: (800) 444-4445 or (805) 927 2000.

Lava Beds National Monument, PO Box 867, Tulelake, tel: (916) 667-2282. Ice caves, cinder cones, lava flows and other volcanic phenomena. Open year-around.

Sutter's Fort State Historic Park, 2701 I Street, Sacramento, tel: (916) 445-4422. Restored to look as it did in 1846 when gold was discovered here, many historic exhibits. Tours 10am–4.15pm daily.

National Parks

California has 20 National Parks which come in a variety of guises – National Monuments, National Recreation Areas and National Seashores – which are visited each year by 30 million people. All have helpful rangers as well as great scenic vistas. During the week or in the off-season they are obviously less crowded. For information about accommodations, campgrounds, fishing, horseback riding, backpacking and ranger programs, contact the Golden Gate National Recreation Area, Fort Mason, San Francisco, CA 94123, tel: (415) 556-0650.

Golden Gate National Recreation Area, tel: (415) 556-0560. 44,000 acres (17,800 hectares) around San Francisco Bay. This vast urban park includes ocean beaches, sand dunes, redwood forests, lagoons, marshes, and many historical buildings.

Kruse Rhododendron State Reserve, Plantation Road, north of Jenner on Highway 1, tel: (707) 847-3221. Hundreds of acres in bloom. Open April–May.

Lassen Volcanic National Park, tel: (916) 595-4444. 106,000 acres (43,000 hectares) between Redding and Susanville. Home of Lassen Peak, the largest plug dome volcano in the world; hot springs; boiling mud pots; ski areas; and several lakes.

Lava Beds National Monument, tel: (916) 667-2282. 46,000 acres (18,600 hectares) 30 miles (48 km) south of Tulelake. Self-guiding trails take you to 20 fantastic caves (including relatively recent lava and ice caves), as well as fumeroles and other volcanic wonders.

Pinnacles National Monument, tel: (408) 389-4578. More than 30 sq. miles (78 sq. km) between King City and Hollister. Hiking and climbing are favorite activities on the eroded slopes of an ancient volcano with spire-like rock formations which rise to 1,000 ft (305 meters) above the surrounding toothills.

Point Reyes National Seashore, tel: (415) 663-1092. 65,000 acres (26,300 hectares), one-hour's drive northwest of San Francisco. Colorful cliffs, sandy beaches, languid lagoons, bird rookeries, sea lions barking on the offshore rocks. Point Reyes is the perfect place for an afternoon romance.

Redwood National Park, tel: (707) 464-6101 for park information; (800) 444-PARK for campsite reservations. More than 106,000 acres (42,897 hectares) of pristine redwood country centered on Crescent City. The park has two distinct zones; the redwood forest (with its associated vegetation, streams and rivers) and the coastal zone (with abrupt cliffs, beaches, lagoons and tidepools).

The **Redwood Information Center**, one mile (1½ km) south of Orick on Highway 101, offers a slide show and tours, tel: (707) 488-3461.

Sequoia and Kings Canyon National Parks, tel: (209) 335-2314. 1,324 sq. miles (3,429 sq. km) east of Fresno. Here are grand old groves of giant redwood trees as well as Mount Whitney (tel: 209-565-3373), the highest point in the contiguous 48 states. Kings Canyon is a Sierra Nevada wilderness of granite domes, jeweled lakes, tumbling waterfalls and deep canyons.

Whiskeytown-Shasta-Trinity National Recreation Area, tel: (916) 246-1225. 10,000 acres (40,500 hectares) north of Redding. Named after the three major lakes inside the park, this sportsman's paradise offers camping, hiking, fishing, boating, swimming, picnicking, hunting and water skiing.

Yosemite National Park, tel: (209) 373-4171. 1,189 sq. miles (3,080 sq. km) in central California on the western slope of the Sierra Nevada. Take a scenic walk through the Valley with its leaping waterfalls, rounded domes and towering cliffs, or backpack into the alpine forests. Yosemite, one of the most popular parks in the country, has a splendid hotel, a cafeteria, lodges, cabins and camping facilities.

Riverboat Rides

Lunch, dinner and dance cruises on the *Petaluma Queen*. Information from 226 Weller Street, Petaluma, tel: (707) 778-4398. Sternwheeler cruises on the Napa River by the Napa Riverboat Co., tel: (707) 226-2628. *Delta King* riverboat, the 1920's Sacramento sternwheeler, is now a hotel, restaurant, theater and saloon, tel: (916) 444-KING.

Vineyards & Wineries

In the San Francisco Bay region there are a number of wineries open to visitors in the Livermore, tel: (510) 447-1606 and Gilroy, tel: (408) 779-2145 areas, as well as many in the famed wine country of Napa, tel: (707) 963-1048 and Sonoma tel: (707) 996-1090 valleys.

Napa Valley Wine Train is at 1275 McKinstry Street, Napa, tel: (707) 253-2111 or (800) 427-4124 for reservations. Board a meticulously restored vintage train and ride in elegance through the wine country. There's a gourmet chef on board to prepare decadently luxurious meals – lunch, brunch or dinner.

Visiting the Missions

From the beginning of California's history, the 21 missions set up along El Camino Real by Father Junipero Serra and his successors have played an important role. Today they are major tourist attractions. The most important Northern California missions include:

Mission Dolores in San Francisco, tel: (415) 621-8203. Open daily 9am–4pm.

San Luis Rey, tel: (619) 757-3651. Open Monday–Saturday 10am–4pm, Sunday noon–4.30pm.

San Jose, tel: (510) 657-1797. Monday–Saturday 10am–4.30pm, Sunday noon–4.30pm.

Santa Clara de Asis, tel: (408) 554-4023. Open daily 7am–7pm.

Santa Cruz, tel: (408) 426-5686. Open daily 9am–5pm.

There are other missions in Carmel, Solano, San Rafael, San Luis Obispo, San Juan de Bautista, and San Luis Rey. Originally developed by Spanish clerics with virtual slave labor from local Indians, most of the missions were abandoned and fell into decay after the passing of the Secularization Act in

1834 and were forgotten for almost half a century. Helen Hunt Jackson's 1880 book about mistreatment of the Indians, *A Century of Dishonor*, revived interest in the buildings whose architecture thereafter became a much-emulated style.

Whale-watching

The California gray whale, up to 50 ft (15 meters) long and weighing as much as 40 tons, migrates down the coast – a 10,000 mile (16,093 km) trip – between December and February and back north again in March and April. The best observation points are from Mendocino Headlands State Park; Russian Gulch State park; Jughandle State Reserve north of Caspar; Todd's point (Ocean View Drive, south of Noyo harbor); and MacKerricher State Park, south of Cleone. Two companies in Monterey – Monterey Sports Fishing, tel: (408) 372-2203 and Randy's Fishing Trips, tel: (408) 372-7440 – organize excursions between January and March.

Nightlife

Evening diversions in California are as varied and all-encompassing as the state itself. Visitors can entertain themselves with events that range from world-class operas and musicals, theater and symphonies to first-rate comedy and funky live blues, jazz and rock'n'roll.

To track down nightlife, you would do best to refer to the local newspaper as a guide to what's on in town. In San Francisco, the Sunday *Chronicle & Examiner*'s "Pink Pages" will apprise you of most of the Bay Area's activities. In the tourist areas of most towns you will usually find a free alternative local paper. In San Francisco, for example, the newspaper the *Bay Guardian* has comprehensive listings

Theater

Theater performances fall roughly into two groups: touring companies that bring to San Francisco big Broadway productions or major revivals, and Bay Area-based companies that offer a range of productions from Shakespeare to experimental net works.

The price of tickets, particularly at the Broadway houses, can be prohibi-

tive. As a result, **Stubs** on Stockton between Geary and Post, tel: (415) 433-7827, does a booming business selling half-price tickets for theatrical and musical performances. Open from Tuesday Saturday noon–7.30pm. Stubs accepts cash only. Discount tickets are allowed for current bookings only.

The larger theaters, ranging upwards from about 600 to 2,000 seats, usually house Broadway road companies, with occasional local productions. They are:

Curran Theater, 445 Geary, tel: (415) 293-9001.

Golden Gate Theater, 25 Taylor, tel: (415) 473-3800.

Orpheum Theater, 1192 Market Street, tel: (415) 749-2228.

Theater on the Square, 450 Post, tel: (415) 433-9500.

Small repertory companies (99 to 500 seats) include:

American Conservatory Theater, Meson and Geary, tel: (415) 749-2228. The largest San Francisco resident company, ACT has earned a national reputation for consistently good productions and an unimaginative choice of plays. ACT doesn't take risks with new material, preferring to run uncontroversial pieces by well-established playwrights.

Berkeley Repertory Theater, 2025 Addison, Berkeley, tel: (415) 845-4700. Started as a repertory company, it grew slowly but steadily in the 1970s until its own theater was set up in 1980. More daring than ACT, the Rep offers excellent productions of contemporary drama, Noel Coward revivals and occasional premieres of better-known playwrights. With three-quarters of its seats subscribed by the start of each season, tickets are often sold out.

The Eureka, 2730 16th Street, San Francisco, tel: (415) 558-9898. This company presents politically and socially relevant works, including many world and US premieres.

The Magic Theater, For Mason, Building D, San Francisco, tel: (415) 441-8822. A campy, crafty crew that favors things that have never been done before. There are occasionally impressive partnerships between the production people and the playwrights – Michael McClure and Sam Shepard have premiered plays at the Magic.

Dance

The Bay Area has two major ballets. The **San Francisco Ballet** performing at the San Francisco Opera House, Van Ness and Grove in Civic Center, tel: (415) 621-3838, is over 50 years old and well-known for traditional choreography, consistently excellent productions and classical form. Members of the San Francisco Symphony perform with the ballet. San Francisco was the first ballet company in the country to perform the *Nutcracker Suite* as a Christmas event. Season runs December–May.

Across the Bay the **Oakland Ballet** has been challenging San Francisco Ballet's dominance, building a reputation on innovative and young dancers who make up in dedication and energy what they lack in classical form. By reviving Diaghilev classics with original sets and costumes, western ballets of Copeland-Loring collaboration, and presenting the work of new California choreographers, Oakland is gaining national attention. Season runs September–December.

The **Dance Coalition**, 2141 Mission, San Francisco, tel: (415) 255-2794, publishes a comprehensive monthly calendar covering all forms of dance in the Bay Area – classical, modern, jazz, ethnic, folk and tap.

For modern and contemporary dance shows, try the **New Performance Gallery**, 3153 17th Street, San Francisco, tel: (415) 863-9834. Founded by two modern dance companies in order to have a house of the right size and dimensions for their own performances, the Gallery has expanded to encompass new works from other local choreographers, experimental pieces from various local companies, and a touring program that periodically brings small new companies to San Francisco.

Two other performance series are worth noting: **The San Francisco Opera House** is home to visiting national and international ballet companies including the Joffrey Ballet, American Ballet Theater and Stuttgart Ballet, among many others. For details write or call the box office to receive information about upcoming performances: San Francisco Opera House, PO Box 7430, San Francisco 94120, tel: (415) 861-4008.

The **University of California** brings a fine mix of classical, modern and ethnic dance touring companies to its Berkeley campus, Zellerbach Auditorium, Bancroft and Telegraph, tel: (415) 642-9988, as part of its "Cal Performances."

Opera & Music

In addition to the San Francisco Symphony (the pre-eminent local orchestra), Oakland, Marin, Berkeley, San Jose, Sacramento and Santa Cruz have resident companies. The Bay Area offers more chamber music groups, per capita, than any other area in the States, and a wide range of Asian and Indian music offerings are presented as well.

The San Francisco Opera is the largest and most fashionable arts organization in San Francisco, an opera-loving city since Gold Rush days. Locals claim the Opera, the second largest in the United States, is the best in the world, and even some international stars would agree.

Public and private money support the Opera and six other opera companies in the Bay Area with unprecedented enthusiasm.

Oakland Symphony, tel: (415) 465-6400 has a reputation for young, dynamic, artistic direction and solid, popular programming.

Sacramento Symphony, 14th and L streets, Sacramento, tel: (415) 916-0800. Plays chamber concerts and an outdoor summer series, in addition to its regular season.

San Francisco Conservatory of Music, 1201 Ortega, San Francisco, tel: (415) 564-8086. Offers professional chamber music as well as student recitals in its small intimate Hellman Hall. With graduates like Isaac Stern to its credit, the Conservatory is widely regarded as the best West Coast music school.

San Francisco Opera, Grove and Van Ness avenues, San Francisco, tel: (415) 864-3330. Perhaps best known for its casting which stems from the loyalty of great, international opera stars. It has successfully revived and restored to its current operatic repertoire a number of little known masterpieces.

San Francisco Symphony, Davies Symphony Hall, Van Ness and Grove, San Francisco, tel: (415) 552-8000. Plays a summer pops series, a Beethoven Festival and the Mostly Mozart Festival each year, in addition to its regular season.

San Jose Symphony has earned a reputation for strong, accessible programs since 1972.

Movies

Only the large cities have theaters that specialize in foreign films, subtitled for American audiences. In addition, universities often screen such classics on campus. In San Francisco these theaters are specially listed in the Datebook (pink) section of the Sunday newspaper. Among them are the **Clay**, **Lumiere**, and **Bridge**.

A number of movie theaters in recent years have discovered a solid market for revivals of old classics. The ticket price for these movie theaters is a couple of dollars less than the first-run theaters. Most revival movies are shown on a double bill (two movies for the price of one). In San Francisco the most noted revival theater is the **Castro**, a renovated 1930s movie palace complete with gilded ceiling, balconies and a live organist on weekends. The **Pacific Film Archive** in Berkeley (part of the University of California) takes a scholarly approach to films. Here you will see particularly obscure masterpieces, often in conjunction with lectures by people involved in making them. Other revival houses include the **UC Theater** in Berkeley, the **J Street Theater** in Sacramento, and the **Stanford** in Palo Alto.

For a complete listing of current movies, the local newspaper is the best resource.

Festivals & Events

Important Dates

In Northern California check out the *San Francisco Chronicle* or the *Bay Guardian* or the local paper in specific areas. Listings for more specialized events will appear in smaller local papers. If you have time before your visit write to the California Division of Tourism, 801 K Street, Sacramento, CA 95814, fax: (916) 322-3402 and request a free copy of *Golden California: Special Events*.

Here are just a few of the popular festivals and events in California:

January

Annual Stockton Ag Expo, Stockton, tel: (209) 466-5271. Agricultural products on display.

Graffiti USA '50s Festival, Modesto, tel: (209) 576-2222. In George Lucas' birthplace.

Memorial Polar Bear Swim, Cayucos, tel: (800) 4LB-STAY. Near Year's Day plunge into the Pacific.

Old Time Fiddle Contest, Cloverdale, tel: (707) 894-2067.

Sacramento Symphony Pops Series, tel: (916) 756-0191.

San Jose Craft Festival, San Jose, tel: (619) 737-0075.

Santa Cruz Fungus Fair, tel: (408) 429-3773. Feast on 150 mushroom varieties.

Tiburon Children's Film Festival, tel: (415) 435-1234.

Village Affair, Carmel Valley, tel: (408) 659-2261. Booths with food and wine.

Winter Music festival, Lake County, tel: (707) 263-6658. Bands and soloists.

Yosemite Chefs Holiday, Yosemite National Park, tel: (209) 454-2020.

February

Annual Crab Race, Crescent City, tel: (800) 343-8300. Rent a crab or bring one.

Antique American Indian Art Show, San Rafael, tel: (805) 652-1960.

Black History Month celebrations, Yountville, tel: (707) 944-8844 *and* Earlimart, tel: (805) 849-3433.

Chinese New Year. Call local tourist bureaus for information. Large celebrations in San Francisco, smaller ones in other communities.

Fiesta Italiana Crab Feed, Guerneville, tel: (707) 869-0623.

Mardi Gras, San Luis Obispo, tel: (805) 541-2183.

Mardi Gras Jazz Festival, Pismo Beach, tel: (800) 443-7778.

Masters of Food & Wine, Carmel, tel: (800) 682-4811. International chefs give lessons.

Pollyanna Doll Show & Sale, Petaluma, tel: (707) 763-5237. Dolls, teddy bears, toys, puppet shows.

Whiskey Flat Days, Kernville, tel: (619) 376-2629. Parade, rodeo, carnival, arts & crafts.

Winterfest, Chester, tel: (916) 258-2426. Dog sled races, snow sculptures, concert.

March

Whale Festival, Mendocino. With chowder and wine tastings, art shows, whale videos etc. Early March.

African Cultural Festival, Oakland, tel: (510) 763-3962.

Bay Area Music Awards, San Francisco.

California Spring Polka Festival, Auburn, tel: (916) 889-1626. Dancing, food & drink.

Camelia Festival, Sacramento, tel: (918) 447-2286.

Dixieland Festival, Monterey, tel: (408) 443-5260.

Saint Patrick's Day. San Francisco, Los Angeles and San Diego. Parades and celebrations.

San Francisco International Film Festival, San Francisco, tel: (415) 931-FILM.

Snowfest Winter Carnival, Tahoe City, tel: (916) 583-7625.

Storytelling Festival, Mariposa, tel: (209) 966-2456. Three days of workshops and performances.

Steinbeck Month on Cannery Row, Monterey, tel: (408) 649-6645. Celebrating the late author's birthday.

Whale Festival, Fort Bragg. With chowder, beer tastings, comic show, gem and mineral exhibits. Whale walk. Late March.

April

Annual Flea Market, Folsom, tel: (916) 985-7452. More than 300 antique vendors from all over the US attend this enormous affair.

Annual Teddy Bear Convention, Nevada City, tel: (916) 285-5804.

Big Sur International Marathon, Big Sur, tel: (408) 625-6626.

Cherry Blossom Festival, San Francisco, tel: (415) 563-2313.

Fort Tejon Dragoon Living History, Lebec, tel: (805) 248-6692. Volunteers recreate civilian and military life of 1865.

Hart Canyon Rendezvous, Twin Oaks, tel: (805) 832-4669. Mountain men traditions, customs and weapons.

Kern County Fair Horse Show, Bakersfield, tel: (805) 833-4900.

Italian Street Painting, San Luis Obispo, tel: (805) 528-6492.

Living History Day, Petaluma, tel: (707) 778-0150. Sheep shearing, brick-making, craft demonstrations.

Sacramento Valley Scottish Games, Roseville, tel: (916) 737-2277.

Shasta Dixieland Jazz festival, Redding, tel: (916) 225-4354.

Tour of Spring Gardens, Mendocino, tel: (707) 937-2435.

May

Balloon and Wine Festival, Temecula, tel: (714) 676-5090.

Bay to Breakers, San Francisco, tel: (415) 777-7770. The world's largest (not longest at 7½ miles/12 km) footrace.

Bicycle Tour of the Lost Coast, Ferndale, tel: (800) 995-8356.

Cajun Crawfish Festival, Vallejo, tel: (707) 427-1060. Arts and crafts, barbecue, music.

Calaveras County Fair & Jumpinhg Frog Jubilee, Angels Camp, tel: (209) 736-2561.

California Festival of Beers, San Luis Obispo, tel: (805) 544-2266. While still fairly small, this festival is the largest regional beer-tasting event in the country.

Carlsbad Village Faire, Carlsbad, tel: (619) 729-9072. California's largest one-day street faire.

Cinco de Mayo, San Francisco, Los Angeles and San Diego. Mexican festivities.

Cross Country Kinetic Sculpture Race, Arcata to Ferndale, tel: (707) 725-725-3851.

Holy Ghost Festival, Ferndale, tel: (707) 786-9640. Portuguese community celebrations.

Living History Day, Petaluma, tel: (707) 778-0150. Return to the 1840s.

Napa Valley Sensational, Napa, tel: (707) 257-0322. Vintners, restaurants, farmers, musicians, entertainers, artists.

Redding Rodeo, Redding, tel: (800) 874-7652. Week-long events.

Russian River Wine Fest, Healdsburg, tel: (800) 648-9922.

Sacramento Dixieland Jubilee, Sacramento, tel: (916) 372-5277. An international jazz festival.

Salinas Valley Fair, King City, tel: (408) 385-3243. Rodeo, carnival, craft exhibits.

William Saroyan Festival, Fesno, tel: (209) 229-7866. Historic walk, bike races, writing contest.

June

Carnaval San Francisco, San Francisco, tel: (415) 826-1401. Mardi Gras parade and activities.

Festival at the Lake, Oakland, tel: (510) 464-1061.

Haight Street Fair, San Francisco.

Garberville Rodeo, Garberville, tel: (707) 923-2613.

Lesbian and Gay Freedom Day Parade, San Francisco.

Living History Days, San Jose, tel: (408) 287-2290. Civil War battles, parades, dancing.

Murietta Settlers' Days, Murietta, tel: (909) 677-7916. Hot Springs.

Tour of Nevada City Bicycle Classic, Nevada City, tel: (916) 265-2692.

Vintage 1870 Father's Day Auto Show, Yountville, tel: (707) 944-2451. Cars, cars, cars.

Wagon Train Dance, Placerville, tel: (916) 677-8000. Celebrating the early settlers.

July

Art in the Redwoods festival, Gualala, tel: (707) 884-1138.

Barbecue & Sheep Dog Trials, Boonville, tel: (707) 895-3011.

California Rodeo, Salinas, tel: (408) 757-2951.

California Wine Tasting Championships, Greenwood Ridge Vineyards, tel: (707) 895-2002.

Festival of Weeds & Wallflowers, Weed, tel: (916) 938-4624. Arts and crafts, entertainment, giant picnic.

Fourth of July. Celebrations and fireworks, state-wide.
Frontier Days & Rodeo, Willits, tel: (707) 459-5248.
Gilroy Garlic Festival, Gilroy, tel: (408) 842-1625.
Mendocino Music festival, Mendocino, tel: (707) 937-2044. Jazz, opera, chamber music.
Modesto Air Fair, Modesto, tel: (209) 578-4377. Display of model and fullsize planes, fly-by, World War I memorabilia.
Mozart Festival, San Luis Obispo, tel: (805) 781-3011.
Solano County Fair, Vallejo, tel: (707) 644-2206. Horse-racing, livestock exhibits, carnival.
Summer Nights in Nevada City, tel: (916) 265-2692. Arts and entertainment on the streets.
Wine Festival & Liberty Ride, Sonoma, tel: (707) 938-6791. Tastings and bike ride.
World's Largest Salmon Barbecue, Fort Bragg, tel: (707) 964-6598.

August

Annual Mateel Woman's Music Festival, Garberville, tel: (707) 923-3368. Dance, music and the arts.
Festa Italiana, Sacramento, tel: (916) 424-8259. Music, culture, dancing.
History Week, Folsom, tel: (916) 985-2707.
Humboldt County Fair, Ferndale, tel: (707) 786-9511. Horse races, contests, sheep shearing, carnival rides.
Indian Fair Days, North Fork, tel: (209) 877-2115. Native crafts, tribal dances, food.
Japanese Cultural Bazaar, Sacramento, tel: (916) 446-0121. Cultural displays, food, games.
Jefferson State Fair, Crescent City, tel: (707) 464-9510. Food, entertainment, carnival rides.
Lake Tahoe Starlight Jazz Festival, South Lake Tahoe, tel: (916) 542-4166.
Nevada County Fair, Grass Valley, tel: (916) 273-6217. Food, rides, livestock, displays.
Oakland Chinatown Street Festival, Oakland, tel: (510) 893-8979.
Plumas County Fair, Quincy, tel: (916) 283-6272. Entertainment, auto races, logger show.
Reggae on the River, French's Camp, Garberville, tel: (707) 923-3368.
Renaissance Pleasure Faire, Novato,

tel: (415) 892-0937 or (800) 52-FAIRE.

September

A la carte, A la park, San Francisco, tel: (415) 383-9378. Sample food from the city's fine restaurants and enjoy live music in Golden Gate Park.
California State Fair, Sacramento, tel: (916) 263-3000. Exhibits, carnival, food, entertainment.
Monterey Jazz Festival, Monterey, tel: (408) 373-3366.
Oktoberfest, Big Bear Lake, tel: (714) 866-5634. Weekends between Labor Day and the end of October.
Oktoberfest, Mariposa, tel: (209) 966-5217. Bavarian food and entertainment.
Paul Bunyan Days in Fort Bragg. Tel: (707) 961-6300.
Mendocino County Fair & Apple Show, Boonville, tel: (707) 895-3011.
Railroad Days, Portola, tel: (916) 832-4131. Celebration of railroad heritage with parade, games, contests.
Redwood Summer Games, Garberville, tel: (707) 923-9248. Three day events for people with disabilities.
Sausalito Art Festival, Sausalito, tel: (415) 332-0505.
Sonoma Valley Shakespeare Festival, Sonoma, tel: (707) 996-2145. Picnics with the Bard.
Summer Theatre festival, Ferndale, tel: (707) 725- 2378. Comedies and musicals.
Winesong, Mendocino, tel: (707) 964-5168. Food and wine tasting, music.

October

Annual Cotton Festival, Corcoran, tel: (209) 992-4514. Street party, parade, barbecue, country western dancing.
Columbus Day Celebration, San Francisco, tel: (415) 434-1492.
Cowboy Poetry, Chester, tel: (800) 326-2247. Western dancing, too.
Daow Aga Pow-Wow, Brockway, tel: (800) CAL-NEVA. Native American music, food, crafts.
Fleet Week, San Francisco, tel: (415) 395-3923. Foreign and US ships assemble.
Half Moon Bay Art and Pumpkin Festival, Half Moon Bay, tel: (415) 726-9652.
Hangtown Jazz Jubilee, Placerville, tel: (800) 457-6279. Ten bands in ten places.
Harvest Fair, Fort Bragg, tel: (707) 961-6300.

Japanese Cultural Festival, Palo Alto, tel: (415) 326-4454.
Octoberfest, Sacramento, tel: (916) 442-7360. German beer, food, music, dancing. Also at Mariposa, tel: (209) 966-5217; Mammoth Lakes, tel: (619) 934-9451); and Lakeport, tel: (800) 525-3743)
Raindance festival, Squaw Valley, tel: (209) 332-2909. Percussion instruments, ethnic food and dances, artwork.
Summer Theatre Festival, Ferndale, tel: (707) 725-2378.
Tomato Fest, Los Banos, tel: (800) 336-6354. Food, flea market, carnival, auto racing.
Zucchini Festival, Angels Camp, tel: (209) 754-6477. Contests, food, music, crafts.

November

Annual Teddy Bear Exhibit, Lakeport, tel: (800) 525-3743. Display of 600 teddy bears.
Carlsbad Village Faire, Carlsbad, tel: (619) 729-9072.
Carols in the Caves, Napa Valley, tel: (707) 224-4222. Seasonal music in winery caves.
Cornish Christmas, Grass Valley, tel: (916) 272-8315. Choirs and cloggers in costume.
Cowboy Poetry, Chester, tel: (800) 326-2247. Readings and western dance.
Holiday Crafts Festival, Weaverville, tel: (916) 623-2760. Food, wine, music, crafts.
Also at Santa Cruz, tel: (408) 423-5600.
Kern Island Artsfest, Bakersfield, tel: (805) 323-7928. Music from *mariachi* to gospel and performing arts.
Latin/Native American Christmas Art Fair, San Jose, tel: (408) 280-1460.
Light the Old Oak Tree, Danville, tel: (510) 837-4400. Carolers, choirs, bands at ceremony.
Mountain Man Rendezvous, Felton, tel: (408) 335-3509. Recalling fur trappers and traders of the 1840s.
Mushroom Festival, Mendocino, tel: (707) 937-5397.

December

Celebrity Cooks & Kitchens Tour, Mendocino, tel: (707) 961-6300.
Christmas Festival, Mendocino, tel: (800) 726 2780. Horse-drawn carriage rides, Dickens' readings etc.

Dickens Christmas Celebration, Lake Arrowhead, tel: (909) 653-3899. Costumed carolers, choirs, dramatizations of the books.

El Dorado County Christmas, Placerville, tel: (800) 457-6279. Lighted trees, carolers, reindeer.

Festival of Lights, Yountville, tel: (800) 959-3604. Town lit up for a month-long festival.

Hometown Christmas, Fort Bragg, tel: (707) 961-0360. Community carols, lighted truck parade.

The Nutcracker. Tel: (415) 431-1210. Performed by the San Francisco Ballet and Oakland Ballet.

Open House and Carolers, Ferndale, tel: (707) 786-4477.

Similar celebrations in village of Murphys, tel: (800) 225-3764.

Spirit of Christmas Crafts Fair and Exhibition, Santa Rosa, tel: (707) 575-9335 for details.

The Gay Scene

San Francisco's nationally-renowned gay scene is centered around the Castro and Mission districts where most of this specialized night life is concentrated. The city's version of Mardi Gras is fulfilled on the last Sunday of June by the annual Lesbian/Gay Pride Celebration which culminates in an enormous Market Street parade with colorful floats and outrageous costumes or lack thereof. In September or October is the Castro Street Fair and the area also sees wild Halloween celebrations and a candlelight march in November to honor Harvey Milk, the former gay city supervisor who was murdered at City Hall in 1979. Gay bars and nightclubs such as The End Up, Dekadence and Rawhide II thrive in the SoMa district and Cafe Flore, Metro and many others draw the crowds in the Castro district. A growing number of theatres cater to gay audiences. Listings for these and other events can be found in such publications as the *Sentinel* and the *Bay Area Reporter* while immediate information about current activities is available by calling the Lesbian/Gay Switchboard at (510) 841-6224.

Shopping

Where to Buy

From elegant malls to farmer's markets, Northern California offers a wide array of shopping opportunities. In San Francisco alone there are 20 distinct shopping areas. The most famous is probably **Union Square**, where most of the large, prestigious department stores are located, including Neiman-Marcus, Macy's and Saks. A block away is **Maiden Lane**, a cute pedestrian street with boutiques, stationery stores and an outdoor cafe. **The Galleria**, a collection of 60 specialty shops, restaurants and services housed under a vaulting glass dome modeled after Milan's Galleria Vittorio Emmanuelle is also nearby.

Visitors will find an abundance of shopping in the **Fisherman's Wharf** area. The shopping area extends from Pier 39 to Ghirardelli Square and includes the Cannery, the Anchorage and a host of street vendors. Once a cargo wharf, Pier 39 now offers two levels of shops, restaurants, amusements and free outdoor entertainment by some of the city's best street performers. Both the Cannery and Ghirardelli Square are converted factories. The Cannery was once a Del Monte peach canning plant, and Ghirardelli once housed a chocolate factory. The Anchorage, a colorful, modern shopping complex, is also located along the Northern Waterfront. Along with specialty shops and galleries, each complex offers unique landscaping, live entertainment, open-air walkways and breathtaking views of Alcatraz, the Golden Gate Bridge and the Bay.

The **Embarcadero Center** is also located on the waterfront, east of Pier 39 near the Financial District. This is San Francisco's largest mall with about 175 shops, restaurants and nightclubs in four complexes between Sacramento and Clay streets.

Other shopping areas in San Fran-

cisco tend to reflect the character of the neighborhood. They include Columbus Avenue and Grant Street in North Beach (Little Italy), Grant Street in Chinatown, Castro Street between 20th and Market and between Market and Church, Haight Street along the Golden Gate Park Panhandle, Union Street at Cow Hollow, and Japan Center.

In the **East Bay**, visitors will find a distinct collegiate shopping atmosphere along vendor-laden Telegraph Avenue in Berkeley, and Berkeley's famous "Gourmet Ghetto" along Shattuck Avenue, as well as a stretch on College Avenue up near the campus. Other locations in the Bay Area boasting boutiques, restaurants and specialty stores include Solano Avenue in Albany, Piedmont Avenue and Jack London Square in Oakland, University Avenue in Palo Alto (Stanford's toned-down "Telegraph Avenue") and the entire business district of Sausalito.

In **Sacramento**, Pavilions at Fair Oaks Boulevard near Howe Avenue is the city's most exclusive shopping area featuring boutiques and upscale restaurants. Downtown Plaza between 4th and 7th streets has been recently expanded to more than 100 shops plus a seven-screen cinema complex. Arden Fair, just east of downtown, includesd Nordstrom's and Sears. At nearby **Folsom** are dozens of factory outlet stores.

Numerous big shopping malls, each comprised of scores of stores, have sprung up outside such towns as **Vacaville** (the Nut Tree on Interstate 80); **Monterey** (The American Tin Cannery Outlet, 125 Ocean View Avenue); **Gilroy** (The Pacific West Outlet, State Route 101 At Leavesley Road); and **Truckee** (Donner Pass Road and Highway 89 in Tahoe). The Stanford Shopping Center, at the edge of the **Palo Alto** university campus is also popular.

Clothing Chart

The following table gives a comparison of American, Continental and British clothing sizes. It is always best to try on any article before buying it, however, as sizes may vary.

Women's Dresses/Suits

American	Continental	British
6	38/34N	8/30
8	40/36N	10/32
10	42/38N	12/34
12	44/40N	14/36
14	46/42N	16/38
16	48/44N	18/40

Women's Shoes

American	Continental	British
4½	36	3
5½	37	4
6½	38	5
7½	39	6
8½	40	7
9½	41	8
10½	42	9

Men's Suits

American	Continental	British
34	44	34
—	46	36
38	48	38
—	50	40
42	52	42
—	54	44
46	56	46

Men's Shirts

American	Continental	British
14	36	14
14½	37	14½
15	38	15
15½	39	15½
16	40	16
16½	41	16½
17	42	17

Men's Shoes

American	Continental	British
6½	—	6
7½	40	7
8½	41	8
9½	42	9
10½	43	10
11½	44	11

Flea Markets

Flea markets in the Bay Area are outnumbered only by yard sales. They are held on weekends, admission is generally free, and there are bargains galore! Sellers range from those old-timers who make a living selling discounted new goods and antiques, to people who think they have too much junk in their attic or garage. The most common items at flea markets are used household items, but you can also spot brand-new stereo equipment, designer clothes, farm tools, food, arts and crafts, puppy dogs and stuffed teddy bears. Bargaining is expected. Most of them accept cash only; no checks or credit cards.

Alameda Penny Market (tel: 552-7206), the best of the flea markets, held on weekends at the Island Auto Drive-In, three blocks south of the Alameda Tube from Oakland. Minimal admission charge.

San Jose Flea Market, at 12000 Berryessa Road (tel: 408-289-1550) is one of the largest in the United States. About 2,000 booths fill 40 acres (16 hectares) with every imaginable kind of merchandise. There are shady rest areas, refreshment stands, kiddie rides, and live entertainment. Open Wednesday, Saturday and Sunday. Small parking fee.

Marin City Flea Market at 740 Donahue Street off US 101 (tel: 332-1441) in Sausalito is the place to pick up something inexpensive which you'll love. Open only on weekend.

Other flea markets which deserve mention include the **Castro Valley Market** at 20820 Oak Street in Castro Valley Boulevard (tel: 582-0396) and the **Solano Flea Market** (tel: 825-1951) at the Solano Drive-In, Solano Way and Highway 4.

Sport

Backpacking

General backpacking information is given in the "The Great Outdoors" article in the features section of this book. The following information tells you how to obtain a wilderness visitor's permit before you set out for any trip.

To get your permit, write in advance, detailing your plans, to the National Park or Forest Service. If you don't have enough time to write and receive a permit in the mail, you may call the park or forest; most will take phone reservations one week in advance. And if you decide to take a truly last minute trip, or if all the advance permits are taken, you can show up at the Visitors' Center the morning of, or the day before, your trip. The Forest Service saves half of its permits for a first-come, first-serve basis, and so do most of the parks.

Bicycling

San Francisco's Golden Gate Park and the bridge designate routes for bicycles only on weekends (tel: 666-7200). Rental shops line Stanyan Street, at the entrance to the park, and can be found throughout the Marina area. Shops also have route maps. Tourist offices in most other places will have maps of suggested bicycle routes.

Angel Island (tel: 546-2815) offers some of the best views for a cyclist. The terrain, however, may discourage the novice.

The Alum Rock Park Trail, tel: (408) 259-5477 runs for 13 miles (21 km) near San Jose. Stop alongside the 60-ft (18-meter) waterfall or the old mineral springs marked by rock grottos. The Cal-train service will transport both you and your bike from San Francisco to Alum Rock.

A gusty wind is likely to speed your progress across the Golden Gate Bridge. So pedal (carefully) over to Sausalito, browse, grab a bite, and return along the breezy bridge path. The west sidewalk is open weekends and holidays to cyclists.

The colorful coast ride of California has something for every rider. The trail traverse 50 miles (80 km) of spectacular surf and sand, from Santa Cruz north to Half Moon Bay. Begin and end anywhere. The easiest stretch extends from Highway 1 between the tourable Pigeon Point Lighthouse and Pescadero Beach. Or paddle backwards in time along the 3-mile (5-km) Monterey Path of History, a well-marked route lined with old adobe structures (tel: 408-649-3200).

There's also good bicycling in the wine country, through the foothills of the Sierras to Yosemite Valley; between two beautiful and fairly remote volcanic mountains – Shasta and Lassen; and along the famous (and flat) garden bowl of the US – the San Joaquin and Sacramento Valleys.

Traveling through the wine country

is a little like traveling through southern France. There is plenty of good bread, cheese, and wine, and restaurants seem to pop up along the roadside like sunflowers.

The bicycling section of the Sierra Club (there are several in the Bay Area) can tell you about good routes, and so can experienced salesmen in the bicycle shops. You need to plan your trip in advance so you can reserve campsites in popular forest areas and parks. For information on the state parks call a toll-free number (800) 952-5580. For a bicycle map of the Pacific Coast, write Cal Trans, 1129 N. Street, Sacramento, CA 95814. The California Department of Transportation established a Pacific Coast Bicentennial Bicycle Route in 1976 and designated special sections in the state parks for cyclists.

Boating

San Francisco Bay is challenging even for the most experienced sailor. If you're experienced, you can try the windsurfing off Crissy Field, between the Marina Green and the Golden Gate Bridge. Ocean kayaking is popular with men and women of all ages. Some of the best sailing in the world can be enjoyed without ever going beyond the Golden Gate. Lessons, equipment, sail and power boat rentals are listed in the *Yellow Pages*. You also can choose to float in smaller vessels and calmer waters like Stow Lake in Golden Gate Park, tel: (415) 752-0347. Canoes to negotiate the Russian River from Healdsburg, can be rented from W.C. Trowbridge, tel: (707) 433-4116.

Sailboarding is popular from San Francisco's Pier 39 and at Waddell Creek in Santa Cruz.

San Francisco's City Parks and Recreation Department (tel: 666-7024) oversees 52 public areas with a variety of facilities in addition to the Golden Gate Park complex.

The Golden Gate National Recreation Area encompasses 35,000 acres (14,000 hectare) and 69 sq. miles (178 sq. km) of waterfront. It contains facilities for bicycling, birding, *bocce* ball, exercise, fishing, hang gliding, hiking, running, jogging, swimming, and walking. For general information, tel: (415) 556-0560.

Bowling

Bocce ball, lawn bowling and indoor bowling are all popular in San Francisco. For information about the first two, tel: (415) 666-7200.

Rock 'N' Bowl, 1855 Haight Street, tel: 826-2695 each Friday and Saturday, 9pm–2am. For your entrance fee you get bowling, shoes, pool games and you can listen/watch rock videos on 25 screens.

Diving

Diving off the Northern California coast is only for those who are willing to brave large waves and poor visibility. About 80 percent of all divers are in search not of beautiful underworld visions (the visions are there, although most of the time you can't see them), but of abalone and fish. Salt Point is a good place to find abalone, as is Humboldt Bay at the northern end of the state; and you can spear ling cod and halibut just about anywhere. Remember that you must have an abalone iron for prying abalones off the rocks and that red abalones must be at least 7 inches (18 cm) long before you can take them. The season runs from December–July, excluding the month of April.

Dive shops in the Bay Area rent diving equipment by the day, week or weekend.

Fishing

California leads the nation in the sale of fishing licenses. Trout and steelhead run in the upper Klamath near the Oregon Border, and for two of the finest fishing streams in the country, toss a line into Fall River or Hat Creek in the Burney Basin northeast of Redding. The McCloud and Upper Sacramento rivers just north of Lake Shasta also offer good, easily accessible fly fishing, as does the Truckee River from Truckee to Pyramid Lake, just north of Tahoe.

Eagle Lake in the northeastern part of the state has more than 300 Forest Service campsites and numerous chances to catch a giant Lahontan cutthroat trout. Lake Pillsbury, northeast of Ukiah, has 115 campsites for fishermen and Lake Siskiyou near Mount Shasta has more than 200 campsites.

You must have a valid California fishing license to fish in the state, but

they are easily obtainable at nearly all sporting goods stores and local offices of the California Department of Fish and Game.

Fresh water fishing is available at the Lake Merced Boating and Fishing Company, just south of the city at 1 Harding Road where Skyline Boulevard and the Great Highway that runs along the ocean come together. Large trout are stocked in the 360-acre (146-hectare) lake which is open year-round. Boats, licenses, bait and tackle are available. For information, tel: 753-1101.

Before you go to Lake Merced, you might want to practice at the Fly Casting Pools near the Anglers' Lodge in Golden Gate Park, off Kennedy Drive, near the Buffalo paddock, tel: 666-7200.

Deep Sea Fishing

Deep sea fishing boats leave San Francisco's Fisherman's Wharf on regular schedules. Catches include salmon, seabass, halibut, rock fish, bonito, shark and albacore. You can rent equipment and you need a fishing license. Your catch can be smoked, packed and shipped to most places for you. Plan for wind and some rough seas. Bring along motion sickness preventatives and warm clothing. Check the *Yellow Pages* for sport fishing trips.

From Half Moon Bay, Fisherman's Wharf, Sausalito, Berkeley, Emeryville, Bodega Bay and various seaside villages further north, fishing party boats leave on regular schedules in search of salmon, seabass, halibut, rock fish, bonito, shark and albacore. (Look in the Yellow Pages under "Fishing Parties".) Remember that the Pacific Ocean can be rough and seasickness is often a problem. Also, the weather offshore is usually windy and rarely warm enough for sunbathing.

Golf

Golf is a year-round sport in California, and just about every town has a municipal golf course.

Pebble Beach in Carmel is California's world-famous championship golf course. Green fees, like everything else about this semi-private club, are expensive. But the setting, along the rugged Pacific Coast, and the course itself are truly beautiful. To make sure you can reserve green time, stay overnight in the lodge. For reservations tel: (408) 624-3811. If you want some serious lessons, Ben Doyle, the mentor of Bobby Clampett, teaches golf in the Monterey area, tel: 408-624-1581.

Another top golf course in a country club setting is Silverado Country Club (tel: 916-255-2970) located in Napa, the heart of the wine country. It's a 36-hole course complete with a Southern Plantation style lodge and separate cabins.

In addition to private golf and country clubs, San Francisco has four public golf courses: Harding Park Golf Course is on Lake Merced (Harding Road off Skyline Boulevard); Lincoln Municipal Golf Course overlooks Golden Gate Park (Lincoln Boulevard and Clement Street); the Golden Gate Park Golf Course (47th Avenue and JFK Drive); and the Jack Fleming Golf Course (Harding Road off Skyline Boulevard).

Other notable public courses include Tilden Park (Berkeley), Cypress Point (Monterey), Sea Ranch (below Mendocino on the North Coast), Franklin Canyon (Rodeo), Mountain Shadows (Rohnert Park) and Dry Creek.

San Francisco boasts four beautiful municipal courses, one with the Golden Gate Bridge as a backdrop. Although it's often possible to pick up a partner, call ahead for reservations. These courses are very popular. Rental equipment is generally available.

The Golden Gate Park Course, 47th Avenue at Fulton, is 9 holes, 1,357 yards (1,234 meters), par 27. Reservations: tel: 751-8987.

Harding Park, south of the city at Skyline and Harding Park boulevards, includes two courses. Fleming, tel: 661-1865, is 9 holes, 2,316 yards (2,105 meters), par 32, and Harding, tel: 664-4690 is 18 holes, 6,637 yards (6,040 meters), par 72.

Lincoln Park Course, 34th Avenue and Clement Street, tel: 221-9911, is 18 holes, 5,081 yards (4,620 meters), par 68. Situated on a cliff, views of the Bay and the Bridge are spectacular.

Group Runs

America is on the run. Jogging has been a fitness fad for years now, and the running shows no sign of letting up. Part of the thrill is the joy of competition; if you'd like to join the race, here are a few of the Bay Area's biggest group runs:

Bay to Breakers, tel: 777-2424. California's largest footrace follows 7-mile (12-km) course from one side of San Francisco to the other. Mid-May.

Nimitz Run, tel: 642-3551. There are two scenic courses: a 3-mile (5-km) flat run on Treasure Island, and a 6-mile (10-km) course around Treasure Island and hilly Yerba Buena Island. Mid-May.

St Jude Run for Kids, tel: 800-632-0512. This 6-mile (10-km) scenic run starts and ends at The Anchorage, 2800 Leavenworth Street. Mid-June.

San Francisco Marathon, tel: 681-2322. The scenic course takes in the sights of the city while avoiding most of the hills. End of July.

Bigfoot-Bigheart, tel: 864-7400. This 6-mile (10-km) race through Golden Gate Park is a benefit for Catholic Social Service. Mid-September.

Bridge-to-Bridge Run, tel: 951-7070. The benefit for Big Brothers & Sisters is an 8-mile (13-km) run along the San Francisco waterfront. Late September/early October.

Seagull Run, tel: 765-5088. Two races are open – the 3-mile (5-km) and the 6-mile (10-km); both around Treasure Island. Mid-October.

Golden Gate Marathon, tel: 392-4218. Sponsored by the YMCA, the full marathon ends at the Larkspur Ferry Terminal in Marin County, and the half-marathon in Sausalito. End of October.

Zoo Run, tel: 661-2023. Some 2,000 runners wind their way through one of the most unusual courses imaginable – 3½ miles (5½ km) through the San Francisco Zoo. Mid-January.

Hang Gliding

There's more hang gliding in California than any other state because the good coastal winds are consistent. One of the best spots to watch or participate is the 200-ft (60-meter) cliff at Fort Funston, just south of San Francisco, at the end of the Great Highway near Lake Merced. Computerized up-to-the-minute wind condition information is available, tel: 333-0100. See the *Yellow Pages* of the phone directory for lessons and equipment rentals.

The Owens Valley, east of the Sierras, is home of the Cross Country

Classic, a hang gliding event held every July that attracts enthusiasts from all over the world. Its flight record is 158 miles (254 km), and every year more than a few flyers go over 100 miles (160 km).

The once-in-a-lifetime flight to make if you are an experienced hang glider is from Glacier Point, just above Yosemite Valley. You can jump off the point in the early morning and take a leisurely ride down 4,000 ft (1,220 meter) to the valley floor below. While falling, you can explore some of Yosemite's famous rock spires and granite walls.

The best site for coastal ridge soaring is Fort Funston, just south of the San Francisco zoo. If you need to learn the sport, there are a dozen hang gliding schools in Northern California. Look for schools in the *Yellow Pages* under "Hang Gliding."

Horseback Riding

Rentals are no longer available, but you can take lessons at the Riding Academy in Golden Gate Park, John F. Kennedy Drive and 36th Avenue. For information, tel: 668-7360.

Jogging

Although there are jogging paths designated in Golden Gate Park and along the Marina Green, the entire city seems to be one big joggers' paradise. You can stick to the waterfront and avoid the hills, but one of the biggest events of the year is the Bay to Breakers run in which the most serious and the most silly participate. Check the free *City Sports* magazine, as well as the daily papers, for all kinds of jogging, striding and walking events.

Kite Flying

In the meadows of Golden Gate Park, on the beaches, and especially in the Marina Green area, this is serious stuff. It's also colorful and fun. Specialty shops sell kites, including one on Pier 39 which features demonstrations out front on the Fisherman's Wharf promenade.

Sailboarding

Sailboarding is also for the experienced, since the Northern Pacific is rarely calm. At Pier 39 in San Francisco, equipment can be rented cheaply by the hour; double the price if you insist on going beyond the break-water into the San Francisco Bay (where they will insist on escorting you in a boat). South of San Francisco, Waddell Creek in Santa Cruz is a popular sailboarding spot, with the right waves and weather.

Skiing
SKI TOURING

Lovers of snow and the soft, sensual silence of a black and white alpine landscape go into the mountains in winter. Because of relatively mild weather, some say the Sierras may be the best mountains to ski tour in the world. Spring is the best time to ski tour and the most spectacular route is down the central spine of the Sierras on the John Muir trail. This is a sport for the experienced: those with good equipment, good map sense, and the ability to build a snow cave; there are few huts in the Sierras where travelers can take shelter from a storm.

Sierra Ski Touring offers guided tours, including the Sierra high route and the White Mountains (east of the Sierras, in the desert) which have perfect intermediate terrain. For brochures, write Sierra Ski Touring, Box 9, Mammoth Lakes, CA 93546.

If you want to learn how to ski tour, or cross country ski (see entry below) contact the Kirkwood Ski Touring Center, tel: (209) 258-8864), 1 mile (1½ km) south of Kirkwood (a downhill ski resort near Lake Tahoe).

CROSS COUNTRY SKIING

Cross country skiing (as it's called when you ski-tour for only a day) is fast becoming popular as an alternative to the long lines at downhill ski resorts, and in the Tahoe Area there are numerous official cross country ski trails offering packed snow and advance runs. Most people forego official trails, and just take off and hike through the snow to a hill or lake. Not having to pay for ski-lift tickets makes the price right. Also, cross country skis can be rented at almost every ski shop for about one-third the cost of downhill skis.

DOWNHILL SKIING

Downhill skiing in Northern California is great if you're from the East Coast (where trails are icy and crowded) but not so if you've skied in the Rockies or the long, leisurely trails of Europe. On weekends and holidays most California resorts have long lift lines and many of the trails are frighteningly crowded. During the week this changes and skiing can be spectacular (although deep powder snow rarely lasts).

There are two main ski areas in Northern California – around Lake Tahoe, about 3½ hours from the Bay Area, and at Mammoth Mountain on the eastern side of the Sierras, about 8 hours from San Francisco. For descriptions of the ski areas see the "Lake Tahoe" and "Sierras" sections.

Sky Diving
If falling from a plane with a parachute is your cup of tea, California is for you; there are more drop zones here than in any other state. Many of these schools use Accelerated Free Fall, a training technique that allows a student to make his first jump from an altitude of 10,000 ft (3,050 meters).

Falcon Parachute School, 11 miles (18 km) south of Los Banos and about 3 hours south of San Francisco, is one of the best-loved sky-diving schools in the state.

Crazy Creek, 18896 Grange Road, Middletown, CA 95461 on State 29, north of Calistoga, tel: (800) 987-SOAR. Gliding and skydiving instruction, flights and drops available.

Soaring
It's possible to get the feel of gliding without actually endangering your life; just plain gliding – being towed up 3,000 ft (915 meters) in a motorless fiberglass airplane and then catching an updraft to 10,000 ft (3,050 meters) and flying 15 minutes before landing. At the Calistoga Soaring Center (1546 Lincoln Avenue, Calistoga, CA 94515), a pilot will take you up over the wine country.

Tennis
Tennis is one of the most popular participatory sports in America and in it California leads the nation. There are public tennis courts in every town, usually at the local high schools and parks. In the city of San Francisco alone there are 142 public tennis courts (tel: 558-4532). You can reserve one simply by sitting on the sidelines and waiting patiently for a court to become free.

The courts are free except for the 21 located in the Golden Gate Park Tennis complex. Here, reservations are required on weekdays, but it's first-come, first-serve during busy weekends. For general information, tel: 666-7024. For Golden Gate Park information, tel: 753-7101. For reservations, tel: 753-7001.

If you're serious about tennis, and wouldn't mind improving your game while on vacation, check out John Gardiner's Tennis Ranch in Carmel Valley. It's the first tennis ranch in the States and offers a tennis clinic for non-members, Sunday–Friday. The clinic includes intensive instruction through videotape, gourmet meals, beautiful accommodations, breakfast in bed and general pampering. For reservations and information write PO Box 228, Carmel Valley, California 93924. Closed on Thanksgiving and Easter.

Sacramento has 225 tennis courts. For information tel: (916) 277-6054.

Water Slides
At Oakwood Lake Resort, 874 East Woodward, Manteca, tel: (209) 239-9566, water sliding is just one of the water sports to enjoy. With eight slides in all, Oakwood offers tubular shapes for fast, yet safe, sliding. For nonsliders, Oakland provides paddle boats, canoes, and an outdoor roller-skating complex.

The four water slides in Milpita, 1200 South Dempsey Road, tel: 408-263-6962, seem almost as steep as waterfalls; some with 360-degree turns! Half-hour sessions, or all day economical tickets. Free parking and changing rooms.

At Windsor Water Works, 8225 Conde Lane, 6 miles north of Santa Rosa, tel: (707) 838-7760, four slides are open daily in the summer. Half-hour sessions or day rates. There's also a pool and picnic area where you can play volleyball or horseshoes.

Spectator
Baseball
Baseball season runs from April–October. In Northern California, the San Francisco Giants play at Candlestick Park (tel: 467-8000). This is a cold, colossal coliseum with whipping winds you won't believe. (Be sure to bring a sweater and a windbreaker!) Express

buses make the trip to the park easier, tel: 673-6864.

The Oakland Athletics (known as the A's) play in the Oakland Coliseum, warmer, sunnier, and much more mellow.

Over the years, the two teams have scored similar success stories, their yearly attendance is about the same, and their fans are equally fanatic. They both play about 80 home games each year. Other than the weather, both teams provide a similarly enjoyable American outing. Prices are the same, as are starting times (1.05pm for afternoon games, 7.35pm for evening games), length of games (three, sometimes four hours), and quality of the hot dogs and beer.

Basketball

The regular National Basketball Association (NBA) season runs from October–April, with championship playoffs continuing in June. The Golden State Warriors play 41 times during the season at the Oakland Coliseum Arena, tel: (510) 638-6000. Tuesday and Thursday night games start at 7.35pm; Saturday night games start at 8.05pm.

The Sacramento Kings play at the Arco Arena.

Football

The National Football League (NFL) season begins in September and runs through December. There are pre-season games in August and post-season playoffs in January. There is only one professional football team in Northern California, the San Francisco 49ers, who play at Candlestick Park. For current information, tel: 468-2249.

There are only eight home games so tickets are seldom available.

College football is not professional, but it is accessible. Stanford University's (tel: 497-1021) season runs from September–November; games start at 1pm or 1.30pm. University of California at Berkeley (tel: 642-5150) has six home games during the season.

Horse Racing

Not only can you sit and watch sleek horses out to trot, but you can wager small sums on your favorite filly and win oodles of money... if you're lucky. Luck (and a love of horses) draws thousands of racing fans to the two Bay Area tracks, Golden Gate Fields in the East Bay and Bay Meadows on the Peninsula. There are usually nine races a day (five days a week) during the season, and you can gamble as much as you like on any race.

Bay Meadows, off Highway 101, tel: 574-7223, is the oldest, busiest and one of the most beautiful ovals in the United States. It is located in San Mateo. The thoroughbred horses race from mid-September to early February, quarter horses run from mid-February to early May, and the San Mateo Fair offers an assortment of horses (thoroughbreds, Appaloosas and quarter) the first two weeks in September. The first race is either at 12.30pm or 1pm and there are special 4pm races on Fridays. The track is open Wednesday–Sunday. Dress code enforced in turf club.

Golden Gate Fields, off Highway 580 in Albany, tel: 526-3020. The highlight here is the thoroughbred racing, early February through late June, Tuesday–Saturday. Post times and admission are similar to Bay Meadows.

Hockey

California has two professional hockey teams, the Los Angeles Kings, who play at the Great Western Forum in Inglewood, and the younger San Jose Sharks, who play at the San Jose Arena. Hockey season runs from October–April.

Tennis

The Transamerica Men's Open Tennis Championship is held at San Francisco's Cow Palace each year. Tel: 469-6065 for information.

The Virginia Slims Women's Tennis Tournament is held either in San Francisco or Oakland each year. Tel: 296-7111 for information.

Further Reading

General

Behind the Mask of Innocence, by Kevin Brownlow. Alfred A. Knopf, 1990.
California: A Guide to the Golden State, Federal Writers Project. Hastings House, 1939.
California Festivals, by Carl & Kathy Kincade. Landau Communications, 1992.
California Political Almanac, edited by Dan Walters. Pacific Data Resource, 1990.
California Spas, by Laurel Cook. Foghorn Press, 1992.
California's Missions, edited by Ralph B. Wright. Hubert A. Lowan, 1978.
San Francisco Almanac, by Gladys Hansen. Presidio Press, 1980.
The Missions of California, by Melba Levick & Stanley Young. Chronicle Books , 1988.
Unknown California, edited by Jonathan Eisen, David Fine and Kim Eisen. Collier Books, 1985.
Walks and Tours in the Golden Gate City, by Randolph Delehanty. Dial Press, 1980.

People

Ambrose Bierce, The Devil's Lexographer, by Paul Fatout. University of Oklahoma Press, 1951.
Autobiography, by Ansel Adams. Little, Brown 1985.
Big Dreams: Into the Heart of California, by Bill Barich. Pantheon, 1994.
Citizen Hearst, by W.A. Swanberg. Charles Scribners Sons, 1961.
The Hearsts, by Lindsay Chaney & Michel Cieply. Simon & Schuster, 1981.
Life and Good Times of William Randolph Hearst, by John Tebbel. E.P. Dutton & Co, 1952.
The Literary World of San Francisco, by Don Herron. City Lights Books, 1985.
The Literary World of San Francisco & Its Environs, by Don Herron. City Lights, 1985.
The Madams of San Francisco, by Curt Gentry. Doubleday, 1964.
The Times We Had: Life with William Randolph Hearst, by Marion Davis. Bobbs Merrill, 1975.
Tree Talk : The People and Politics of Timber, by Ray Raphael. Inland Press, Covelo, 1981.

Geography & Natural History

California Patterns: A Geographical and Historical Atlas, by David Hornbeck. Mayfield, 1983.
California Wildlife Map Book, by Vinson Brown and David Hoover. Naturegraph Publishers, 1967.

California: The Geography of Diversity, by Crane Miller and Richard Hyslop. Mayfield, 1983.

Coast Walks, by John McKinney. Olympus Press.

Outdoor Adventures, by Tom Sienstra. Foghorn Press, 1989.

Spring Wildflowers of the San Francisco Bay Area, by Helen Sharsmith. University of California Press, 1965.

Walks of California, by Gary Ferguson. Prentice Hall Press, 1987.

Where to see Wildlife in California, by Tom Taber. Oak Valley Press, 1983.

History

Berkeley: The Town and Gown of It, by George Pettitt. Howel North Books, 1973.

California: A Bicentennial History, by David Lavender. W.W. Norton, 1976.

A Century of Dishonor, by Helen Hunt Jacson. Scholarly Press, 1880.

A Companion to California, by James Hart. Oxford University Press, 1978.

The Days of the Great Estates, by David F Myrick Trans-Angelo Books, 1990.

Inside the Walls of Alcatraz, by Frank Heaney. Bull Publishing, 1987.

Oakland: The Story of a City, by Beth Bagwell. Presidio Press, 1982.

Ordeal by Hunger, by George R. Stewart. Henry Holt, & Co., 1936.

San Francisco as It Was, and It Is, by Paul Johnson and Richard Reinhardt. Doubleday, 1979.

The San Francisco Earthquake, by Thomas Gordon Stein & Day, 1971.

A Short History of San Francisco, by Tom Cole. Monte Rosa, 1981.

The True Story of the Design and Construction of the Golden Gate Bridge, by John Van der Zee. Simon & Schuster, 1986.

Other Insight Guides

The 190 books in the *Insight Guides* series cover every continent and include 28 titles devoted to the United States, from Alaska to Florida, from Seattle to Boston.

Insight Guide: Southern California. An in-depth look at the missions, the movie stars and the people of Southern California.

Insight Guide: San Francisco. An insider's look at one of America's most fascinating cities.

Insight Guide: Los Angeles captures the energy and glamour of America's movie capital.

Insight Pocket Guides

Insight Pocket Guide: Southern California. Personal recomendations make the most of a brief trip.

Insight Pocket Guide: Northern California. A local host offers hand-made itineraries for a short stay.

Insight Pocket Guide: San Francisco. Tours and tips help you turn a brief stay into a memorable one.

Index

343

T

U